IN THE SHADOW

To Lois,
In solidaty.

ATLANTIC
MIGRATIONS
— AND THE —
AFRICAN
DIASPORA

Jessica B. Harris, Series Editor

IN THE SHADOWS OF THE BIG HOUSE

Twenty-First-Century Antebellum Slave Cabins
and Heritage Tourism in Louisiana

Stephen Small

University Press of Mississippi / Jackson

The University Press of Mississippi is the scholarly publishing agency of the Mississippi Institutions of Higher Learning: Alcorn State University, Delta State University, Jackson State University, Mississippi State University, Mississippi University for Women, Mississippi Valley State University, University of Mississippi, and University of Southern Mississippi.

www.upress.state.ms.us

The University Press of Mississippi is a member of the Association of University Presses.

First printing 2023
∞

Library of Congress Cataloging-in-Publication Data

Names: Small, Stephen, 1963– author.
Title: In the shadows of the big house : twenty-first-century antebellum slave cabins and heritage tourism in Louisiana / Stephen Small.
Other titles: Atlantic migrations and the African diaspora.
Description: Jackson : University Press of Mississippi, 2023. | Series: Atlantic migrations and the African diaspora | Includes bibliographical references and index.
Identifiers: LCCN 2023012294 (print) | LCCN 2023012295 (ebook) | ISBN 9781496845559 (hardback) | ISBN 9781496845566 (trade paperback) | ISBN 9781496845573 (epub) | ISBN 9781496845580 (epub) | ISBN 9781496845597 (pdf) | ISBN 9781496845603 (pdf)
Subjects: LCSH: Slaves—Dwellings—Louisiana—Natchitoches—History. | Slaves—Louisiana—Natchitoches—History. | Plantation life—Louisiana—Natchitoches—History. | Heritage tourism—Louisiana—Natchitoches. | Oakland Plantation (La.)—History. | Magnolia Plantation (Natchitoches Parish, La.)—History. | Melrose Plantation (La.)—History.
Classification: LCC E443 .S635 2023 (print) | LCC E443 (ebook) | DDC 917.63/65—dc23/eng/20230411
LC record available at https://lccn.loc.gov/2023012294
LC ebook record available at https://lccn.loc.gov/2023012295

British Library Cataloging-in-Publication Data available

CONTENTS

PREFACE

I first became interested in museums as racialized institutions in the early 1990s when I began working as a guest curator in a gallery on transatlantic slavery at the Merseyside Maritime Museum in Liverpool.[1] The Transatlantic Slavery Gallery opened in 1994 and in 2007 was expanded to become the International Slavery Museum (Tibbles 1994). The content initially proposed for the gallery—especially the images and narrative for the exhibits—was a source of contention between museum professionals and key sections of the local Black community, with vigorous opposition in particular from Black women about the distorted and hostile images of Black women that already existed in other museum exhibits, especially in Liverpool (Gifford et al. 1989). There were disagreements over the scope of the exhibit—should it focus just on the slave trade, as the financial donor first intended, or should it document African culture before European invasion? Should it also focus on the legacy of slavery? "We're still living in slavery," said some local Black people, "so why just look at the past?" Some people objected to the idea of an exhibit on slavery at all. Why spend money on a museum and the past, when there were so many objectionable stereotypes of Black people in television, films, and entertainment, and so much inequality and discrimination in schools, employment, and politics at present?

And it wasn't just Black people who took exception to the proposed gallery. Many white people asked why there should be such a focus on the role of the British in slavery. After all, they claimed, the British brought civilization to Africa, abolished the slave trade, and forced other nations to do the same; Great Britain also had much better race relations than other nations, including the United States and South Africa. My involvement in this gallery directly influenced the path that my future research took.

I relocated to the United States in 1995, and in spring 1996, I began empirical research at heritage tourist venues in Georgia. At that time, Georgia was finalizing preparations for the Olympic Games and a massive advertising campaign promoting southern heritage was underway to entice visitors and tourists to remain in the state after the games were over. I was surprised by the images of plantation mansions and gardens in the promotional literature and glossy magazines circulating in the state. I was startled to learn that so many mansions from slave plantations still existed, along with a host of ancillary buildings. And I was stunned to discover that a number of these buildings were slave cabins—shacks, huts, and hovels—that had formerly housed so many enslaved persons. As I took part in tours—from "the Antebellum Plantation" at Stone Mountain to Alexander Stephens State Park in Crawfordville, and from Bulloch Hall in Roswell to Hofwyl-Broadfield Plantation in Brunswick—I was shocked by the ways in which slavery and its injustices were so effortlessly circumvented or completely obliterated. Leaflets, colorful brochures, novels, tours, and tour guides highlighted the grandeur and architecture of the mansions, the beauty of the gardens, the honor, civility, and gentility of elite whites, and mourned the loss of a so-called golden age in which "cotton was king," that was now "gone with the wind." White people (especially elites) were everywhere and Black people nowhere. Overall, Black lives, aspirations, and contributions, along with Black suffering, struggles, resistance, and resilience, were marginalized, anaesthetized, erased, or annihilated. All in all, this constituted a grand narrative of praise for southern plantation owners and southern history. Fortunately, I found sustained and spirited challenges to these images in some of the exhibits organized and managed by Black people at the Harriet Tubman Museum in Macon, and the Negro Heritage Tour in Savannah, for example.

As I continued my research, I discovered that at least several hundred original slave cabins existed as part of heritage tourist sites across the entire South. For me they were a palpable, perplexing, and fascinating legacy of slavery. They seemed to capture so many contradictions about slavery and its legacies: the physical juxtaposition of the dilapidated cabins with the luxurious mansions; the marginalization and trivialization of slavery and the cabins as compared with the meticulous attention and glorifying focus on elite white lifestyles and mansions presented by tour guides; and the relative prosperity and privilege enjoyed by white people in the 1990s as compared with Black people in southern society more generally. Here was a massive tourist infrastructure, employing tens of thousands of people, attracting millions of visitors, which provided, to my first impressions, a thoroughly distorted overall picture of slavery as both paternalistic and benign, and the enslaved as contented and faithful.

Slave cabins became an increasingly central focus of my research. They formed part of the first project on plantation heritage sites in the South that I undertook with my colleague and cowriter Jennifer L. Eichstedt (Eichstedt and Small 2002). In that study, we identified slave cabins at about one-third of the more than 120 plantation museum sites that we visited in Virginia, Georgia, and Louisiana, and commented on the relatively minor role they played in the sites' narratives. After that project, I began a more systematic study of slave cabins. I spent several months traveling throughout the South, identifying slave cabin locations at a wide range of public and private heritage sites. These visits included Nottoway Plantation, Oak Alley, and Laura Plantation on the River Road (between New Orleans and Baton Rouge) in Louisiana; Springfield Plantation in Mississippi; Kingsley Plantation and "The Last Slave Cabin" in Florida; Br'er Rabbit Museum and Archibald Smith Plantation House in Georgia; Boone Hall and the Aiken-Rhett House in South Carolina; Horton Grove and Latta Plantations in North Carolina; and the Booker T. Washington National Monument in Virginia and Hampton National Historic Site in Maryland. I even visited the so-called Uncle Tom's Cabin (Josiah Henson Cabin) in Maryland.

I decided to focus on Natchitoches, Louisiana, because of the concentration of original slave cabins and other spaces in which the enslaved slept or lived at prominent tourism sites, the key role that the cabins seemed to play in heritage tourism at the three major heritage sites, and because it was clear to me that Louisiana, especially areas outside New Orleans, was relatively neglected in the literature on slavery and its legacies, compared to other regions in the South. I was also gripped by the fact that significant numbers of legally free people of color across Louisiana themselves owned enslaved people and that Natchitoches was home to one of the most significant group of owners—the so-called Cane River Creoles.[2] I felt strongly that a more comprehensive understanding of the legacies of slavery had to engage with a wide geographical terrain, and with the troubling issue of people of color owning Black people.

It will be a revelation to most people that hundreds of original antebellum slave cabins still exist across the US South, many of which are currently incorporated into the extensive heritage tourist infrastructure of that region. Surprisingly, most of them are in excellent physical condition, mainly because they have benefited from substantial preservation, renovation, reconstruction, and refurbishment. Many of these cabins are no longer in their original location and have, in fact, been relocated multiple times over the last 150 years for purposes of habitation or exhibition, or because they were abandoned or discarded. Many people will be astonished at the ways the cabins are marginalized at so many sites across the region. Some people will be shocked to discover that African Americans were living in such cabins in recent decades. In all probability, many of these cabins are still occupied by African Americans or others.[3]

These facts raise important questions about the legacy of slavery in the United States today; about the nature and role of heritage tourism across the South; about the relatively limited attention paid in heritage tourism to slavery and slave cabins as compared with the attention devoted to elite whites and their accommodations; and about the ways in which gender shapes the organization of the sites, including representations of Black women. As I have argued elsewhere, the practices and priorities prevalent at heritage sites reveal far more about contemporary social values than they do about the facts of history (Small 2015). Overall, they provide insights into practices of remembering and forgetting. They expand our understanding of differential access to resources and the underlying power imbalances of such access. In this regard, they have value to social analysts of racialization and US institutions. Nowhere is this more obvious in the United States than in the public discussions—characterized by tensions, antagonism, and conflicts—over Confederate monuments, which have been so prevalent in the United States, especially since 2015. I believe this book makes a significant contribution to these discussions.

ACKNOWLEDGMENTS

I would like to thank the many people who contributed directly and indirectly to this book, and who have been steadfastly at my side on this scholarly journey. Staff and librarians in Natchitoches were overwhelmingly supportive and greatly facilitated my access to all aspects of the heritage sites, and to information, documents, and contacts that proved extremely valuable for this research. In particular I would like to thank Mary Linn Wernet, the librarian at the Cammie Garrett Henry Research Center at Northwestern State University, Natchitoches, who was welcoming and extremely generous in providing access to a wide range of primary documents. I would also like to thank Rolonda Teal for her insights, advice, and encouragement.

Kathryn Benjamin, Amy Wolfson, and Rob Connell, graduate students at University of California, Berkeley, undertook library and online research on many aspects of the project and spent several weeks carrying out empirical research on plantation heritage sites along the River Road and beyond. They also read several initial drafts of sections of the manuscript and provided important feedback. Alexis Martin did significant library and online research, as did Sofia Franco, who also provided feedback and edited sections of the manuscript. Amy Tran-Calhoun did research visits in and around New Orleans and provided useful feedback on a draft of one of the final chapters.

Lynne Bush did an outstanding job editing the manuscript and helping me beat it into shape. She spotted many instances where I was able to refine my analysis. Her recommendations were astute, insightful, and elegant. I have benefited greatly from her knowledge, skills, and experience. She also consistently encouraged me to get the book to press. Patricia Wong carried out extensive online research and undertook tremendous editing in the final stages of the manuscript. She worked with energy and determination to ensure comprehensiveness and consistency, and to remove many of the inelegancies. I benefitted from her meticulous attention to detail. Erin Winkler and Rebecca C. King-O'Riain each provided feedback on a chapter of the book. My particular thanks to Ana Araujo who generously read the entire manuscript and gave me excellent feedback on the substance and framing of the arguments and on historical specificities in Louisiana and South Carolina.

I benefited from conversations with colleagues and friends at the Institute for the Study of Societal Issues and the Department of African American Studies, including Troy Duster, David Minkus, and Ula Taylor. Their feedback alerted me to a number of important issues, and both broadened and deepened my approach to the overall argument, its nuances, and its implications.

Many friends, colleagues, and interlocutors across the diaspora have shared information, insights, and criticisms, directly and indirectly, which have helped me sharpen my understanding and clarify when I analyze issues of the kind raised in this book. They reminded me of both the common and unique issues that arise when we analyze slavery and its legacies in different locations across the African diaspora. They also recommended publications and information that were beneficial. This group includes Kwame Nimako, Jennifer Tosch, Mano Delea, Sandew Hira, and Sitla Bonoo; in the United States, Camilla Hawthorne, Michael Hanchard, and Trica Keaton; in Liverpool, Jimi Jagne, Leona Vaughn, and Charles Forsdick. Kwame Nimako in particular motivated me to develop a far broader and deeper analytical frame than I had prior to meeting him in 2006. My involvement and lectures at the Black Europe Summer School, since its first meeting in 2008, have provided me with tremendous insight.

I want to thank colleagues, students, visiting scholars, and staff at the various institutions where I presented papers on the issues raised in this book. This includes the Institute for the Study of Societal Issues and the Center for Race and Gender, both at the University of California, Berkeley, Louvain University in Belgium, the National Archives in Suriname, in Curaçao at the invitation of Jeanne Henriquez, and at the Annual Conference of the Organization of American Historians in Seattle, Washington, in March 2009.

My partner and wife, Angela Lintz Small, carried out onsite research in Natchitoches, reviewed documents and interviews, and provided insightful feedback and analysis. She has been my consistent interlocutor and motivator.

Some of the material in this manuscript has appeared in much shorter form and in regard to Louisiana, more generally in a variety of publications. This includes: "Confederate Memorials, Plantation Museums, and Slave Cabins: Public History of Slavery in the United States," in Jessica Moody and Stephen Small, "Slavery and Public History at the Big House. Remembering and Forgetting at American Plantation Museums and British Country Houses," *Journal of Global Slavery* 4 (February 2019): 36–48; "Social Mobilization and Public History of Slavery in the United States," in *Eurocentrism, Racism and Knowledge: Debates on History and Power in Europe and the Americas,* ed. Marta Araújo and Silvia Rodríguez Maeso (London: Palgrave Macmillan, 2015), 229–46; "Still Back of the Big House: Slave Cabins and Slavery in Southern Heritage Tourism," *Tourism Geographies: An International Journal of Tourism Space, Place and Environment* (September 2012): 1–19, https://doi.org/10.1080/14616688.2012.723042; "Multiple Methods in Research on 21st Century Plantation Museums and Slave Cabins in the South" in *Rethinking Race and Ethnicity in Research Methods*, ed. John H. Stanfield II (Walnut Creek, CA: Left Coast Press, 2011), 169–89.

Funding for the research came from University of California, Berkeley, from the Department of African American Studies, and from several grants, including from the Townsend Center for the Humanities.

Committee for the Protection of Human Subjects Protocol #2008-3-68

IN THE SHADOWS OF THE BIG HOUSE

INTRODUCTION

The antebellum cabins, huts, houses, hovels, shacks, and ruins that used to be inhabited by enslaved families and have been incorporated into the heritage tourism plantation sites of twenty-first-century Natchitoches are the physical and institutional embodiment of social forgetting and social remembering. Still juxtaposed physically against the so-called big houses once occupied by the most prosperous master-enslavers and mistress-enslavers of the antebellum period, slave cabins remind us of the subordinated and exploited status of enslaved Black people throughout the late nineteenth century;[1] and they highlight the continued uses to which the history of that subordination has been subjected in the contemporary period.[2] They are the *cumulative institutionalization of neglect* and in the context of heritage tourism, they provide insights into the dynamics of public history, and the past and present struggles that such dynamics reflect. These include political, ideological, and cultural struggles shaped by race, class, and gender. Their existence as part of twenty-first-century southern heritage tourism offers powerful insights into the nature of representations and discourses of slavery across these sites; and bringing slave cabins to the foreground of analysis affords greater opportunities to illustrate issues of resource imbalances and the framing of slavery at heritage sites than does a consideration of plantation main houses alone.

The concept of a "twenty-first-century antebellum slave cabin" captures some of the contradictions reflected in the sites at the start of the twenty-first century, including temporal dimensions (built in the antebellum period, still in use today), spatial dimensions (behind the big house), and racialized dimensions (elite whites in the big houses and mansions, enslaved Blacks in the cabins), which convey irrepressible dimensions of authority, power, and resource imbalances. This study enables us to compare how and why discourses, texts, and images at the sites focus inordinately on elite white lifestyles as compared with slavery, slave cabins, and the lives of enslaved people;[3] to assess the role and significance of white ethnic identity (in this instance, French Creoles and Anglo-Americans) and class privilege; to investigate

3

the treatment of gender and especially the limited representations of Black women; and to explore some of the ways in which Black voices (in narratives, folktales, memoirs, religion, and music) and Black visions (in art and sculpture) can extend and enhance the depth and range of representations at the sites. It also provides an opportunity to examine the role of the state (including the federal government) in the management, organization, and funding of contemporary southern heritage tourism sites. Finally, it reveals how racialized discourses operate at the sites, including how tactics of evasion, erasure, and euphemism enable sites to avoid addressing dimensions of slavery that may leave some visitors uncomfortable.

. . .

In the years leading up to the Civil War, when the enslaved population was at its peak in Natchitoches Parish, there were 9,434 enslaved persons legally owned by more than 600 free residents in Natchitoches (1860 census).[4] Enslaved people in Natchitoches, as across the South, lived in a range of structures and locations. Like the majority of enslaved persons in Louisiana, those in Natchitoches lived in rural areas in structures made of log, wood, *bousillage*, or brick.[5] Many lived in structures built for other purposes, such as kitchens, blacksmith or carpenter shops, or barns. Others lived inside the so-called big houses of their master-enslavers and mistress-enslavers at the plantation. Most of the rest lived in houses in towns, often in attics, basements, or other rooms inside, or attached to, their master-enslavers' homes (Wade 1964). Some enslaved people lived alongside rivers in makeshift and flimsy accommodations, and still smaller numbers of fugitives and maroons lived in forests, bayous, or swamps, in more ephemeral accommodations (Diouf 2014; Scott 2005; Hall 1992).[6] It is likely that enslaved persons in antebellum Natchitoches lived in more than 1,880 dwellings.[7] We do not know the precise number living in each of these different types of dwellings, but it is most likely that the majority lived in unattached structures made of wood, log, or bousillage.

By the start of the twenty-first century in Natchitoches, the vast majority of antebellum slave cabins and quarters were gone.[8] In the fieldwork I carried out between 2007 and 2011, I identified sixteen slave cabins—that is, unattached structures built exclusively for enslaved persons—that had been incorporated into the heritage tourism industry in the parish.[9] These cabins date originally to the mid-nineteenth century. I also visited several cabins around the parish located on private and public land. Local residents insisted that there were many others scattered across the parish, but these cabins did not play a role in heritage tourism and are not examined in this book. The primary focus of this book is the sixteen slave cabins, as well as the other spaces in which the enslaved lived, slept, or worked, located at the three most popular heritage tourism sites in Natchitoches: Oakland Plantation, Magnolia Plantation Complex, and Melrose Plantation.

If we accept this estimate of almost 1,800 dwellings for enslaved persons in 1860, that means that just under 1 percent survived into twenty-first-century heritage tourism. What happened to the rest of them? Many of the cabins simply collapsed during slavery, as they were not built to last. Many cabins were destroyed deliberately during the Civil War, for example, by Union or Confederate troops who used them for fuel in cold and desolate winters. Other cabins were destroyed by troops or thieves as a result of malice or in anger when plantations were ransacked. Still others were taken apart so that their materials could be repurposed. For example, more than thirty years after the main house at Magnolia Plantation was destroyed during the Civil War, some of the former slave cabins were taken apart and their bricks used to help rebuild it.[10] A number of cabins were destroyed by natural catastrophes, including floods, fire, or hurricanes; others simply deteriorated with the passage of time. Some were destroyed or allowed to collapse due to embarrassment, guilt, or shame.

The majority of cabins that survived the Civil War were modified, extended, adjusted, altered, or generally improved after slavery ended, and continued to function as accommodations in a period when Black people had relatively more control over their private spaces (that is, as compared with times of slavery). Alterations to the cabins continued throughout the twentieth century. Since I completed the research for this book, many cabins in heritage tourism—in Natchitoches and across Louisiana—continue to be modified or reconstructed, and several sites have built replica cabins in order to highlight the lives of the enslaved. For example, Oak Alley Plantation built six cabins in 2014 and Whitney Plantation also built or reconstructed cabins.

During my research in Natchitoches, a number of plantation sites were open to the public for heritage tourism, and the three major sites in the parish housed purpose-built slave cabins that could be visited, including some that could be entered. There were two cabins and the ruins of a third at Oakland Plantation, eight cabins at Magnolia Plantation, and five cabins at Melrose Plantation. The majority of them were made of wood and log or a combination of wood, log, and bousillage, and eight were made of brick. All of them had deteriorated considerably over time and some had sustained great damage in the past. Fewer than half of these cabins were in their original locations, having been physically moved around their original plantation sites or relocated to different sites for a variety of reasons. It is only as a result of deliberate intervention that these cabins were preserved and restored. Their impressive physical condition at the start of the twenty-first century was the result of extensive renovations over the course of the previous twenty-five years.

In addition to these purpose-built slave cabins, there were other structures and spaces on these plantations in which enslaved persons slept or lived for substantial periods of time during and after slavery. These included rooms and spaces in the main houses and kitchens at all three plantations and other buildings, such as a blacksmith and carpenter shop and barns.[11] There were also several buildings in the town of Natchitoches with spaces in which enslaved people regularly slept or lived. For example, Tante Huppé House still had a former servants' quarters extension to its building. Many of these outbuildings were incorporated into heritage tourism, but the main houses at the plantations played a far more prominent role in heritage tourism than any of the other buildings.[12] This range of buildings and spaces in which enslaved people lived or slept constitutes what I call a *continuum of coerced accommodations* for the enslaved—a concept that directs our attention beyond the binary of "slave/nonslave" accommodation typical of most analyses.[13] The concept also highlights a number of important issues, including physical and social proximity between networks of families (Black, white, and other) on the plantations, issues to which I will return later in the book.

This book examines how a group of cabins built for the sole purpose of housing enslaved African Americans under antebellum chattel slavery survived to become a central part of the heritage tourist infrastructure of the twenty-first century. I was primarily concerned with understanding the social organization of the sites, the nature and distribution of the slave cabins and other spaces in which the enslaved lived or slept, and the representations of slavery and slave cabins at the sites. What information was provided to visitors about slavery and slave cabins? What was said about the elite white inhabitants of the plantation? How was ethnic identity among whites articulated and expressed? How did gender shape the representations, and what was said about white women, Black women, and women of mixed origins? And what images could be seen of these women?

A central question involved the extent to which Black voices and Black visions of slavery (as described above), slave cabins, and their legacies were incorporated into presentations at the sites. I was particularly attentive to ways in which the voices and visions of Black women were expressed, elaborated, or silenced. For example, what did we hear at the sites from Black women?

In this book, I also provide important historical background information—for example, brief histories of the plantation experiences during slavery and Jim Crow legal segregation—and I describe the incorporation of the cabins at the three sites into the regional tourist industry over time. I argue that consideration of slave cabins raises fundamental issues about racialization, representations and discourses, gender, white ethnic identity, and the role and influence of the state in ways that are far more immediate and revelatory than a focus on slavery alone. It also allows for a more direct consideration of the role of Black voices and visions, not least of which because we are far more likely to hear from Black women and men in the cabins than anywhere else.

My research revealed marked differences in the incorporation of information about slavery and slave cabins even within a single locale. It also revealed how common elements of white racial identity across the South can become fractured or rearticulated depending on the specifics of locality. Overall, I consider how past patterns of racialization, especially in their institutional, material, and ideological forms, are manifested in the present configuration of the sites, and the nature and scope of the public history presented there. And the book as a whole provides the opportunity to explore issues of resource imbalance, material inequality, and access to power.[14]

RESEARCH CONTEXT

At least several hundred slave cabins—and almost certainly far more—still existed across the South at the start of the twenty-first century (Moody and Small 2019; Modlin et al. 2018; Mooney 2004). Some of them were incorporated into the tourist infrastructure of plantation museums—at both public and private sites—while many others stood alone on private or public land. Scholars from various disciplines have analyzed plantation heritage sites, and the field of heritage studies in particular is an important and growing field of intellectual inquiry. A focus on legacies of slavery—including race and racism—is a central feature of these studies. Research has been undertaken by public historians, sociologists, and museum specialists on representations of slavery at contemporary plantation heritage sites. Some research has been carried out by cultural studies analysts and geographers. The primary focus of this work has been on the role, operation, and functioning of these sites in the present rather than the past (Araujo 2020, 2014; Modlin et al. 2018; Small 2015; Buzinde and Santos 2009; Adams 2007; Eichstedt and Small 2002). These include studies of individual sites and some comparative studies within or across states and the region as a whole (Small 2012; Harrison 2008;

Adams 2007; Matrana 2005; Mooney 2004; Walsh 1997). There is significant recent work on Louisiana and elsewhere (Moody and Small 2019; Bright, Alderman, and Butler, 2016). Some of this work examines innovations in representing slavery, including theatrical and performative activities (Benjamin and Alderman 2017); and some of it is archaeological (MacDonald and Morgan 2007; Brown 2006).

Analysis has been undertaken within the theoretical traditions of public history and collective memory as well as by scholars of representations, images, and discourses (Bright and Carter 2016; Eichstedt and Small 2002; Handler and Gable 1997; Walsh 1997; Goodwin et al. 1984). Some recent studies analyze the views, opinions, and actions of site owners, managers, tour guides, and visitors (Walcott-Wilson 2020; Modlin et al. 2018; Bright and Carter 2016). Many of these studies explore the ways in which heritage tourist sites that focus on the southern past discuss (or avoid discussion of) slavery, racial segregation, and injustice by focusing on the narrative strategies used and the ways in which explicit images and language work alongside evasions, erasures, euphemisms, or circumlocutions (Moody and Small 2019; Carter 2015; Eichstedt and Small 2002. See also Trouillot 1995). There has also been interrogation of stereotypes and images of Black women (Dill and Zambrana 2009; McElya 2007).

Some research has addressed the public debates and power struggles over the establishment, operation, and content of information at these sites; the prevalence of representations that privilege Confederate interpretations; and the ways in which heritage tourism is inextricably linked to commercialization, gender ideologies, and the changing racialized nature of political power (Clinton 2019; Alderman 2018; Cook 2017; Horton and Horton 2006; Brundage 2005, 2000; Yuhl 2005; Savage 1999; Shakel 1999; West 1999; Campbell and Rice 1991). There are other writings that discuss the intense and sometimes controversial contemporary debates over museum exhibits on slavery and monuments that celebrate or commemorate the Confederacy (Landrieu 2018; Horton and Horton 2006; Brundage 2005, 2000; Yuhl 2005; Shakel 2003; Goldberg 2002; Savage 1999; West 1999; Campbell and Rice 1991). These are debates with significant precedent in the twentieth century (Wallace-Sanders 2008).

Most research on contemporary plantation heritage sites fails to address the twenty-first-century antebellum slave cabins themselves in any detail, though several studies mention slave cabins as a secondary aspect of their analysis (Harrison 2008; Matrana 2005; West 1999). Rehder (1999) described some cabins across Louisiana in the 1990s, and there is one book that compares slave cabins across counties in Maryland, but this is almost forty years old (McDaniel 1982). There are several dissertations in which slave cabins receive some attention (for example, Wolcott-Wilson 2020; Harrison 2008; Handley 2004). These studies have brought important perspectives to our understanding of the role of plantation heritage sites today and of slave cabins both historically and at present. However, we still lack detailed information, analysis, or understanding in several other important areas and we know far more about slave cabins in the past than in the present.

Few studies of heritage sites have focused directly on slave cabins or on the ways in which treatment of the cabins compares with treatment of slavery more generally. In earlier work, my colleague and I provided comprehensive coverage of race and representations at plantation heritage sites and drew attention to the existence of slave cabins and to the *symbolic annihilation* of these cabins (Eichstedt and Small 2002). The distinction between slavery in general and slave cabins in particular is important because representations of slavery at plantation heritage sites without reference to slave cabins frequently remain limited in scope, while a focus on cabins in detail can provide more revealing aspects of the assessment of slavery.[15] We do not know much about the physical condition of the slave cabins or about the condition of their exteriors and interiors in the twenty-first century. We do not know much about the objects, artifacts, and information provided inside cabins nor how many are in their original location or have been relocated. We lack any significant recent work on the influence of gender ideologies in the organization, framing, and presentation of slavery and slave cabins at tourist sites. We do not have any recent books on how slave cabins function as part of heritage tourism in the twenty-first century either individually or collectively. There is no up-to-date book on any individual slave cabins per se and none that compare slave cabins of several types across sites in one region or across regions. And we do not know much about the social significance of the cabins today, the nature and format of presentations about them, or how such presentations fit into sites' presentations as a whole. I have undertaken research on several of these issues in Louisiana (Moody and Small 2019; Small 2015, 2012).

Since I completed research on these issues in Natchitoches in 2011, there have been some significant changes in the parish, in Louisiana, and across the South. This has included improvements in the range of representations of both slavery and the cabins in all three areas just mentioned (Clinton 2019; Brundage 2018; Alderman 2018; Alderman and Bright 2017; Cook 2017). There has also been a dramatic increase in public discussion of slavery and its legacies in the United States, especially since 2015. Some horrific crimes and several highly visible racist incidents have forced the issue into public discussion and have also highlighted current racial antagonism, tensions, and conflict.[16]

The majority of research for this book took place in Natchitoches between 2007 and 2011 and I intend it to stand as an analysis of the situation in the parish at that time. I continued to carry out empirical research on similar sites across Louisiana through 2016 with several research assistants, and I have continued to monitor developments in Natchitoches since that time (Moody and Small 2019; Small 2015). The epilogue to this book addresses developments since 2011 and considers the implications for my primary research findings. In that regard, the evidence in this book can be used to compare what was in place then with developments in the parish—and elsewhere—since that time.

WHY NATCHITOCHES?

Natchitoches is both a town and a parish in the northwestern region of Louisiana. The population of the parish in 2009 was 17,635, including 7,263 whites (41.3 percent) and 9,599 African Americans (54.6 percent). The remainder of the population included Native Americans, Hispanics, Asians, and people of mixed racial origins. The land in this region was originally inhabited by Native Americans before being colonized by the French in the eighteenth century (Din 1999; Dollar 1998). French culture prevailed, and chattel slavery was introduced. For a short while the Spanish became dominant (Burton and Smith 2008; Mills 1977). After Napoleon I recaptured the territory, he sold it to the United States in 1803, and in 1812, it became a state (Din 1999).

Slavery was by far the most important institution in the economic growth, unfolding wealth and inequality, and political and social relations of Natchitoches. Slavery began early in the colony, and the massive expansion of farms and plantations was achieved primarily through the labor of enslaved people (Burton and Smith 2008; Din 1999). The richest and most politically powerful men in the colony, and later the parish, all owned enslaved people or benefited directly from such ownership. Shortly before slavery was legally abolished, the US Census data for 1860 listed 9,434 "slaves" in Natchitoches (Blake 2002). At that time, the Prud'homme and Hertzog families, which owned two of the three sites described in this book—Oakland and Magnolia—were among the wealthiest master-enslavers in the parish.[17] The Metoyers, the owners of the third site, had attained their maximum wealth (and ownership of humans) some decades earlier, and by the 1830s, their wealth and holdings had already diminished significantly (Mills 1977). Today, Natchitoches

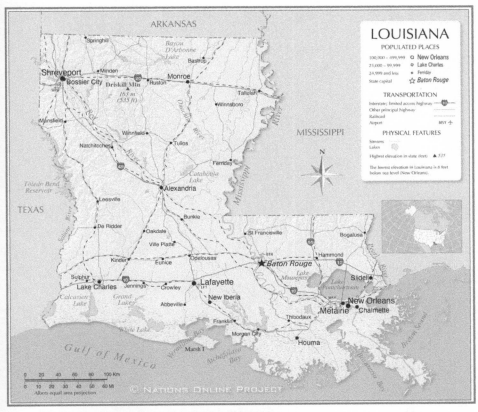

Map of Louisiana showing Natchitoches. © Nations Online Project.

systematically markets itself in heritage tourism as the oldest French establishment in the Louisiana Territory (Historic Natchitoches 2007).

Between 2007 and 2008, I visited more than thirty-five plantation heritage
sites in nine states to identify a location that might yield important insights.[18]
Natchitoches was selected for several reasons. First, at the start of the twenty-
first century, Natchitoches was a major tourist regional center that received
thousands of visitors each year, the majority of whom came especially for
heritage tourism. Heritage tourism highlighted several themes—first, the
lifestyle and legacy of Creole families and culture, with a particular focus on
architecture, including both European families and those of mixed African
and European origins. A second theme was the distinctive, multitier racial
hierarchy that prevailed in the region, which led to the growth of a significant
group of legally free Creoles of color, some of whom were themselves master-
enslavers (Mills 1977). As I mentioned above, one of these families—the

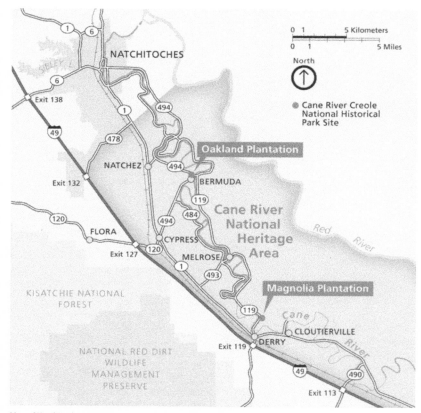

Map of Natchitoches showing three plantations. © National Park Service.

Metoyers—rose to great wealth and status, attaining the dubious status of being the largest master-enslavers among legally free people of color in the South (Mills and Mills 1973). A third theme highlighted agricultural plantations and the working communities and lifestyles associated with them, including farming, machinery, and work culture. A fourth theme was the significance of individuals who were notable locally or nationally, including Louis Juchereau de St. Denis and John Sibley. Several exceptional women also ranked highly among these community notables, including Cammie Henry, Marie Thérèse Coin Coin, Clementine Hunter, and Kate Chopin.[19] There was also a limited amount of information on Native American individuals.

Second, Natchitoches had a significant number of twenty-first-century antebellum slave cabins that were actively incorporated into its heritage tourism infrastructure. Third, the sites revealed striking variations in their treatment and representations of slavery and the slave cabins; and they also reflected different modes of management. At the Oakland and Magnolia plantations, both managed by the National Park Service (NPS), the slave cabins were highly represented in the promotional literature and websites. They were available for self-guided tours, and park rangers and volunteers had information at hand about the nature of the cabins and the history of the enslaved persons who lived in them. At Melrose Plantation, which is owned and operated by the nonprofit Association for the Preservation of Historic Natchitoches (APHN), the slave cabins were in principle accessible to visitors, but they were difficult to recognize as slave cabins per se. As will be explained, they were primarily identified in the site's promotional literature and website as cabins occupied by the white writers who visited for short periods in the 1920s and 1930s. During my research, typically no information was provided or available on the range of enslaved persons who lived in the cabins in the antebellum period, or the Black workers, servants, cooks, maids, and nannies who lived there in the postbellum period, or throughout most of the twentieth century. In this book, I explore and explain how these differences in ownership and/or management across the sites came about and how they gave rise to such contrasting representations of slavery and slave cabins.

Fourth, there was a rich set of primary data and evidence about the cabins and the plantations to which they belong. This included data from official sources (such as local, regional, and federal government records), manuscript collections, and family sources (household records). There were extensive archaeological and architectural records and the sites themselves had a wealth of information that covered many periods in their history and documented the activities of the sites since their incorporation into heritage tourism in the last quarter of the twentieth century. There were also significant newspaper and media accounts of the sites. While most of these sources and records were created by and for the people in power—overwhelmingly elite or educated whites (especially men)—there were also significant sources left by Black people (including oral testimony, folklore, and material culture such as art and painting). These data enabled me to describe many aspects of heritage tourism across Natchitoches and document the historical trajectory of the plantations and cabins and their incorporation into heritage tourism in the parish.[20] Details about sources and methods are described in the appendix.[21]

Finally, slavery and its legacy in Louisiana have not attracted anything like the scholarly attention devoted to other areas in the South, especially the upper South. There is a significant literature on New Orleans and on people of mixed racial origins in that city (Vidal 2019; Devore 2015; Stanonis 2006; Dominguez 1986). New Orleans is not representative of the state as a whole, however, and this literature does not address issues outside that area.

This focus on New Orleans may have inadvertently distracted attention from fundamental issues to do with slavery and its legacy elsewhere in the state. For example, we do not have the nature and range of studies of slavery for Louisiana that exists for, say, Virginia or North Carolina; nor does the literature cover the array of issues (e.g., family, social relations, resistance, and gender) covered in other states. With one or two exceptions, there are few studies of gender in Louisiana outside of New Orleans (Malone 1992). In terms of plantation heritage sites, until recently, there was little work on Louisiana as compared with the South, and there is minimal work on Natchitoches, as compared with other areas in Louisiana. [22] Even for analyses of slavery in Louisiana, there is far more literature on sugar plantations, as compared with cotton plantations (Follitt 2005; Scott 2005; Rodrigue 2001; Conrad and Lucas 1995; McDonald 1993; Sitterson 1953). In this book, I bring both more attention to Louisiana, as compared to other states in the South, and to Natchitoches, as compared to other areas of Louisiana.

. . .

The first, overarching goal of this book is to describe the nature, role and significance of the sixteen twenty-first-century antebellum slave cabins in the social organization of heritage tourism and public history in Natchitoches at the start of the twenty-first century and to highlight how they are connected to a range of other structures and spaces across the plantations (such as the main house, kitchens and other workspaces) in which enslaved people slept or lived. I describe the nature of heritage tourism and public history generally in the parish; the number, distribution, and condition of the slave cabins at each plantation; I detail how far more attention is devoted to the lives and culture of elite whites at that site than to Black people; and I compare the attention given to slavery in general with attention given to slave cabins (and other structures and spaces in which the enslaved slept or lived). This last distinction is important because, as I argue later, a focus on slave cabins and other structures and spaces in which the enslaved slept or lived requires consideration of issues that are frequently left unaddressed in a focus on representations of slavery alone. These issues include the material conditions of the enslaved, the contingencies of labor and family relations—including blood and family relations with white people—and multiple dimensions of the racialized hierarchy that existed, as well as important elements of Black people's social values, both past and present. I also consider how, at sites where the cabins were discussed explicitly, it was the separate and distinct slave cabins that dominated representations, while other locations in which the enslaved regularly lived were neglected. I discuss why this narrow focus prevents us from exploring equally salient issues. And overall, I raise questions about power and access to resources as I consider who made—and continues to make—decisions about the issues that are most prevalent in representations at the sites.

The second goal is to assess what representations of slavery and slave cabins at the sites tell us about the reconfiguration of the past and the rearticulation of history at present. How are historically rooted institutions and structures of racialized and gendered inequality and power reproduced in the contemporary period? And how was the history that prevailed at the sites—their emphasis, themes, stories, and details, as compared to some other possible emphasis, themes, stories, and details—shaped by these patterns of inequality? I consider how certain aspects of southern history and society are institutionally incorporated into tourism and other aspects omitted. I also consider broader questions of collective memory (how certain aspects of southern history are willfully remembered and others willfully forgotten). Discussion of gender is again central. I explore some of the debates that have taken place over the role and functioning of slave cabins and their place in the tourist industry in Natchitoches. For example, what discussions took place when the sites were being established, and what suggestions were made about what should be done with the cabins? Who was involved in these discussions? Which suggestions were implemented and why? Who was responsible for incorporating them in the ways that they existed during the period of research? What were the consequences and outcomes?

The third goal is to describe the historical trajectory of plantations and cabins over the 130-year-period between the Civil War and the 1990s, including the transformation of many of the cabins during the immediate postbellum period and into the twentieth century. Why, when, and how did most cabins disappear? Which cabins survived and why? What initiatives were undertaken in the 1960s and 1970s to save the few that remained, restore them, and put them on exhibit? And who led such initiatives? These questions and issues have been a low priority for researchers of Natchitoches Parish and the data we have at present are limited. But here I begin to outline some key elements of this history. The historical patterns at Oakland Plantation and Magnolia Plantation reveal many similarities, with cabins occupied through the 1960s and 1970s, at which point they were identified for restoration and exhibit. Melrose Plantation reveals a markedly different pattern in that many cabins were identified and restored as early as the 1920s (though not for exhibit), with some that continued to be occupied through the 1950s.

The fourth goal addresses an important issue in the history of US slavery that is largely neglected in heritage studies—the thorny issue of people of mixed European and African origins (typically called "mixed-race" or "mulatto") who were master-enslavers. During slavery, they were scattered across the South, but in far higher numbers and relatively higher status in Louisiana than in the rest of the South (de la Fuente and Gross 2020; Schweninger 1996; Berlin 1984). These questions have attracted far more attention in the Caribbean and Brazil (Heuman 1981; Degler 1971). A great deal has been written about this group under slavery, but not much about how they are represented in heritage tourism in the twenty-first century.[23] In this book, I attempt to rectify that situation by describing what information was provided and how it was framed.

Four important themes recur throughout the book. The first is how gender ideologies and practices structure the social organization of the sites. This includes the presentation of the sites and the cabins, the gender division of labor in management and administration, and the immediate historical antecedents to both of these. How did gender ideologies shape the treatment and presentation of slavery and the slave cabins? What role did gender play in the organization and management of the sites? What images and discourses of gender, and of Black women in particular, were presented at the sites, for example, in website information, promotional leaflets and literature, texts and images in buildings at the sites, and during guided and unguided tours? And what roles did gender play in the processes leading up to the current situation? This last question, of course, requires consideration of irrepressible dynamics of race and gender under slavery and Jim Crow segregation (Glymph 2020; Jones-Rogers 2019; Berry 2017; Fuentes 2016; Morgan 2004; Fox-Genovese 1998). Race and gender relations figure prominently, irrepressibly, in both historical and contemporary processes and power struggles (Yuhl 2005; Brundage 2000; West 1999; Clinton 1982). The concept of "intersectionality" highlights the many dimensions of such institutionalized relationships and their implications, and I bring this concept to the foreground in my analysis (Jones-Rogers 2019; Collins and Bilge 2016; Collins 1991).

The second theme concerns the role of ethnic identity in representations of elite whites. I explore how the historically fractured ethnic identity of whites in Natchitoches—among Europeans with Spanish, French, and Anglo ancestry and identity—was represented and framed in a range of information and exhibitions at the sites. I call this *the Natchitoches twist*, because this emphasis is different from the tendency to play down ethnic differences of this kind in other states in the South. In Louisiana in general, and Natchitoches in particular, distinction, antagonism, or conflict among whites of different European origins played a significant role in the establishment and growth of the colony and state throughout the early antebellum period (Hall 1992). For most of that period, whites of French descent dominated the parish. Ethnic tensions continued to play a role in the antebellum and postbellum period, by which time Anglo-Americans became the dominant ethnic group in the parish. At the sites in this study, ethnic differences, especially the history and legacy of the French presence and culture, were highlighted as points of distinction and interest. These ethnic differences were expressed as positive contours of the cultural presentations at the sites, including the ethnic identity of master- and mistress-enslavers, the architecture of the buildings, including cabins, and the cultural practices of both enslavers and the enslaved (from family structure, language, and religion to food, music, and clothing). It is not by accident that one of the first things potential visitors to Natchitoches learn is that it was the first permanent settlement in the Louisiana Purchase (as cited in a wide array of tourist leaflets produced in the parish). In Natchitoches, we see how a monolithic "white" southern identity is resisted, and multi-ethnic white identities are presented. How and why was this done? Who fueled such efforts and with what consequence for the representation and treatment of slavery and slave cabins?

A third theme involves consideration of Black voices and Black visions. I examined how much information, evidence, and data from Black people played a significant role at the sites. For example, Black people (and some of mixed origins) were the majority of occupants at these sites; they lived in the majority of dwellings. When visitors receive information from websites, promotional literature, signs, and placards at the sites, and tour guides during tours, do we hear from Black people? In other words, to what extent do we hear Black voices (from narratives, biographies, folktales, songs, and religious texts) and see Black visions (in art, sculpture, and drawings), including the voices and visions of Black women? Do we read or hear their views of life as enslaved people, what legal abolition of slavery meant to them, and what life was like after slavery ended? Do we hear about what life was like under Jim Crow segregation, including the impact and consequences of industrialization and the Great Migration? Do we see images of Black men, women, and families in photographs, art, and drawings? If so, do they convey the range of experiences at the sites? Are Black people at these sites individualized or humanized? And how does information about the main house compare with information about the slave cabins and the other spaces in which the enslaved lived or worked? The significance of Black voices and Black visions for a more accurate understanding of the lives of the enslaved has long been highlighted (Mitchell 2020; Craft and Craft 1999). Their importance in Louisiana has also been highlighted (Jackson 2012; Eakin and Logsdon 1968).

A fourth theme concerns the role and influence of the state at each site. By "the state," I mean the federal government and the state of Louisiana. Two of the three sites in Natchitoches (Oakland Plantation and Magnolia Plantation) are owned and managed by the National Park Service. The third site (Melrose Plantation) is owned and managed by the Association for the Preservation of Historic Natchitoches. What role did the state play in shaping treatment and representations of slavery and the slave cabins? What was its impact in terms of information, knowledge, resources, and social connections? How did the state become involved in the establishment of the sites? Given the significant differences across the three sites in their treatment of slavery and slave cabins, I argue that Oakland Plantation and Magnolia Plantation engaged in practices of *relative incorporation*, while Melrose Plantation engaged in *symbolic annihilation* of the slave cabins.[24] To what extent is state involvement (or otherwise) a decisive factor in this differential treatment?

ORGANIZATION

In this introduction, I have provided a brief summary of the history of slave cabins and their contemporary deployment in the Natchitoches heritage industry. I highlighted the social importance of slave cabins and how analysis of them can provide an understanding of issues of racialization, class, gender, and power in the realm of public history and collective memory. I summarized the goals of the book, listed a number of key themes that will be addressed and provided a definition of twenty-first century slave cabins and slave quarters as a *continuum of coerced accommodations* lived in by the enslaved. I described the importance of Natchitoches as the site of study and briefly mentioned research methods and data for this book. What follows is organized into five chapters.

Chapter 1 provides a brief history of slavery and slave cabins in Natchitoches, the changing role of cabins in the postbellum period and later, details of their incorporation into heritage tourism in the 1970s through 1990s, and an overview of heritage tourism and slave cabins in Natchitoches at the start of the twenty-first century. The chapter highlights the range of factors and prominent themes that influenced heritage tourism in the parish at the start of the twenty-first century and identifies some of the key actors central to the promotion of these themes.

The next three chapters describe and examine the slave cabins and other structures and spaces in the *continuum of coerced accommodation* at each of the sites during the period of research. The first sections of each chapter describe the respective plantation and its cabins under slavery and Jim Crow segregation and the transformation of the cabins from accommodations for the enslaved into accommodations for legally free Black people, and their incorporation into heritage tourism in the 1970s. Later sections describe the social and physical organization of heritage tourism at each particular site at the start of the twenty-first century.

For example, chapter 2 describes and evaluates Oakland Plantation, paying particular attention to the three slave cabins at the site. It also discusses the servants' quarters in the main house—the so-called mammy room—along with the cook's cabin, the carpenter's cabin, and the *pigeonniers* (dovecotes). A fascinating aspect of Oakland Plantation is that it is an example of one long, unbroken chain of ownership by a single family. This site was owned by the same family—the Prud'hommes—for 160 years. We can thus ask whether what happens to slave cabins is different when ownership continues unbroken.

Chapter 3 describes and assesses the buildings at Magnolia Plantation, the second site organized and operated by the National Park Service. Its final section describes the social and physical organization of heritage tourism at the site, paying particular attention to the eight brick slave cabins. Magnolia is the only heritage site in the parish that has slave cabins made of brick, an uncommon construction material in the parish, the state, and across the entire South. It is also the only site in which all the cabins are in their original location and in a grid pattern. It also discusses the blacksmith shop, the slave hospital/overseer's cabin, and the gin barn.

Chapter 4 describes and evaluates the buildings at Melrose Plantation. Given the complex history of the site and its owners, this chapter covers a far wider range of material than the previous two. It describes the tremendous social significance attached to the cabins in the early twentieth century by Cammie Henry and her establishment of a writers' colony in the 1920s. It then describes their incorporation into heritage tourism in the 1970s. The final section details the social and physical organization of heritage tourism at the site, paying particular attention to the five slave cabins at the site; that is, the Bindery (a gift store at the time of my research), the Weaving House, the Ghana House, the Female Writer's Cabin, and the Yucca House. Four of these buildings were made of log and Yucca House was made of bousillage. This chapter also discusses the main house, the kitchen ruins and the African House. I describe how and why slavery and slave cabins at Melrose are represented in radically different and far more complex ways than at the previous two sites. I also consider the significance of the site being managed by a nonprofit organization.

The conclusion provides a summary of the major findings and reflects on some of the key issues for Natchitoches, and their implications more generally. It is followed by an epilogue. A methodological appendix provides more detail on the methodology, concepts, theories, research methods, and data collected for this project. A bibliography of primary and secondary sources is also provided.

Chapter One

SLAVERY AND HERITAGE
IN NATCHITOCHES

ESTABLISHMENT AND GROWTH OF SLAVERY

The area around what is now known as Cane River had been the focal point of Native American settlements for hundreds of years prior to the arrival of Europeans and before it was colonized by the French in the eighteenth century (Dollar 1998; Gowan 1976). The Natchitoches band of Caddo Indians lived where Natchitoches is currently situated, and the location was a center for a network of trade routes (Din 1999). The Cane River region was also populated by the Natchitoches Caddo, the Yatasi Caddo, the Adaes, and the Doustioni. When Europeans arrived, they recognized the area's geographical advantages and used it as the basis for colonial forts and later plantations that exploited enslaved labor. The French arrived in the region in 1714 and established Fort St. Jean Baptiste. Shortly thereafter, the Spanish established a presidio known as Los Adaes, situated fifteen miles west of Natchitoches. The town of Natchitoches grew up around Fort St. Jean Baptiste, and the tobacco and later cotton plantations that developed there used the town as their base.

Natchitoches proved to be both a secure and a profitable place for the Europeans to settle. Louis Juchereau de St. Denis, one of the town's founders, forged strong trade and defense alliances with the Spanish and with various Native American tribes. The trade provided the French with a nearby market for their goods. Access to the Red River allowed farmers in the area to ship agricultural goods to New Orleans and other downriver settlements. Natchitoches grew under the leadership of St. Denis, who led the town until his death in 1744. The fort had always been the center of town, and area farms and businesses had grown up in its shadow. In 1788, a small Catholic church was erected at the corner of what became Front and Church streets, and the population of Natchitoches moved north around it. In doing so, Natchitoches established a new town center and ensured that the town would survive the loss of the fort. This migration laid the foundation for the current city's National Historic Landmark district.

By the 1780s, the plantation culture by which the region has long been known was growing in earnest. In the early days, plantations primarily produced tobacco and indigo, but this changed with the invention of the cotton gin in 1793, which made the widespread production of cotton possible. Cotton quickly became the preferred cash crop of local planters (Din 1999). From the earliest opportunity, white planters and their families sought and purchased enslaved Africans to work the land, quickly creating a large, enslaved population in the region (Din 1999; Taylor 1974). The capture and enslavement of Africans by Europeans and Americans was already well-established in the region by this time and there were ample opportunities for the growing number of master-enslavers in the Natchitoches area to buy enslaved persons and acquire land. New Orleans was already on its way to becoming the largest port in the South.

The first Africans transported and enslaved in the Natchitoches region were forced there in 1735 (Mills 1977); by 1776, the number of people of color rose to 1,021, of whom only eight were legally free (ibid., 23). Black men, women, and children were put to work in a wide range of areas, with the majority in agricultural labor for commercial production, including crops like indigo, tobacco, and, eventually, cotton. They also worked in crops that were staples in their diets, such as corn. In addition, this labor force worked in several skilled trades such as blacksmiths and carpenters (for men) and domestic work such as cooks, maids, and nannies (for women).

At the same time as the exploitation of African and African American labor for profit rose, so did the exploitation of Black female bodies for sex and reproduction of the enslaved labor force. As elsewhere in the South, sexual relations in Natchitoches between whites (mainly men) and Blacks or Native Americans (mainly women) developed in a context of extensive and entrenched power imbalances and coercion (Hodes 1999; Jordan 1968). One of the most obvious consequences of these relationships was the emergence of a population of mixed African and European origin. This new group was initially enslaved, but over the decades, enough of them accessed legal freedom to emerge as a distinctive and relatively powerful group with an identity and group affiliations separate from the Blacks (Schweninger 1996). During the colonial era, it was culturally acceptable among the European settlers for white male planters to enter into lengthy relationships with enslaved African or Native American women, despite both French and Spanish legal bans on racial mixing. This acceptance reflected patriarchal power, the remoteness of the settlements from established pillars of European authority, and the difficulty of effective enforcement of prohibitions. At the same time, white men's almost unfettered access to the bodies of Black and Native American women was condoned.

As more and more children from these relationships were granted their legal freedom, they formed a small but significant group of people that blended aspects of French, Spanish, African, and Native American cultures. They were increasingly called *gens de couleur libres* (free people of color). Their presence became common across the state of Louisiana and the evidence indicates they were accepted by whites to a far greater degree in Louisiana than elsewhere in what became the United States (Berlin 1984).

Eventually some of these gens de couleur libres became successful planters, owning large numbers of enslaved persons, sharing their fortunes with their extended families and/or passing them on to their children, and consolidating their position as a distinctive group (Schweninger 1990). One of these powerful families in Natchitoches—the Metoyers—traces its origins to Marie Thérèse Coin Coin, a Black woman whose place of birth (Africa or Louisiana) remains unclear (Mills 1977). While enslaved, she had a number of children fathered by a white Frenchman who then legally freed her. Her family grew to become the largest legally free family of color who owned enslaved persons in the United States.

Marie Thérèse Coin Coin's experience was unusual but not unique (Schafer 2013). It reflected common patterns of sexual relations between white men with power and enslaved women of color in the South, and especially in the lower South (Hodes 1997). Many women in these relationships received various benefits in kind, including preferential labor duties and often access to legal freedom. Their children often fared even better. In other words, most of the legally free people of color who became wealthy and/or owners of enslaved persons across the South, or who secured top economic positions during slavery, were of mixed ancestry, and most "were the children or grandchildren of White planters or merchants and slave women" (Schweninger 1990, 35). Some rose to what can only be described as a dubious but spectacular success, given the racial system of the day and the obstacles confronting them (Leslie 1995; Alexander 1991).

This was not the experience of most Black women or many women of mixed origins, the vast majority of whom remained enslaved, unaccustomed to privilege, and subject to the whims and caprices of their white male owners. Across the South, as a whole, only a small percentage of the economic upper class of legally free people of color was female, that is, around 13 percent, and most of them had become legally free mainly via self-purchase. But "more than one-third of the most prosperous group in the Deep South

(36 percent) were free women of color, often mulatto women who had lived with White men or inherited estates from White merchants or planters" (Schweninger 1990, 45). The descendants of this group of people in the Cane River region became known as the Cane River Creoles, and some of them continued to occupy the same land where their ancestors' plantations stood into the twenty-first century (Shiver and Whitehead 2012).

From the moment Europeans arrived in the area, the economics, politics, and culture of the French dominated the region and town of Natchitoches, suppressing Native Americans and introducing increasing numbers of enslaved Blacks (both Africans and African Americans) (Burton and Smith 2008). The Spanish wrested control of the colony from the French in 1763 before it was briefly returned to the French, under Napoleon I, in 1801. Napoleon I then sold Louisiana to the United States in 1803, and the territory that was to become the State of Louisiana (in 1812) was first named the Territory of Orleans (Din 1999). By this date, the national and ethnic differences left by the French and Spanish presence—what I call *the Natchitoches twist*— were well embedded. The Louisiana Purchase was the largest peaceful land acquisition in US history, containing territory that eventually comprised parts of fifteen states and two Canadian provinces, stretching from the Gulf of Mexico to Canada. For this land the United States paid around $15 million. It was regarded as a crowning achievement for President Thomas Jefferson. From this time on, the number of whites who were not of French or Spanish origin dramatically increased and became known as "Anglos."

During these developments, the enslaved population in Natchitoches became larger through both natural increase and forced importations. In 1785, the total population of Natchitoches was 756 (Biographical Memoirs 1890). By 1810, it was 2,870, of whom there were 1,213 Caucasians, "181 free colored," and 1,476 enslaved (ibid.). By 1830, there were 3,802 whites and 3,571 enslaved; by 1850, there were 5,466 whites and 7,881 enslaved; and by 1860, there were 6,306 whites and 9,434 enslaved (Blake 2002; Mills 1977; Menn 1964).

At the same time, white men continued to take sexual advantage of enslaved Black and other women of color and the population of mixed origins continued to grow. As they developed a separate identity, many in the population of mixed origins also actively sought relationships with one another rather than with Blacks or whites. This was especially the case among the legally free population that gained access to wealth and power (Schweninger 1990). By the middle of the nineteenth century, some individual families of mixed origins matched and surpassed local whites in wealth, plantation size, and sometimes in the numbers of enslaved persons they owned (Mills 1977).

The number of legally free people of color in Natchitoches remained small for some time. For example, in 1776, out of a population of 1,021 people of color, there were only 8 legally free among them (Mills 1977, 23). By 1810, their numbers had increased to 181; by 1820, to 415; by 1840, to 657; by 1850, to 881; and by 1860, to 959 (ibid., 79).

Over time, the small farms owned by white people grew into larger plantations, which were further consolidated, and increasingly concentrated in the hands of a smaller and smaller elite (Burton and Smith 2008). This transformation occurred steadily under the Spanish and French. It advanced rapidly under the Anglos once Louisiana became a state in 1812 (Malone 1992).

Anglos had begun settling in this region long before the Americans controlled it, and they had been encouraged to do so by the Spanish. The democratic, secular government of the United States and multiple elements of its culture were very different from those of the Catholic monarchies that had previously governed the territory. Powerful Natchitoches whites clashed with the American government and Anglo plantation owners over issues of public land, church and state, political representation, and the status of the gens de couleur libres (Mills 1977). They also clashed over matters of language, culture, etiquette, and social interactions, including gender mores (Shugg 1939; Biographical Memoirs 1890). In the end, Natchitoches' powerful Creole elites were forced to make compromises with the US government, and Anglo cultural elements became predominant.

The transition to American control also provided benefits for the established elites. For example, the United States brought the region renewed military importance. Two forts were built in Natchitoches, as it was on the border between Spanish Texas and the United States. For example, Fort Claiborne was established in Natchitoches shortly after the Louisiana Purchase, but was replaced in 1822 by Fort Jessup, located more than twenty miles west of town (Burton and Smith 2008). American arrival also led to the rapid expansion of slavery across Louisiana and, as the nineteenth century progressed, Louisiana became one of the largest markets for the purchase of enslaved persons from the upper South (Finley 2020; Deyle 2005; Tadman 1989). New Orleans grew dramatically, fueled by the economics of its "slave auctions," by the concentration and distinctive requirements of sugar production, and by its port (Conrad and Lewis 1995; Tadman 1989).

The arrival of the Anglos also changed the nature of slavery in Louisiana, including in Natchitoches. Under French plantation owners and their Creole descendants, slavery in Louisiana displayed characteristics distinct from slavery elsewhere in the South and from what it became under the Anglos. Scholars have documented distinctive laws, customs, and customary rights for both the enslaved and for (white) women (Taylor 1974; Shugg 1939). It has often been stated that these resulted in better treatment for the enslaved as compared with their counterparts outside Louisiana (Taylor 1974; Shugg 1939). For example, they highlight the far more varied racial hierarchy that existed in the state, with the emergence of a significant and powerful intermediate caste of gens de couleur libres (Foner 1970). All these characteristics were manifest in Natchitoches (Burton and Smith 2008; Mills 1977).

The privileges extended to people of mixed origins, especially the children of rich white fathers, or of wealthy parents who were themselves of mixed origins, were also distinctive. It was first suggested that these privileges arose from the mores of French and Creole culture, including a greater willingness than Anglos to recognize the soul and humanity of Black people rather than treating them as nothing but chattel. Yet, it's clear that white patriarchy played a significant role, as rich white fathers ensured that their children benefited from their wealth. And it's also clear that people of mixed origins, especially those that were legally free, worked collectively and often through families to maintain their distinctive status (Small 1994a, b; Berlin 1984).

Labor practices and legal codes under the French and the Anglos were different from one another, although the actual labor extracted was determined more by the labor requirements of the crop—whether sugar, cotton, or other—than the cultural practices of the master-enslavers (Follett 2005; Scott 2005; McDonald 1993). One of the changes that occurred with the arrival of Anglos related to legal manumissions. Under the French, the number and rate of manumissions of the enslaved was higher than elsewhere in the United States (Berlin 1984). But restrictions on legal manumissions became more and more severe as the nineteenth century unfolded, and access to legal manumission decreased significantly once the Anglos arrived (Berlin 1984; Taylor 1974). Other laws were changed too. Protestants increased significantly in number in the state, and there were changes in architecture and food consumption. Some things remained the same: for example, rates of mortality among the enslaved did not decrease.

Even with Anglo predominance, significant aspects of French culture persisted during the antebellum period in many areas, especially in New Orleans, in Cajun country, and in Natchitoches (Johnson and Yodis 1998; Dorman 1996). This was evident in the forms of religion, architecture, music, language, and food (Edwards and Kariouk 2004; Edwards 2002; Sexton et al. 1999), all of which would later serve these areas well for tourism later (Stanonis 2006; Mills 1977). It was also evident in traditions of Black culture—in the transformation from African to African American culture—which would also play a major role in tourism, not least of which in music, religion, and food (Stanonis 2006).

Of the Anglo-Americans who poured into Louisiana, some were rich planters searching for new lands to cultivate as plantations for profits; others were poor and working-class whites, seeking their fortunes and realizing their dreams of becoming planters and owning enslaved persons themselves (Malone 1992). Many brought enslaved Black people with them. Between 1830 and 1839, Louisiana's population increased 63 percent (Malone 1992). In 1835, enslaved persons were imported into Louisiana from other states in massive numbers, and the ratio of enslaved to free was 50.8 (Malone 1992, 29). The total Louisiana population continued to expand in the 1840s, despite the Panic of 1837 that plunged the South and the nation into a depression (ibid.). By the 1850s, immigration had slowed down in Louisiana.

The white population of the state increased from 21,244 in 1803 to 73,383 in 1820. It increased to 89,441 in 1830 and 158,457 in 1840. By 1850, whites numbered 255,491 and by 1860, they were 357,456 (Berlin, 1984, Table B, 398–99). The enslaved population went up from 12,920 in 1803 to 69,064 in 1820. In 1830, the enslaved numbered 109,588, and in 1840, they were 168,452. By 1850, they numbered 244,809, and by 1860, there was a total of 331,726 (ibid., Table A, 396–97). Similar patterns developed in Natchitoches. From a small population in 1803, the number of whites increased consistently through the early and mid-nineteenth century. By 1850, there were 5,466 whites in the parish (Sixth Census). The enslaved population of Natchitoches also rose consistently. By 1850, there were 7,881 enslaved persons in the parish (3,967 males and 3,914 females). By 1860, there were almost 9,500 enslaved persons in the parish, along with 621 master-enslavers (1860 Census). By this time, a small clique of established families had become the most powerful in the region, including the Prud'hommes, the Hertzogs, and the Metoyers.

Louisiana became one of the largest purchasers of enslaved persons, and New Orleans one of the largest markets for buying and selling Black bodies, bringing in thousands of enslaved persons from Virginia, Delaware, and Kentucky. New Orleans became the largest "slave market" in what was called the inter-state trade, or the domestic slave trade (Scott 2005; Johnson 1999). There were also significant numbers imported illegally from abroad. Although the United States legally abolished the international slave trade in 1808, the nation continued to transport hundreds of thousands of enslaved persons into the nation for decades afterwards.

The vast majority of nineteenth-century "chattels" were transported into Louisiana with migrating owners and professional dealers after 1810 or were the descendants of such enslaved people (Malone 1992, 251; Tadman 1989). In Natchitoches, however, the majority of enslaved persons were born and raised in the parish (Mills 1977). The remoteness of the parish from the economic power of New Orleans and the sugar parishes, and its far more limited waterway access, were significant deterrents to importation.

In Natchitoches, the Anglos had a significant impact in another way, by removing the Great Raft, a hundred-mile-long logjam situated on the Red River, north of Natchitoches (Mills 1977). From prehistoric times, this massive obstruction had made river travel any farther north nearly impossible. Removal of the logjam also had the unforeseen effect of making the main channel shift gradually away from Natchitoches. The river shifted direction in 1832 and had, by 1835, left Natchitoches with little trade, and "a small waterway" (Miller and Wood 2000, 18). The river bypassed the city almost completely by the 1870s, leaving Cane River open to riverboat traffic only during the rainy seasons. What was left of the river was later dammed to make the oxbow lake that exists there now. One of the consequences of this change is that Natchitoches developed far more slowly than other towns on the river, and thus by the twentieth century, its architectural and cultural style more closely resembled its colonial and antebellum origins than did other cities and towns in the area. This historical accident thus provided the town with one of the more appealing cultural and architectural landscapes in the region.

SLAVERY IN THE ANTEBELLUM PERIOD

Antebellum slavery in Louisiana and Natchitoches shared much in common with slavery elsewhere in the US South—its most distinguishing feature being the prevalence of chattel slavery and the economic exploitation of enslaved Black labor. Enslaved persons were primarily defined by African ancestry and were subordinated to all whites with the power of law, political and social authority, and when necessary, violence and brutality. Enslaved persons were bought and sold at will. Families were broken up, and whipping, branding, and physical abuse were quotidian and endemic (Burton and Smith 2008; Taylor 1974; Shugg 1939). Black women were subjected to the range of subordinations arising from the gender division of labor under slavery, including being victimized by sexual predators (Jones-Rogers 2019; Fox-Genovese 1988). Although economics was the primary motivation, racist ideologies, many articulated with reference to Christianity, were the most common and consistent rationalizations (Scott 2005). Paternalism was also endemic—a situation in which master-enslavers conceptualized enslaved Africans and their descendants as subordinate, dependent, and juvenile family members, rather than simply chattel (Mills 1977; Phillips 1920). Often held up as an ideology inherently superior to the brutality of Caribbean slavery, paternalism nonetheless included the not-so-savory aspects of brutal exploitation, violent punishment, and sexual predation (Jones-Rogers 2019; Genovese 1976). So it was in the US South, so it was in Louisiana, and so it was in Natchitoches.

However, the parish revealed features distinctive from elsewhere in the South, arising mainly from its French cultural background and population, its multitier racialized system, the long-established, interlocking network of families that dominated the parish, and its remoteness from the main seats of political and military power in the state. These differences included a distinctive legal system for governing slavery and the enslaved (including the rights of some white women to own enslaved property) and a racial hierarchy that recognized three distinct racialized groups: whites (all free), Blacks (overwhelmingly enslaved), and "people of color" (both legally free and enslaved) (Dorman 1996; Hall 1992; Dominguez 1986; Foner 1970). This also meant a significant social and economic role for legally free people of color that owned enslaved persons. This cultural distinctiveness included Catholicism, French language, architectural styles, the layout of plantations, and different types of crops. These features led to an isolated and unique social order (Dollar 1998; Mills 1977).

Slavery was the basis for the economic success of white people in the parish and it thrived in antebellum Natchitoches. The political and legal system was designed to serve the economic interests of master-enslavers in particular and to ensure the social and political superiority of whites in general. There were large numbers of enslaved workers on plantations and in other areas of work, primarily in agriculture. The size of the enslaved population in the parish increased steadily over the course of the 1800s and reached its peak in the 1850s and 1860s.

According to US Census data for 1860, the total population of Natchitoches was 16,697. This population included 6,304 "Whites," 959 "free colored," and 9,434 "slaves" (Blake 2002). According to Blake's calculations based on the Slave Schedule of 1860, there was a total of 621 "slave owners," including approximately 41 persons owning 50 or more enslaved persons (for a total of 3,622 slaves, or 38 percent of the parish total). Among those who owned at least 50 enslaved persons, the average holding was around 83.3 persons (Blake 2002; Menn 1964). A transcription of the Slave Schedule by Blake provides a list of these 41 slaveholders (Blake 2002). At the same time, 580 persons owned less than 50 enslaved persons (for a total of 5,812 enslaved persons, totaling 62 percent of the parish total). Thus, the majority of enslavers in the parish owned less than 50 enslaved persons and many had a small number of enslaved persons.

The majority of enslavers were, of course, white and male. For example, in 1860, among those master-enslavers who owned 100 or more enslaved persons were J. B. Blanche, Jnr, with 130 enslaved; W. W. Brazeale with 123; Marco Giva-novich, with 135; A. Lecompte with 234; J. Prudhomme with 120; Narciss Prud-homme with 104; Ph. Prudhome with 145; John Smith with 186 and Ambroise Sompayos with 104 (the total number is 11 owners with 100 or more) (Menn 1964, 294–301).[1] Thus, the largest owners were A. Lecompte with 234 and John Smith with 186. Among those owning less than 100 enslaved persons at this time can be found John Blair with 51; Suzette Buard with 55; Daniel Brown with 56; Joseph Henry and Company with 60; J. F. Hertzogg with 64; S. M. Hyams with 69; W. V. Lambre with 62; and Achill Prudhomme with 81. There are also several women listed as owners of enslaved persons, including Widow Czette Roubiew with 61 slaves; Suzette Buard with 55; Cockfield and Mrs. Benoist with 60; and Eugenia Lance with 62. And then there is Maria Bryan listed with 171 enslaved persons, but Menn suggests that she probably owned no land and that the enslaved belonged to Hardy Bryan, who was probably her son (Menn 1964, 294, fn3).

By this time, a small clique of established families, self-identifying as French and Creole (but presumed to be white, without any African ances-try) were the most powerful in the region, including the Prud'hommes, the Lecomtes, and the Hertzogs (Blake 2002; Mills 1977; Menn 1964). These families formed part of an interconnected set of families joined by mar-riage and business interests. For example, Menn identifies at least nine own-ers of enslaved persons named Prudhomme, with Ph. Prudhomme owning 145 enslaved persons and J. B. Prudhomme, 120 enslaved persons. The com-bined ownership of Lecomte family members totaled 680 enslaved persons (Menn 1964, 298).

Alongside this group were Creole families of mixed racial origins, the so-called free people of color. Many of these families—the Cane River Cre-oles—collectively owned several hundred enslaved persons (MacDonald et al. 2006; Mills 1977, 108–9). The Metoyers owned more enslaved persons than any other legally free people of color in the United States, at their peak 287 (Mills 1977, 109). And they wielded power and influence equal to, and often surpassing, that of many white master-enslavers. In the 1860 census, Menn lists "Aurora Metoya" as owning 119 enslaved persons. She was probably a member of the Metoyer family. By this time, however, the family was already in decline and had experienced its peak ownership of enslaved persons in the 1830s and 1840s (Mills 1977).

The majority of the enslaved worked on cotton plantations, and many plantations produced several hundred bales of cotton a year by the 1850s and

1860s. Other crops included "Indian Corn" and sweet potatoes. Plantations also had animals like horses and mules for labor, and cows, swine, and sheep for food. None of the plantations produced sugar.

Throughout the antebellum period, Catholicism remained the dominant religion, and shaped both family structures and lifestyles. French was widely spoken, and architectural styles, the layout of plantations, and daily routines were shaped by French culture. For example, bousillage was the distinctive style of building for many homes and common buildings.

Natchitoches also revealed one other aspect typical of slavery across the state and the South: the flight of the enslaved in a quest to escape bondage. The evidence for Natchitoches is limited because many of the newspapers of the parish are no longer extant, although clearly escape was a constant feature of slavery there (Mills 1977, 119). For example, as early as 1804, enslaved men and women in Natchitoches escaped to Spanish territory, because they were encouraged by the Spanish to believe that they would become free there (Taylor 1974). Several enslaved persons, who had just been newly purchased from North Carolina ran away from John Waddell's plantation, ten miles below Natchitoches (Taylor 1963, 182). There is also evidence of enslaved persons who ran away, including many so-called mulattoes from Cane River plantations, in the 1820s and 1850s. Mills says, somewhat disingenuously, "If runaway slaves were indicative of ill treatment, then perhaps Cane River owners were occasionally harsh" (Mills 1977, 119). Many enslaved persons fled during the Civil War (Ripley 1976). While whites who owned enslaved persons believed their treatment of their "property" was superior to that of owners in other states, this did not translate into appreciation by the enslaved.

THE *CONTINUUM OF COERCED ACCOMMODATIONS*

The slave cabins and other spaces in which the enslaved lived and slept during antebellum slavery in Natchitoches were varied, and on most plantations, cabins were not the first buildings constructed but were typically added as plantations became larger. They were built primarily for the interests of the master-enslavers and with economic profit, social control, and status in mind. But the enslaved used their coerced accommodations for their own purposes to socialize, to rest or recuperate, to sustain culture and religion, and also to plan resistance, escape, and rebellions (Glymph 2008, 2003; Vlach 1993; McDaniel 1982).

By the peak of the antebellum period, the majority of enslaved persons in Natchitoches (as elsewhere in the state) lived in the state's rural areas in a *continuum of coerced accommodations* that involved two clusters. The first cluster comprised purpose-built structures made of log, wood, bousillage, and brick (Miri 1998b; Poesch and Bacot 1997; Yocum 1996; Olmsted 1969). The second cluster involved places and spaces set aside by elite whites within the main house (for example, basements and attics) or in other operational buildings such as external kitchens, blacksmith and carpenter shops, barns, or pigeonniers (Miller and Wood 2000).[2] In the first cluster, it is likely that by 1860, enslaved persons in antebellum Natchitoches lived in more than 2,000 dwellings.[3] We do not know the precise number of enslaved persons living in each of these different types of dwellings, but it seems likely that the largest numbers lived in purpose-built structures made of wood, log, or bousillage. This is suggested by the numbers of purpose-built structures in the antebellum period, and the fact that the majority of workers on most of the plantations were field hands rather than domestic laborers.

Some information on the number of "slave dwellings," especially at the large plantations, is provided in the 1860 census (Menn 1964). For example, in 1860, on a plantation with 130 enslaved persons owned by J. B. Blanche, Jnr, are listed 30 slave dwellings; and on the plantation with 135 enslaved persons owned by Marco Givanovich are listed 30 slave dwellings. The holding of A Lecompte with 234 enslaved persons lists 70 "slave dwellings"; while that of J. Prudhomme with 120 enslaved persons lists 30 slave dwellings. The holding by Ph. Prudhomme with 145 enslaved persons lists 30 slave dwellings, while that of John Smith with 186 persons has 40 slave dwellings and that of Ambroise Sompayos with 104 has 30 slave dwellings (Menn 1964, 294–301). These accommodations refer to separate, purpose-built structures. It is not readily apparent how many people were living in other improvised accommodations or spaces, nor what the conditions of those spaces were like.

The purpose-built slave cabins and quarters at these plantations were used primarily for the enslaved who were field hands. The structures for field hands were usually located a relative distance from the house of the master- and mistress-enslaver and usually close to the fields where the enslaved worked. No separate arrangements were made for men and women, but there were some variations based on family size. Fogel and Engerman argue that in 1860, across the South, the average large plantation had 5.2 slaves per cabin (Fogel and Engerman 1984). In Natchitoches in 1860 the average number of enslaved residents per cabin was 4, and thus it reveals a lower average than elsewhere (Mills 1977, 120). When Frederick Law Olmsted visited the Cane River area in the 1850s and concluded that the colored planters had "large, handsome and comfortable dwellings," he did not mean the cabins (cited in Sterx 1972, 210). Mills maintains that "on plantations belonging to members of the colony, the average cabin housed only three slaves" (1977, 120). He continues, "The housing which was provided for the Cane River slaves was rudimentary, as was most slave housing, and seems to have been typical of that of the late antebellum period, as described by Fogel and Engerman" (ibid.).

The average number of enslaved persons living in each of these purpose-built units is difficult to calculate, in part because the enslaved were often counted over several plantations, they were always on the move, and averages do not reflect highly divergent local situations. One author tells us "We don't know the number of slaves living at Magnolia Plantation at this time because the census includes 'resident slaves' from other Lecomte properties. Inventories from 1840 to 1860 tell us some but not all who worked in specific areas of the plantation" (Keel 1999, 19). It was the same case elsewhere in Louisiana for owners of several plantations, for example, Oakley Plantation in West Feliciana Parish (Wilkie 2000, 54).

Many of these purpose-built structures underwent considerable changes in construction, size, and function over time (Miller and Wood 2000; Miri 1998a, b; Keel 1997; Keel and Miller 1997; Yocum 1996; Hahn and Wells 1991). In the first decades of the colony, when most agricultural units were small farms, the enslaved lived in makeshift accommodations and oftentimes in the same spaces as whites. This reflected the practical and economic realities of the day, especially on smaller agricultural units. As units got bigger and the enslaved population was enlarged, separate spaces were built. And as the primary considerations were economics and social control, cheaply available local material was used for the construction of cabins. This meant wood and bousillage. Some brick cabins emerged in the antebellum period, typically where local brick was economical.

In the second cluster of accommodations there is clear evidence—especially on plantations with main houses large enough to require several domestic servants—of domestics living in a variety of spaces inside the so-called main houses. One example of this at Natchitoches is at Oakland Plantation, where there was a so-called mammy room (also known on the site as a "nanny room"). Also, for most of the time that she was enslaved, Marie Thérèse Coin Coin worked as a house servant and almost certainly lived in the house (Mills 1977, 28). There were almost certainly others like her. Evidence from external kitchens, blacksmith shops, and carpenter shops at sites across Natchitoches is also highly suggestive that they functioned as living space for the enslaved (Miri 1998a; Keel and Miller 1997).

Some enslaved people also lived in homes inside the town boundary, such as those owned by master-enslaver families, including Lecomte, Prud'homme,

Hertzog, and DeBlieux. This typically involved space in the corner of a room, or sometimes a separate room or basement for "house hands." There were main houses with kitchens and servants' quarters, some even with stables, and thus many indications that the enslaved were living in them, or close by. Dean (2001) describes many houses in town belonging to planters that were big enough to have servants, including several houses belonging to legally free people of color. In particular, he mentions Tante Huppé, the home of Suzette Prud'homme in the 1860s, in which "the rear wing used to be the slave quarters" (Dean 2001, 59). Originally this house had two large rooms, galleries, and an outside rear kitchen and carriage house, although restoration took place from 1834 to 1845. It was the largest bousillage house in Natchitoches (ibid.). Some enslaved persons may also have lived in separate buildings adjacent to master-enslaver homes, although evidence on this pattern is not available (Wade 1964).

It is highly likely that some enslaved persons lived alongside rivers in makeshift, flimsy, or ephemeral accommodations, while still smaller numbers, temporary fugitives and maroons, lived in forests, bayous, or swamps on their own, or in small communities (Burton and Smith 2008; Din 1999). Evidence on the accommodations created by maroons (enslaved persons that had escaped, and their free-born children) in the south of Louisiana and in Florida suggests the improvisations that must have occurred (Landers 2000; Gomez 1998; Hall 1992).

These patterns demonstrate how a varied cluster of spaces and places, with living and sleeping places of the enslaved, that is, a *continuum of coerced accommodations*, which began in the colonial period continued well into the antebellum period. During the colonial period, both whites and enslaved lived, slept, and worked alongside one another, often in the same relatively small buildings. There was physical proximity but social distance. As the plantations became larger, the number of separate and distinct spaces for the enslaved to live and sleep increased, but many of them—especially domestic workers—continued to live in the same spaces as the whites, and thus the enslaved were never segregated entirely into separate structures. In light of the division of labor on the plantation, and the economic priorities and labor demands of the master-enslavers and their families, physical separation was not always practical.

The material used to construct purpose-built cabins varied across Natchitoches, Louisiana, and the entire South. Cost was a major concern as the primary goal of building slave cabins was not for the benefit of the enslaved, but for the benefit and aggrandizement of the master-enslaver, which included enhancing his status as a wealthy person by displaying how many chattels he owned (Vlach 1993; Upton 1988). Cheaply constructed cabins usually meant local materials. In some places, brick was cheap—for example, in South Carolina—and in others it was stone—for example, in Maryland and Texas (See Campbell 1989 and McDaniel 1982). Any other cheap material would also do, including locally concocted materials such as "tabby" in Florida and Georgia (Landers 2000). And of course, construction was shaped by the cultural practices and architectural styles of the master-enslavers, as can be seen from a comparison of the English, French, and Spanish areas in Virginia, Georgia, Florida, and Louisiana (Upton 2010; Follett 2005; Landers 2000, 1996; Walsh 1997). In Natchitoches wood, log and the local material bousillage were the primary construction materials.

The construction material of the cabins gives one indication of the likely quality of life experienced by the enslaved. Were the cabins functional in the cold and the heat, and especially in the humidity of Louisiana in the summer? The construction material also suggests whether cabins would survive for any significant period of time. Most cabins succumbed to deterioration or destruction from natural causes—including weather, humidity, storms, insects, and accidents, or destruction by humans (Miller and Wood 2000; Keel 1999; Miri 1998; Yocum 1996; Hahn and Wells 1991).

Evidence about contents of cabins in Natchitoches during slavery is also limited. For other areas of Louisiana and the South, evidence from enslaved persons and from master-enslavers provides important insights (Fleischer 1996; Douglass 1988; Starling 1988). Across the South, we know that master-enslavers and other whites, especially men, frequently went to the slave quarters to monitor activities or for sex (Hadden 2001, 117; Blassingame 1972). We do not have any detailed information for Natchitoches, but if we did, it is unlikely to contradict what we know from other places. For example, it is clear that the cabin residents were able to hide much of what was going on inside the cabins, including material goods and the substance of their discussions (Battle-Baptiste 2011, 2007; Franklin 2001; Rawick 1972). Black people maintained cultural traditions in the cabins in ways unknown or misunderstood by whites, including the expression of African culture, especially religious symbolism (Franklin and Lee, 2019). We cannot form a conclusive picture of what was inside the cabins based on evidence provided by the whites that visited them. More recently, however, there is increasing archaeological evidence about what was inside the cabins. Some of this indicates that Black people had a range of items, including valuables and cultural artifacts (Franklin 2019, 2001; Battle-Baptiste 2011; Singleton 1985). Additional evidence has become available for Natchitoches too (Brown 2008a, 2006).

Inside the cabins was a range of furnishings, including a bed and a chair or stool. Olmsted (1969) suggests that they were sparse. Mills offers similar conclusions, but says the cabins of Cane River were of better quality and bigger than many cabins elsewhere (1977, 120). Some cabins may have had a few decorations on the walls. The Historic Structure Reports (HSR) for several plantations draw similar conclusions on the interiors and interior furnishings (Brown 2008; Miri 1998a). Although lacking significant concrete evidence for Natchitoches, we can gain some insights by drawing on evidence from elsewhere in the state and the South. For example, there is the biography of Solomon Northrup, born legally free in New York, but later enslaved (Eakin and Logsdon 1968).[4] He was enslaved in several parishes close to Natchitoches, and in his biography, he provides some mention of cabins as places of rest and repose for the enslaved from long day's work; as places to harbor those in duress; and as places for the enslaved to socialize (ibid.). Northrup described the cabin where he lived:

> The softest couches in the world are not to be found in the log mansion of the slave. The one whereon I reclined year after year, was a plank twelve inches wide and ten feet long. My pillow was a stick of wood. The bedding was a coarse blanket, and not a rag or shred beside. Moss might be used, were it not that it directly breeds a swarm of fleas.
>   The cabin is constructed of logs, without floor or window. The latter is altogether unnecessary, the crevices between the logs admitting sufficient light. In stormy weather the rain drives through them, rendering it comfortless and extremely disagreeable. The rude door hangs on great wooden hinges. In one end is constructed an awkward fireplace. (Eakin and Logsdon 1968, 104)

This history of slavery and of cabins in Natchitoches raises two issues for my analysis of representations of both in heritage tourism in Natchitoches at the start of the twenty-first century. The first is that there was clearly no simple binary between slave cabins and nonslave cabins, as the enslaved population lived and slept in a far greater array of housing spaces than the cabins alone. Many, in fact, lived in close proximity to whites, frequently in the same spaces, and some whites were no doubt their relatives. The second is that cabins (and other spaces of coerced accommodation) were (and remain) ambiguous places (Small 2012). Whites and Blacks experienced them in very different ways, with different motivations. Whites liked to believe that the enslaved were well-fed, well-kept, happy, and faithful. The evidence indicates otherwise. The enslaved frequently secured additional food and supplies and they had their own goals, ideas, aspirations, and beliefs. We know that much resistance—passive and active—was conceptualized and elaborated inside the cabins, and that Black women were at the forefront of much of this activity (Jones-Rogers 2019; Franklin 2017; Camp 2005; Glymph 2003). They sometimes ran away. The necessary research on these issues for the Natchitoches area has yet to be done. There are many signs that this work will provide a far more critical picture of the nature of antebellum race relations than we currently have framed under the presumed magnanimity of Creole paternalism.

THE CIVIL WAR AND POSTBELLUM PERIOD

The Civil War reached the Cane River region in 1864, when Union general Nathaniel Banks was ordered to move his army out of Union-held New Orleans and capture the Confederate capital of Louisiana at Shreveport in what is known as the Red River campaign (Wells 1990). Union forces pushed through Natchitoches during their advance up the Red River, but before they could reach the area, Confederate forces burned cotton gins and storehouses to prevent their capture. Slave cabins were also burned at this time, and Federal soldiers on the retreat in northern Louisiana burnt buildings of various kinds. According to Johnson, "[b]arns, smokehouses, corn cribs, chicken houses, and cotton gins were destroyed as well as dwellings. Not even the cabins of the Negroes escaped the torch" (Johnson 1958, 225).

Midway to Shreveport, the Union army fell into a Confederate trap, suffering military defeats at Mansfield and Pleasant Hill. Banks began a retreat, setting fire to many communities along the way, including the town of Campti and Magnolia Plantation. No doubt, more cabins went up in smoke. The small town of Grand Encore was also burned down, as were other cabins throughout the state. For example, one mistress-enslaver in Terrebonne Parish relates how the slave cabins on her plantation were torched by soldiers, along with the plantation house, store, and other buildings (Harrison 2006).

Many whites in Natchitoches fought for the Confederacy. For example, "[t]welve companies left Natchitoches parish and joined the Confederate army" (Dunn n.d., 28, Cammie Henry Center). It was their duty, they felt, and their desire. Most of the planters in Natchitoches, including many of the legally free people of color, supported the Confederacy, directly or indirectly. Some served as officers in the Confederate army. Others provided supplies, funds, or knowledge and others encouraged local whites to fight on their side. Chattel slavery had long been part and parcel of their economic success, social status, and culture, and they were not ready to give it up without a fight.

During the Civil War, there was extensive destruction of property, significant loss of life, and financial disaster for many families. Whites suffered but Black people suffered far more (Taylor 1974). They had less political and economic power and were often targeted for random violence by both Southern and Northern whites. Taylor comments that during the Civil War in Louisiana, planters did badly and "the ordinary man in Louisiana" did worse (by which he means whites) (1974, 320–21). But, he adds, "however desperate the condition of whites, it was far better than that of Louisiana freedmen" (ibid., 321).

During the Civil War, most Blacks in Natchitoches and Louisiana remained on the plantations (Messner 1978). The majority of Blacks at Oakland Plantation remained there in large part because they were ordered to do so by the Union forces then stationed in Natchitoches (HSR 2004, 27; Breedlove 1999, 15). But they were not simply passive, as some negotiated for better contracts, wages, and conditions. Most failed, but some succeeded, for example at Oakland Plantation. Writing in the 1970s, Taylor relates that in Natchitoches at the end of the Civil War, "An 'insurrection,' which would probably be called a strike today, occurred on a Natchitoches Parish plantation in December, 1865. The freedmen resisted the authorities, but the only man killed was black" (1974, 92).

However, throughout Louisiana, many Blacks fled at the first opportunity, giving lie to the claim that they were "faithful slaves." For example, so many enslaved persons fled as soon as Union troops arrived that by fall 1862, there were "10,000 black refugees in New Orleans" (Conrad and Lewis 1995, 33). It is possible that some joined the Union forces to fight against the South. Given the volatility of the situation and the very real threat of death, however, the majority stayed put.

Despite the hardships, many Natchitoches Parish communities survived the Civil War. When slavery was legally abolished, all enslaved persons in Natchitoches became legally emancipated and the financial value they represented to the parish's master-enslavers was gone. The master-enslavers had lost the value of their enslaved property, and legal power over life and limb of the enslaved; but the now legally free enslaved had asserted their humanity, and made the next significant step towards self-determination. The constitutional amendments that conferred citizenship and the right to vote upon them were the next step.[5] The postbellum period produced new conditions, opportunities, and challenges in Natchitoches, in Louisiana, and across the South. Whites and Blacks, men and women, all newly positioned themselves in the context of a legal freedom that was deeply entrenched in conditions of political, economic, and social inequality. Though slavery was over, the various elements of Jim Crow segregation were already being developed and expanded. These elements would remain in place—in their distinctively paternalistic manner—in Natchitoches for the next ninety years (Crespi 1999; Malone 1999).

After the Civil War, the plantations remained the primary economic focus of the long-established planter families. Many families that had grown rich during slavery lost their property and wealth. Some plantations were destroyed, and others had their business interrupted to an extent that they could not revive it. Still others faced extensive taxes when the war ended (Shugg 1937). Some plantations and their cabins were lost to families and then broken up. For example, Yucca Plantation, which had been lost to the Metoyers in 1847, passed through the hands of several families, including a change of ownership after the Civil War.[6] By the 1880s, Yucca had been sold to Joseph Henry, and upon his death in 1899, it became the property of his son John Hampton Henry.

Other plantations were consolidated, and some were expanded. Several changed ownership after the war. The plantations operated in much the same way as before, despite some significant changes in structure and operations. Slavery was replaced by sharecropping or tenant farming and most of the so-called freedmen continued to be housed in the old slave quarters of the plantations they had worked on when they were legally enslaved.

Despite the devastation caused by the Civil War, the elite whites in Natchitoches retained significant relative power and influence as well as extensive connections across the city, parish, and state. Like whites elsewhere in Louisiana, they sought to reassert their power and did so with the force of law, all the institutions of the state, and both systematic and random acts of encouragement and persuasion, where possible, but with coercion, violence, and brutality when not. They did so by building on long-established networks of family, community, and business connections cultivated during slavery.

The ravages of the war, combined with low cotton prices, made the Reconstruction period (1865–1877) difficult for all the people of the Cane River region, as it did across the state (Messner 1978; Biographical and Historical Memoirs 1890). The postbellum period in Natchitoches produced many challenges for whites and Black laborers, as the groups negotiated new social, economic, and political relations. At the group level, these negotiations almost always favored the whites in general, and the former master-enslavers in particular. Jim Crow segregation, in practice and under law, became entrenched and encompassing, a means for whites to protect the economic, political, and social privileges over Black people established during slavery (Tunnell 1984; Winters 1963). Although Black people organized collectively to press for their rights and had some successes, they continually lacked the power and resources necessary to ensure that fairness and justice were achieved. That did not begin to happen until the civil rights movement of the 1950s.

There were variations across the South and uneven outcomes. In Natchitoches, for example, white paternalism was the main order of the day, and although Blacks remained subordinate in most regards, the literature suggests that they seem to have avoided the more extreme acts of violence, lynching, and aggression common elsewhere in the state and the South (Dollar 1998). But it was always an underlying threat, and sometimes violence, even extreme violence, occurred in and around Natchitoches (Glymph 2019).

Most of the families that held the biggest or most profitable plantations before the war prevailed, and they were largely able to keep their plantations. This meant mainly the white families and the Creoles that were known and identified as white. This was the case for Oakland and Magnolia plantations. Yucca Plantation, which had been in the hands of the Hertzogs since the 1830s, was sold after the war to the Cancanerau family. It was bought by Joseph Henry, renamed Melrose Plantation, and later, in 1899, became the property of his son and daughter-in-law. During this postwar period, Blacks became mainly tenant farmers and sharecroppers. Whites were determined to maintain political and economic power, and this involved restricting Blacks to second-rate land and to menial jobs (Woodward 1957). As it was in the South, so it was in Louisiana, and so it was in Natchitoches.

Now that Black people were no longer legally enslaved, they were seen by many whites as posing a threat to white authority and supremacy, and there was increased expression of hostility towards Blacks from many sections of the white population. For example, there was strident opposition to educational and political opportunities for Blacks. Some of this reflected the volatility of the situation; some of it reflected the anger of whites who felt their unassailable power was being taken away; some of it reflected the vengeance of whites who had lost property or family members in the war. None of it benefited Black people. Although the extant literature does not provide detailed evidence of systematic or random discrimination, there are some documented cases. And the fact that so few Blacks were able to develop independent businesses or farms is prima facie evidence of the obstacles they confronted.

For example, one author relates that many whites resented the Freedman's Bureau and distrusted them (Dollar 1998, xv). Nor was it exclusively about race or racism. For example, in Natchitoches, Catholics opposed education for Blacks because it spread Protestant and secular ideas (Dollar 1998, 5). There were exceptions. After the Civil War in Natchitoches, four plantations were ready to provide education for those who had been enslaved. Hertzog's was one of them, and he was ready to start a school for the "colored people" (Dollar 1998, 18).

Once again, Natchitoches revealed some differences that reflected its unique brand of paternalism. For whites across the state, "[p]ersuasion, economic pressure, and terroristic methods were used to intimidate Negro voters in 1868" (White 1970, 149). Overall, whites tried to lure Blacks from the Radical Republicans to the Democrats, and across Louisiana many parishes prevented Blacks from voting by reducing the number of polling places in Republican parishes (Taylor 1974, 239). In Natchitoches, the voters were mainly white, so these measures were not necessary, and many polling places were available (ibid.). Blacks in Natchitoches were convinced, persuaded, or coerced not to vote. In 1868, "[i]n some parishes not one Republican vote was cast. E. H. Hosner, Bureau agent in Natchitoches, claimed that a reign of terror interfered with Negro voting except where troops were stationed, and that freedmen were 'assaulted and hanged until nearly dead for carrying Radical voting tickets'" (White 1970, 150).

White League organizations worked to force Radical parish office hold-ers to resign (Taylor 1974, 285). This tactic was also put to use with success in Natchitoches in the mid-1870s. On more than one occasion in that town, whites broke up a meeting of Black Republicans. After some successes in this way, the White League went for larger goals, demanding the resignation of the parish judge and the parish tax collector. They did not resign, "but they left Natchitoches parish in haste," frightened for their lives (Taylor 1974, 285). Blacks were not the only targets; so were their white supporters. Thus, white Republicans were murdered across the state, including one in Natchitoches (ibid., 488).

There was clearly hostility, violence, intimidation, and the murder of Black people in Natchitoches, even if it did not reach the same extent as elsewhere, as for example, with the Coushatta Massacre in Red River Parish (Taylor 1974, 284). Democrats took control in 1877, and redemption from Reconstruction took place. White men tried to do away with white radicals. There were even some Black men elected to political office—like P. B. S. Pinchback, who became governor of Louisiana, and Oscar James Dunn, lieutenant governor of Louisiana—but they did not last long. Once they had lost power, Blacks did not gain political office again until the third quarter of the twentieth century. As Mills points out, "From this point forward, no non-white in the parish was elected to any public position, and their exercise of civil rights was marked by steady regression" (1977, 246). What happened in the rest of the state also happened in Natchitoches—politically, socially, and economically, the status of people of color declined for at least fifty years after 1877.

Overwhelmingly, Blacks and people of color in Natchitoches were denied political rights and had severely restricted opportunities for education, even at the basic level. The whites in Natchitoches, as elsewhere, envisioned Blacks as a subordinate and cheap labor pool and worked hard to ensure that they stayed that way. Blacks resisted and left the plantations in large numbers, as did Blacks elsewhere across the South, to head north and west, looking for better work opportunities and less racial discrimination (Foner 1988). Those who stayed did what they could, relying on their families and networks, and on their churches and religion.

Another significant development after the Civil War was the increasingly unfavorable environment for legally free people of color. As elsewhere in the state, legally free people of color lost more of their power and status, as whites had already been cracking down on them "with unprecedented ferocity in the mid-nineteenth century" (de la Fuente and Gross 2020, 182). Throughout the lower South, "the war and its aftermath spelled disaster for the great majority of free blacks who had, only a short time before, been among the most prosperous blacks in the nation" (Schweninger 1990, 47). In this period after the war, as elsewhere in Louisiana, radical politicians worked hard to reduce any recognition of people of color, no matter how light in complexion. They were largely successful (Mills 1977). Ancestry, rather than appearance or local acceptance by whites with power, became the primary criterion for who was Black and who was white, as the "one-drop" rule became firmly entrenched (Davis 1991). Most of the Cane River Creoles, especially those that had large numbers of enslaved persons, had offered their support to the Confederacy. This did not put them in favor with the white North. Many had experienced great economic losses as a result of the war: "'The road all the way to Natchitoches,' one observer said, describing the area where some of the wealthiest free people of color in the South owned their plantations, 'was a solid flame'" (Schweninger 1990, 47). They also lost their standing with local whites, who now saw them as more of an economic threat and sought ways to prevent their ascendancy.

This process involved changes in laws and in customary practice. For example, during the Civil War, Union commander Banks had declared that it was not practical or feasible to distinguish free people of color and the recently emancipated "negroes" from one another (Rousseve 1937, 98). Thus, "with the rapid decline of their economic fortunes came the disintegration of the pre-war clans of free blacks" (Schweninger 1990, 48). They tried to defend what they had achieved and maintain their positions, but for the most part were unsuccessful. For example, in 1890, the descendants of free people of color organized the "Comité des Citoyens" (Committee of Citizens) to promote and protect their interests, and work against Jim Crow laws (Rousseve 1937, 129). Any limited success for their cause occurred only in New Orleans; one prime example of this struggle is reflected in the 1896 Supreme Court decision *Plessy v. Ferguson* (Foner 2007).

Beyond plantations, other economic developments in the parish included an expanding railway system and a greater array of production and merchandise. The Bank of Natchitoches was founded. Agriculture faced hard times; cotton farming was dramatically and negatively affected, especially as a result of the infestation of the boll weevil throughout the South into the twentieth century.

The limited evidence available suggests that the majority of Black people who had lived in the cabins during slavery continued to live in them after the Civil War ended. They stayed by virtue of necessity, custom, and habit; they also stayed because they had so few viable alternatives, as was the case across Louisiana (Roland 1957, 138). Some families made a number of improvements and extensions, including adding extra rooms or other additions. Some cabins that had housed two families during slavery were now occupied by one family. Some cabins were also modified by white people after the war.

It was clear that the owners were still in charge and put their own interests first, especially when it mattered most. At Magnolia Plantation, for example, after the original plantation house that had been built in 1850 was burned down by Union troops during the Civil War, a reconstruction of the original house was built in 1897, using bricks from some of the slave cabins and from the original house (Hunter 2005, 35; see also Keel 1999, 35). After a change of ownership at Yucca Plantation, two formerly enslaved workers, "Uncle Israel" and "Aunt Jane," stayed on, after remaining there for more than fifty years (see chapter 4). Many other Blacks remained at the plantation as well (Teal 2008; Crespi 2004).

THE TWENTIETH CENTURY THROUGH THE 1970s

The railroad had arrived near Natchitoches in 1881 when the Texas and Pacific Railroad followed the Sabine-Red River divide, four miles from Natchitoches (McLeod 1936). Telephone service was introduced in Cane River in 1906 (HSR 2004, 35). At the start of the twentieth century, cotton prices rose, bringing a brief period of economic success to many of the plantations in the parish (HSR 2004, 35). Prices continued to increase and did so significantly during World War I. But the boom didn't last, and prices crashed in 1919. As the twentieth century unfolded, more modern machinery was introduced to the region (Malone 1996, 145–46, cited in Big House, HSR 2004, 38). This led to massive institutional changes, the growth of mechanization, the incorporation of the South into the national and international economic order, and the dramatic aftermaths of World War I, the Great Depression, and World War II. There were long periods of decreased labor opportunities as a result of mechanization, insect infestations, and economic busts.

Jim Crow segregation, with all its economic, political, and social inequities, remained in employment, education, and housing in Natchitoches throughout this period. For example, as Fischer notes, "White opposition to mixed schooling was virtually universal throughout rural Louisiana," including White supremacists' points of view, and outright condemnation of any education for Black people at all (Fischer 1974, 93). In some cases, white teachers refused to teach Blacks. In other cases where white teachers agreed to teach Blacks, some white communities would not tolerate white teachers in Black schools (Fischer 1974, 95).

There were exceptions, but not many. For example, there were plans to build some schools for Blacks in Natchitoches in the early twentieth century, and some local whites supported these efforts in order to slow down Black migration out of the parish (de Jong 2002, 76). In general, in terms of education for Blacks, "Most whites could tolerate it as long as the races were strictly segregated" (ibid., 93), while "In other northern Louisiana districts whites and Negroes apparently quietly agreed to ignore official directives and maintain separate schools" (ibid., 96). Although current published evidence is slender, I suspect that this was the case in Natchitoches. But it was not always so tacitly accepted. For example, "In Natchitoches, by one account, white boys drove Negro children from a public school and then drove the teacher away" (Taylor 1974, 473).

White farmers and planters in Natchitoches strongly opposed union meetings involving Blacks and intimidated anyone, white or Black, who promoted such activities (de Jong 2002, 110). There were attempts to lynch several people who opposed the status quo (ibid., 113). One case that almost resulted in death exemplifies opposition to labor organizing:

> The authorities in Natchitoches suppressed an LFU meeting and ran the union organizer, Clinton Clark, out of the parish. On the day of the meeting, July 27, 1940, about six hundred blacks had arrived in the town "on mules, horses, in wagons, trucks or jalopies." Whites

believed they were there to demand forty cents an hour for picking cotton and planned to strike if they failed to get it. The mayor warned Clark to leave town lest he wind up floating down the Cane River inside a sack. The police then arrested him, together with six union men from New Orleans. The latter were held for three days, Clark for three weeks. Upon his release Clark stated, "They filled my automobile with gas, gave me an escort to the Texas border, and told me to 'keep moving.'" State attorney general Eugene Stanley had sternly instructed local officials to prevent Clark being lynched. (Fairclough 2008, 53)

Most Black people remained on the plantations, including the three plantations in this study. I could find no evidence of any Black people achieving high-level, high-paying, or high-status jobs in Natchitoches before the 1980s. Jim Crow, even the so-called paternalistic version practiced in Natchitoches, would not allow it. Some Black businesses existed, but they were few in number and were confined to trades primarily associated with Black customers, such as funeral parlors, barber shops, and hairdressers. Some Blacks worked in the food industry, and others, especially women, worked as domestics for white families (Teal 2008).

Black people sought support and comfort in families, community, and churches, and they developed social networks across the state. For example, in Natchitoches, monthly meetings took place at the Bethel Baptist Church to disburse funds to needy members (de Jong 2002, 56). There was some trade union organizing, but the threat of the KKK and related white terrorist organizations cast its shadow even in remote Natchitoches.

The overall result for Blacks was significantly increased outmigration, as many Blacks moved to cities, especially in the North and Midwest, and even to California. Black people continued to leave Louisiana throughout the 1930s. For example, "At the close of the nineteenth century and in the first decade of the twentieth, the rapid development of the lumber and other industries and railroad building absorbed a large part of the most efficient Negro labor, leaving a serious shortage of agricultural labor" (Sitterson 1953, 316). Racist hostility and violence were a continuing factors too, including in Natchitoches (de la Fuente and Gross 2020; Rousseve 1937, 147).[7]

The first NAACP branch in Louisiana began in Shreveport in 1914. New Orleans, Alexandria, Baton Rouge, and Monroe also had established branches by 1925 (de Jong 2002, 67). Activities also took place in smaller communities. A branch of the NAACP also opened in Natchitoches in the early decades of the twentieth century (ibid., 68). But Blacks could only go so far, and some things would not be tolerated, even in paternalistic Natchitoches.

By the 1960s cotton agriculture had become primarily mechanized, "which virtually eliminated the need for tenants and other cheap labor on the South's cotton plantations" (Big House, HSR 2004, 40). The "cotton South" was an integral part of the world economy, and global factors—the availability of cheap labor elsewhere, massive reductions in the cost of transoceanic shipping, and dramatically improved systems of communications—shaped its success.

The overall migration of Blacks away from Natchitoches is clearly revealed in census figures. For example, in 1870, the US Census recorded a white population of 7,312 and a "colored" population of 10,929 (Blake 2002). By 1960, almost one hundred years later, the parish was listed as having 20,082 whites and 15,529 "Negroes." The white population had increased almost threefold, but the Black population only one and a half times, in the hundred-year period.

When the civil rights movement took hold across the state of Louisiana, it had some of its most active campaigners in New Orleans, but it did not have a significant impact on Natchitoches (Sartain 2007).

HERITAGE TOURISM EMERGES

The seeds of tourism in Natchitoches had already been planted deep in its soil long before the twentieth century unfolded. What grew—in the form of a thriving tourist industry by the start of the twenty-first century—is part of the legacy of slavery in the parish. The most important seeds had their origins in the establishment and expansion of French colonization, with its distinctive cultural patterns and multitier racial system. When slavery ended, there was both nostalgia and regret, but how it was experienced and how it was remembered or commemorated varied with families, and by race, gender, and class. White people dominated the public sphere, and Black people were allowed only in the private sphere or their own segregated communities.

The first commemorations and memorials to occur in Natchitoches after slavery were led by families, white and Black, in particular by the women in these families (Clinton 1995; McLeod 1936). They built on traditions established and cultivated during slavery, including family and personal commemorations and memorials, religious ceremonies, and dedications of cemeteries (Brundage 2018; Yuhl 2005). Thousands of women across the South worked "to redeem their fallen nation through memorial associations and Confederate women's groups" (Clinton 1995, 182). Confederate mythmaking was the driving force at the collective level and dominated the public sphere (Brundage 2005; Blight 2002). In 1894, the United Daughters of the Confederacy, established in 1894 in Nashville, Tennessee, became "a power force in the South during the first half of the twentieth century" (Clinton 1995, 182). Once they had established domination in the political, economic, and political spheres, few things were more offensive to whites than Black people commemorating those who had fallen while seeking to abolish slavery. Blacks dared not challenge them or offer their interpretations of the meaning of slavery and the Civil War in public.

Gender roles and expectations among white people, molded by patriarchy, shaped the prevalence of white women in commemorations. White women of all classes had primary responsibility for commemorating their dead husbands, brothers, and sons. Elite white women took the lead—they organized private services and remembrances, and they tended and decorated cemeteries and churches. A long tradition of women tending cemeteries had begun with plantation families much earlier. Other elite white women, excluded by law and custom from the political realm, found fulfillment in formal commemorations (West 1999).

A range of white organizations centered on commemorations emerged, and several set up branches or activities in Natchitoches. For example, the "United Confederate Veterans association of Central Louisiana" was organized in 1887. Among the four vice presidents was Colonel David Pierson of Natchitoches. W. E. Russell of Natchitoches was treasurer; and G. L. Tichel and T. Haller of Natchitoches were two of the eight-person executive committee (Dunn n.d., 21, Cammie Henry Center). In 1879, the Creoles of color formed the St. Augustine Historical Society to preserve a property of cultural significance to them, and they held a Creole Heritage Day festival each January to serve as a homecoming celebration for all Cane River Creoles (Keel 1999). Black people mainly commemorated in their homes and churches.

One person who played a highly influential role in documenting Natchitoches history is Cammie Henry (Becker 2018). Born to a planter family in southern Louisiana, she studied at Natchitoches Normal School, where she met and later married Natchitoches resident John Henry in 1894. They went to live at Yucca Plantation in 1898. By this time, the plantation had been renamed Melrose Plantation by John Henry's father, Joseph Henry. After her husband died in 1918, she began a writer's colony in the 1920s. Some of the most important Louisiana writers and several important southern writers spent time at this colony, including Lyle Saxon, Harnett Kane, Roak Bradford, Ada Jack Carver, and Rachel Field. Also, there was François Mignon—writer, columnist, gardener, close confidante of Cammie Henry and later agent to Clementine Hunter. Mignon's charm and writing skills, it was later revealed, were surpassed only by his mendacity. His entire life he claimed to be a French native who had escaped the Nazis; he turned out to be Frank Minett, born and raised in upstate New York (Ford 1991; see also chapter 4).

The many (white) writers and artists that stayed at the writer's colony generated creative work that became the fuel for the myths that were incorporated into heritage tourism in the twenty-first century (Becker 2018; Macdonald et al. 2006b). Many of them also documented Black life and culture, which was a main focus of their attention (Thomas 1991; Scarborough 1963; Saxon 1950, 1948, 1937). Kate Chopin had briefly lived in the Natchitoches area in the early 1890s, and she collected colorful information and insights that would later appear in her writings (Toth 1999, 1990).

Cammie Henry also identified and relocated a number of log cabins to Melrose Plantation, which she refurbished and used as accommodation for the writers (Cammie Henry Diary 1934; François Mignon collection, BV 115). The cabins were not saved as slave cabins per se, that is, not because of their social significance as the former homes of Black people. Rather, they were saved as examples of a disappearing cultural practice: log cabins.

A curious incident occurred in Natchitoches in the 1890s, which later contributed to tourism in the region; it involved a cabin at Hidden Hill Plantation (later named Little Eva Plantation in the mid-twentieth century). As is well known, Harriet Beecher Stowe claimed that *Uncle Tom's Cabin* was based on many facts of slavery, and even on some real people. Several authors claimed that the plantation in the novel, and the wicked master-enslaver Simon Legree who owned it, were based on a master-enslaver named McAlpine at Hidden Hill Plantation in Natchitoches. A cabin on the plantation was identified as the original Uncle Tom's Cabin and relocated by "A. L. Chapin of Louisiana, and D. B. Darling of Texas" to the World's Fair in Chicago in 1893 (*New York Times* 1898). The cabin was shown at the fair and a small price was charged for entrance. Apparently, it was not a big attraction, and the owners did not take it away after the fair closed. Several years later it was advertised as being for sale, or it would be disposed of. The cabin was never seen again.

After the story of the cabin and its alleged relationship to Natchitoches became known, several writers on Natchitoches, including Lyle Saxon, promoted the story that the cabin was from the region (Saxon 1950; Graves 1930). From the start, however, several local planters insisted that the cabin was a fake, and that Stowe had never even visited the region (DeBlieux Collection, CHC, Folder 101). Its authenticity was rejected (Cane River National Heritage Area Master Plan, n.d.). Promotion of the cabin or the plantation for tourist purposes has never led to anything significant, but its disputed origins are still mentioned. For example, in 2008, I visited the Little Eva

Plantation, a working pecan plantation, which was open to the public. There were several posters and newspaper clippings on display in the plantation store that related details of the story of the cabin from the 1890s and beyond. It is another example of how local incidents become part of local lore and serve to enrich the stories that attract tourists.

Another curious episode in Natchitoches around the time of Cammie Henry's ascendancy involves the "Good Darkie" statue. The statue was erected in Natchitoches in 1927 by Jack L. Bryan, a wealthy white business-man (Daugherty 2019; Handley 2007). The statue is a "life-size bronze com-memorative sculpture" created by Hans Schuler ("One of the most important portrait sculptors working in the USA") for $3,250 (half of his normal fee) (Handley 2007, 99–100). Reputedly the first statue at that time in the entire South to be dedicated to Black people, it was offered by Bryant and celebrated by some whites as a tribute to docile and compliant Negros and meant to be indicative of Black commitment to serving whites. Many local whites endorsed the statue and the idea behind it. For example, the Natchitoches Rotary Club supported the statue "and the message it embodied" (Handley 2004, 103). The statue inspired a poem by Grace Tarleton Aaron, published in the *Natchitoches Enterprise*, which praised it as a symbol of Black faithful-ness, loyalty, and the dedication of "noble slaves" (Handley 2004, 105). But it was also challenged by some whites in Natchitoches as an affront to the town—why should the first statue in town be dedicated to Negroes, they said—and an unwise use of funds. And it was considered by the few Black people who spoke up as an insult and an outrage.

The statue remained on display as a tourist attraction for decades, with some white visitors coming to the town specifically to see it. During this period, it "became the most photographed landmark in town, and appeared in innumerable postcards" (Handley 2004, 107). The fact that its unveil-ing was syndicated in newspapers around the United States helped. As the decades passed, the statue became known locally as "Uncle Jack" and was highlighted as a tourist attraction in newspapers, magazines, annual tourism promotional literature, and coffee-table books.

When the statue was first erected, most Blacks apparently said little to nothing publicly about it—not surprising given the legal, economic, and power inequalities in the town, after several hundred years of slavery, more than seventy years of legal Jim Crow, and the continued dependence of Blacks on white employers. They continued to say little to nothing publicly until the 1960s, when some Blacks threatened to tear down the statue. The African American magazine *Ebony* criticized the statue. The civil rights movement had occurred, Black power and Black nationalism had gained wide currency in the Black population, and Blacks no longer felt that they had to tolerate or remain silent about such insults. In 1968, the statue was moved to storage, and later on, in 1972, to the Rural Life Museum in Baton Rouge, where it has remained ever since. In 2007, I visited the statue at the museum. At that time, it was located out in the open on a traffic circle on the grounds of the museum. Sometime afterwards, it was again placed in storage, rumors emerged that the statue might be stolen and returned to Natchitoches for display in a museum for African Americans that was being developed there (Daugherty 2019).

Stories like these—and other stories more fascinating and cryptic—are the basis of the compelling myths that served as fodder for heritage tourism in the parish. And the people who were keen to see their parish promoted were more than enthusiastic in promoting and disseminating such tales (Macdonald et al. 2006b). Some such stories, even those that are clearly inaccurate, were circulated widely at the tourist sites during my research.

As the twentieth century unfolded, promotion of heritage tourism gained significant ground, not just in Natchitoches but across the South and the nation (Brundage 2005; Yuhl 2005). Because of its remoteness and relative lack of resources compared to other areas in the state (for example, New Orleans) and the South (for example, Charleston, South Carolina, or Savannah, Georgia) Natchitoches was slower than most to act—or did so with less success. The promotion of heritage tourism and architectural preservation were activities in which elite and powerful whites in general, and elite white women in particular, across the South were increasingly becoming active (Brundage 2018, 2000; Yuhl 2005). Elite women continued to play key roles. Annual festivals and Christmas events began in Natchitoches as early as the 1920s, including the very popular Festival of Lights, which began in 1927. Groups with names like the "Ladies in Calico," the "Belles in Calico," and the "Ladies of Natchitoches," became the basis of the Association for the Preservation of Historical Natchitoches (Cammie Henry Center; Natchitoches tourist literature), now the owner of Melrose Plantation.

As the town developed, prominent Natchitoches citizens prevented the destruction of important historic buildings. Others sought a permanent monument and testament to their culture, architecture, and way of life. Working conscientiously, they identified houses deemed to be of historic importance and romantic appeal, promoted annual and holiday events, and produced a wide array of tourist literature. They restored homes and prevented others from being destroyed by the relentless march of industrialization and progress. Overwhelmingly, they focused on the homes of elite, respected, and notable whites—both French Creoles and Anglo-Americans—central to the establishment and growth of the colony and the state. These included families like Badin-Roque, DeBlieux, Prud'homme, Hertzog, and others. These heritage promotion activities paid little or no attention to Black people, with the exception of Marie Thérèse Coin Coin and Clementine Hunter. Not surprisingly, Black people (and probably working-class whites) played little to no role in any of these activities, but attention was paid to legally free people of color and to Melrose Plantation. They also promoted information about exceptional (white) women, such as Cammie Henry and Kate Chopin. These efforts are comparable to initiatives on colonial and antebellum heritage in places like Virginia and South Carolina, and the leaders in Natchitoches had those places very much in mind (Yuhl 2005; West 1999).

These efforts were given impetus by federal and other funds for urban regeneration, and by opportunities for earnings from the promotion of tourism. They often earned awards that generated prestige and further publicity.

From its start, Natchitoches had been celebrated by its elite white residents as a place of southern gentility, accomplished (male-headed) families, civility, and romance. Proud of its uniqueness and its distinctive French cultural heritage, the parish's promoters helped the tourism push gain more and more momentum, and by the 1930s, it started to blossom. Some academic work contributed to the nostalgia and romance, including work by a white graduate student at Louisiana State University in Baton Rouge writing on the history of Natchitoches. She commented that "the new and the old truly meet in this little town so rich in romance and history. The Spanish, French, and American are co-mingled in a most fascinating manner. Over the town there is an atmosphere of peace, calm, hospitality, and congeniality" (McLeod 1936, 103). McLeod described a range of appealing houses in town and reflected on the nostalgia of the period (the 1930s) in ways that were highly selective and highly racialized. The writers at Cammie Henry's colony did a great deal more to promote the parish around the state (Scarborough 1963; Saxon 1950, 1948, 1947; Kane 1945). Others such as Kate Chopin did their piece (Toth 1990, 1998). Several of them helped cultivate Cammie's reputation as a person of good deeds, good intentions, and kind and considerate relations with all people (Kane 1945).

Lucile Prud'homme and several other white women who had formed the Association of Natchitoches Women for the Preservation of Historic Natchitoches also played their part (Big House, HSR 2004, 41). Working with the encouragement of Bobby DeBlieux, the then-mayor of Natchitoches and a key figure in the Natchitoches preservation movement, the family sold its plantation to the National Park Service (see details in chapter 1).

As efforts to preserve and promote Natchitoches heritage gained ground, with recognition among the powerful of the importance of plantations in tourism in Natchitoches, there was no consensus on whether slavery or slave cabins would be addressed. During the almost one hundred years since the Civil War had ended, the economic and political system of racialized inequality and power imbalances remained intact. Whites that promoted tourism in the main ignored or sugarcoated slavery, and the majority of Blacks in the parish, still largely dependent upon white paternalism for low-paying jobs, remained excluded from the heritage promotion business. Overwhelmingly, when the town promoted itself for business or tourist purposes, it ignored or downplayed slavery, while at the same time highlighting its rich culture filled with French and Spanish influences. This is exemplified in Chamber of Commerce literature of the time (Louisiana, Bayou Wonderland leaflet, 1944).

Outside sources were also useful. For example, scenes from the 1959 movie *The Horse Soldiers*, directed by John Ford, starring John Wayne and set in the Civil War period, were shot on location in the parish, and the publicity gave an added impetus to tourism. More steam was generated in the 1980s from the shooting of the movie *Steel Magnolias* in Natchitoches, including scenes at the local Oaklawn Plantation. The star-studded cast of women—Sally Field, Shirley MacLaine, Olympia Dukakis, Dolly Parton, Daryl Hannah, and Julia Roberts—brought Natchitoches back into the media limelight. Bobby DeBlieux, whose tenure as mayor of Natchitoches had already ended, was an adviser to the movie. Having attracted people to the parish to shoot these movies, the movies then provided the opportunity to attract more tourists to talk about the movies having taken place there. Both movies are frequently mentioned in the tourist literature and on the tours. Of course, neither provided as much capital as *Gone with the Wind*, but it was all in the same vein.

In practical terms, the promoters of Natchitoches placed overwhelming attention on elite, mainly white, Creole families and their distinctive way of life. Whether from ignorance, neglect or refusal; from an uncritical acceptance of the well-established southern penchant for foregrounding southern gentility and civility; or from embarrassment, shame, or guilt, the main promoters of heritage tourism in Natchitoches had other ideas in mind than to air their dirty laundry. For example, during discussions in the 1960s and 1970s, there was opposition expressed by some whites in Natchitoches to the plantations having any information on slavery, especially any significant information. Several members of the families that owned the plantations—for example Betty Hertzog of Magnolia Plantation—were hesitant to support critical attacks on their families as former master-enslavers (Thompson 2000). Laura Gates, the superintendent of Cane River Creole

National Historical Park, indicated that when the plantation was being set up for tourism, some people wanted hoopskirts, magnolia, and moonlight (Gates 2002, 39). A congressionally mandated study was completed in 1993, and the Cane River Creole National Historical Park was created in 1994. The family vacated the plantation in June 1998 (Big House, HSR 2004, 42).

FROM CABINS TO QUARTERS

As these events were unfolding in the twentieth century, many Black people continued to live in the cabins, which they modified to better meet their needs. Some families had by now been living in them for decades; eventually, the majority of the residents had not been born enslaved. Overall, the Black residents of the cabins tried to make the best of their situation. It was far from perfect. Racial inequality was widespread and opportunities for Black people were severely limited, but many of their basic needs were met. And it always looked like there were worse situations elsewhere. After all, Blacks were from the local community, and they knew it intimately and felt committed to it. They had developed a history in the community that kept them there, including family, social connections, and church.

Many Blacks continued to live in cabins on or near Melrose Plantation. No doubt some also lived in workspaces like the kitchens, the blacksmith shop, and/or the carpenter shop. Some had remained on the plantation after it changed hands in the 1880s and 1890s. This included "Uncle Israel" and "Aunt Jane" (HSR, Melrose 2005, 14). In fact, Israel and Jane lived in Yucca House up to the 1920s, before the writer's colony got under way. When Cammie Henry got to Melrose in the late 1890s, she found Uncle Israel and Aunt Jane living in two rooms of Yucca House (HSR, Melrose 2005, 16). Like other Blacks at the plantation, they continued to fulfill subordinate labor roles in agriculture, as well as in domestic jobs, such as cooking, washing, and serving. This meant that the majority of cabins on or near the plantation were occupied by Blacks. It is possible some of the Black people also lived in the main house, though we have no concrete evidence of that at this time.

Another resident at Melrose Plantation was Clementine Hunter. She had arrived there around 1900 with her parents and first worked in the fields. Initially they lived in cabins provided on site by Cammie Henry, and Hunter probably also lived in the main house for some time. And later on, after Cammie had died and Hunter had become a noted artist, she lived in her own cabin, which was still on site when I completed research (Shiver and Whitehead 2012; Shelby 2000). The evidence indicates that that cabin was not previously a slave cabin and had been built sometime during the twentieth century. While she lived in this cabin, she also included slave cabins in her work, such as Ghana House and African House. Black people continued to occupy these living spaces at Melrose Plantation until at least the 1960s. But the whites, except for François Mignon, pretty much terminated their residence after Cammie died in 1948.

By the 1920s, Cammie Henry had already more actively begun the process of saving some log cabins (including those that had previously been slave cabins) and moving them to her plantation (Cammie Henry Diary 1934). They were transformed into habitations exclusively for white residents. There were also some cabins in the recently established local art colony, which were not slave or tenant cabins, but reproductions. For example, funds collected from membership fees and donations paid for the building of a log cabin on Washington Street in 1925 that became the headquarters of the Natchitoches Art Colony. The cabin was constructed as an "authentic log cabin type by two of the few woodsmen who still knew that craft" (Mcleod 1936, 112).

Some Black people also continued to live in servants' quarters in the town of Natchitoches in the late nineteenth and throughout the twentieth centuries. Black labor, especially female labor, did most of the domestic work for wealthy white families, and there were lots of wealthy white families in Natchitoches during the entire period. During slavery, there were many houses in town belonging to planters that were big enough to require servants, including several that belonged to legally free people of color who also owned enslaved persons (Dean 2001). Many of the legally free people of color lost their properties after the Civil War, and they fell into and remained in white hands, even if they changed hands among families.

One example is Tante Huppé House. Antoine Prud'homme presumably built it for his daughter Suzette, circa 1851 (Dean 2001, 59). We are told that "Until her death in 1861, Suzette lived alone, but the cousins, aunts, uncles, nephews, and nieces used the house as a town one and servants were imported from the country where the various Prud'homme plantations were located" (Dean 2001, 59). By the start of the twenty-first century, the house still had eighteen rooms and there was an original Punkah over the dining room table.[8] Also, "the rear wing used to be the slave quarters" (ibid.).

However, the vast majority of cabins disappeared—as did many plantations across the region—although exactly when and how is yet to be documented (Matrana 2005; Rehder 1999). As stated earlier in this chapter, some were destroyed during the Civil War, others in the period immediately after it, and still others as the twentieth century unfolded. Bobby DeBlieux, born in 1933, remembered many cabins along Cane River when he was a child, but he said they had soon begun to disappear, probably as a result of deterioration and natural disaster (author interview, 2007. See also DeBlieux 1993, 1986). For example, at Magnolia Plantation in 1939 a tornado severely damaged the Cottage Buard, the eight remaining cabins, and the gin barn (Keel 1999, 21). During a tour along the Cane River that Bobby DeBlieux took me on in spring 2008, he pointed out where many cabins had existed when he was a child. He also took me to some very dilapidated cabins that still had residents. And he pointed out that his family house—Tante Huppé (a hotel at the time)—still had a servants' quarters and let me in to take photographs.

The evidence available suggests that between 1945 and 1960, a large number of the then-existing cabins and tenant houses were torn down by plantation owners, as were many other plantation buildings, such as barns (Keel 1999, 21). By the 1950s, most cabins, it seemed, had disappeared from sight and those that remained were in very bad shape. Some survived because they were never discovered during this long historical period, or only discovered recently. Cabins at the Oakland and Magnolia plantations were in very significant disrepair, as evidenced in the many existing photos of them at that time.

Carrying out research in Louisiana during the late 1950s, one author indicated that while some of the quarters of the past still existed at that time, they were not representative of the quarters of the past. He argued that the simple fact they survived suggests that such cabins had enjoyed better than average construction. He added that most of the surviving cabins were of brick, and that this was not the most common type of construction. This must have been in southern Louisiana (Taylor 1974; see also Vlach 1993, 162).

HERITAGE TOURISM IN THE TWENTY-FIRST CENTURY

By the start of the twenty-first century Natchitoches had become a major heritage tourist center with tens of thousands of visitors each year. An extensive landmark district was located within the city of Natchitoches. Promoting itself as the oldest permanent settlement in the Louisiana Purchase territory, Natchitoches boasted historic buildings, natural resources, social and cultural events, museums, and interpretive centers and activities (Historic Natchitoches 2007). The buildings and historic structures included plantations and houses, churches, and forts, as well as parks, lakes, and forests (Badin Rocque 2006). Many plantations remained open to the public year-round and many private houses opened to the public for special events, including the long-established Festival of Lights each Thanksgiving and Christmas.

Bobby DeBlieux played a significant and enduring role in all of this. An article in the local paper in 1979 described Natchitoches Historic District as "Louisiana's Answer to Williamsburg," and indicated that "It is interesting to note that within the Historic District of Natchitoches are found more colonial buildings than were in Williamsburg when the Rockefellers started their project for Virginia" (ibid., n.p.). It mentioned that under Bobby De-Blieux as mayor, the City Council had passed ordinances creating the district on the local level with "strict guidelines," keeping preservation in the old town west of river, and the new town development in the area east of river. Bobby DeBlieux said about his job as mayor: "I think it is my responsibility to see to it that our town grows but grows with livability." And "We don't want growth for growth's sake alone; we want to have a good place to live, an environment that is desirable, and a city where we can still bring up our children in a place with good schools and good opportunities" (ibid., n.p.). "I will, as mayor, always remember that it must not be any more important than the development of new jobs in the community," he said about the historic district.

DeBlieux was elected president of Museum Contents Incorporated by a local group. Its goal was to save important documents in private collections that were going to be dispersed. One major project was restoration and relocation of Roque House to the banks of Cane River in the middle of the Historic District. The bousillage house cost "a pile of money" to move physically to the historic district, but DeBlieux and his organization raised the funds to do it. This led to him becoming involved in Tante Huppé House and efforts to secure funds for the reconstruction of Fort St. Jean Baptiste.

Perhaps his greatest accomplishment was the acquisition of Magnolia Plantation. According to the same article, Museum Contents, Inc.

> just inherited 13 acres on [sic] the famous Magnolia Plantation on Cane River which contains eight brick slave quarters, the plantation store, the overseer's house, which is a raised cottage of the boussilage construction, the blacksmith shop with tools, the pigeonnaire, several outbuildings and the most magnificent thing of all, the only cotton press in the United Sates [sic] left standing on its original site. (ibid., 1979)

The Hertzog family donated the site but kept the main house. Bobby De-Blieux became very popular in Natchitoches—"this is our favorite son," said the article.

François Mignon had been forced out of Melrose Plantation when the plantation was sold in the 1970s, but he remained in the area, lending his support, providing information, writing newspaper articles, and promoting the work and painting of Clementine Hunter. Clementine Hunter had become a bigger and bigger local celebrity. The number and value of her works significantly increased, and her popularity was widespread (Lyons 1998). In 1974, the then-extant buildings of Melrose were declared a national historical landmark. Oakland and Magnolia would soon become tourist sites. And the scene was set.

The National Park Service played a central role in many of these activities. It had brought extensive resources to Natchitoches in the form of finances, personnel and management, technical advice, and research. Its influence was both powerful and extensive, and its presence had beneficial effects throughout the city and region. The National Park Service was able to build its work on a well-established foundation, as a wide range of heritage tourism activities was already established and had been cultivated by a network of experienced and active individuals, groups, and organizations long before the National Park Service became involved in the 1970s (Cane River Creole Heritage Area n.d.). Many of these organizations continued to play a central and frequently independent role alongside the National Park Service.

As mentioned in the introduction, heritage tourism in Natchitoches highlighted several themes. First was the cultural legacy of the French and of (elite) French Creole families, including architecture, language, religion, and food, as well as laws associated with their presence. A second theme was agricultural plantations and the working communities and lifestyles associated with them, including mention of antebellum slavery and postbellum periods. A third theme was the distinctive, multitier racial hierarchy that prevailed in the region, including the growth of significant groups of legally free people of color who themselves became master-enslavers. And a fourth theme was the emphasis placed on local notables, especially those who achieved national or international acclaim. Natchitoches includes several exceptional women who rank high among these community notables, including Marie Thérèse Coin Coin, Cammie Henry, Clementine Hunter, and Kate Chopin.[9]

During the research period, the region boasted Cane River Creole National Historical Park (which included Oakland and Magnolia plantations), Cane River National Heritage Area, the Natchitoches National Historic Landmark District, six other National Historic Landmarks, three Louisiana State Historic Sites, and the National Park Service's National Center for Preservation Technology and Training. A wide range of organizations also existed to promote and coordinate heritage tourism in the parish, including the National Park Service, the Creole Heritage Center, and several other preservation organizations that have ensured the historical integrity of the area. There

was a series of websites that advertised and promoted the parish. The result
was a beautiful region with enduring traditions and cultural landscapes that
recalled Louisiana's complex history, presented through the enhancing lens
of elite culture, the distorting lens of paternalism, and a blind eye to any
blemishes in the portrait. While this approach clearly pleased a large number
of people, it left many others dissatisfied, displeased, or downright angry.

Chapter Two

OAKLAND PLANTATION

Oakland Plantation is one of the two sites in Natchitoches owned and operated by the National Park Service (NPS). NPS bought the property to convert it to a national historic site, describing the family home and seventeen original outbuildings as the most complete Creole plantation in the South (Miller and Wood 2000, 21).

The US Congress established Cane River Creole National Historical Park (CRNHP) in November 1994. In 1998, NPS acquired a portion of the plantation for public interpretation, including all the then-standing structures (Haynie 2002, 96). It was purchased from the Prud'hommes, the local Creole family who had owned it for at least eight generations. The park consisted of Oakland Plantation and portions of Magnolia Plantation, both located along Cane River in Natchitoches Parish, Louisiana (Magnolia Plantation Complex is discussed in chapter 3). At that time, the park's physical resources consisted of sixty-three historic structures, impressive plantation landscapes, family and plantation records, and an extensive collection of tools, equipment, furniture, and personal items (CRNHA, Draft Management Plan, 2001).

Along with the other parts of the CRNHP, the Oakland Plantation site demonstrates the history of colonization, frontier influences, French Creole architecture, cotton agriculture, slavery and tenancy labor systems, changing technologies, and evolving social practices over the course of more than two hundred years. During the research period, the site gave guided tours of the main house (and front garden area), introduced a cell phone tour of the site (which began in 2010), and provided opportunities for self-guided tours of the grounds, which allowed visitors access to a series of buildings, including a cook's cabin, two intact slave cabins, and the remains of a third. A map was provided to assist with the self-guided tour. The cell phone tour allowed visitors to dial a number and follow an audio guide to various places at the site, and a narrator provided a brief description at each stop.

The website for the plantation (accessed June 8, 2011) provided a succinct introduction to the range of attractions for heritage tourism:

Though Oakland contains a fine example of a raised Creole plantation Main House, even more important are the 27 historic outbuildings still standing on the property. This rare wealth of buildings allows visitors to more completely understand life on a plantation. Prior to the Civil War, large plantations often were more like small villages than farms. Though plantations focused on producing cash crops such as rice, sugarcane, tobacco, or cotton, it was necessary for them to also grow food crops and raise poultry and livestock to support their large populations. A portion of the fields was often reserved for corn, potatoes, or other staple foods. Enslaved laborers were usually allowed to tend small personal gardens in their free time. Chickens, cattle, hogs, and turkeys were raised by most plantations.

and

Oakland Plantation continued to be passed down from one generation of Prud'hommes to another and parts of it are still farmed today. The Prud'homme family sold the core of Oakland Plantation to the National Park Service in 1997, and the last family left the land in 1999. It is now one of the two units of Cane River Creole National Historical Park. Cane River Creole National Historical Park is in the process of restoring Oakland Plantation to its appearance circa 1960. Its goal is to portray Oakland as a working plantation and offer insight into the everyday lives of all of the people whose lives centered around this fertile ground for 200 years.

Heritage tourism at Oakland Plantation had several distinctive features. First, since its designation as a heritage site in the 1990s, the NPS and successive park superintendents have made it clear that the site would cover all aspects of the plantation experience, including all the outbuildings and the wide range of residents at the sites—from the elite whites to poor whites and the enslaved in various capacities. In other words, the park would not focus solely on the main house and the elites that occupied it. In an interview in 2002, Park Superintendent Gates related: "It is the responsibility of NPS to discuss slavery and Reconstruction. When two plantations included among their property lists 175 and 275 enslaved people, respectively, it would be ludicrous to think that our interpretive program would not discuss the issue" (Gates 2002, 40–41). These views were emphasized during an interview I conducted with Superintendent Gates in August 2010. She said, "Most people who come to the park come to visit the big house. We are still trying to expand their vision of the past. We need to consistently remind the park staff about this. We want the site to be more inclusive" (author interview, August 2010). She made it clear that the site was under constant review and that she welcomed research as a way to review and improve all aspects of the site.

Second, the fact that the plantation was held in the hands of one family—the Prud'homme family—for more than eight generations is communicated clearly and consistently at the site. Unbroken ownership for such a lengthy period is uncommon at plantation heritage sites across the South and in that respect the site is distinctive. During their ownership, successive generations of the Prud'homme family created and kept extensive records, artifacts, and other items. These items—more than 250,000 of them—were purchased by the NPS when it acquired the plantation. A major portion of this acquisition includes extensive documentation of the history of the site, and a massive collection of primary documents is currently held at the NPS regional headquarters in Natchitoches. Most of these documents focus on the twentieth century (interview and visit to archives, August 2010). A large collection of nineteenth-century documents for the site is located at the University of North Carolina at Chapel Hill. The NPS collection also has several hundred artifacts, including metal crosses and other religious artifacts, baskets, and saddles.[1] It offers great opportunities for studying the role of gender, and the experiences of Black women and men at the site, for example, in terms of the records of transactions, work tasks, and other quotidian activities. Some of the artifacts are Native American. The collection consists of an impressive array of primary material, most of which has not yet been reviewed and evaluated in any detail. Collectively, the wide range of items conveys clear evidence of the dynamic process of Creolization in the region (Hall 1992).

Third, the site had an impressive range of buildings and structures, many of which dated to the first half of the nineteenth century. This included the main house (also called the "big house"), the plantation store and post office, two pigeonniers (dovecotes), the doctor's cottage, an overseer's house, a roofed log corn crib, a carriage house, a wash house, a mule barn that was originally a smokehouse, a carpenter's shop, the cook's house, two slave cabins (the north and south cabins), and the remains of a third slave cabin. All these buildings have significant historical value, both architecturally and in terms of the social relations they reflect in the history of plantation life. The site offered a guided tour of the main house, the cell phone tour, and options for self-guided tours. The main house (and its front garden) got most attention and was the only guided tour at the site, during which visitors were told about the architecture, the elite white inhabitants and their lives, and the furniture and other interior items unique to the house. The cell phone tour began at the welcome pavilion and then traveled through ten stops, including the main house, doctor's cottage, overseer's house, slave/tenant cabins, and plantation store. Visitors could also do a self-guided tour that provided the widest latitude and flexibility for visiting the site. Of course, these options could be combined in various ways.

It is the slave cabins and the treatment of slavery at the site that are of most concern to this book, specifically, the north cabin and south cabins, listed collectively on the site map as "Slave/Tenant Quarters and Ruins," and Gabe Nargot's cabin ruins. These three cabins are original to the site, although they were moved to new locations around the site for functional purposes when it was operational as an agricultural unit, and subsequently for purposes of tourism. The plantation had several other structures in which enslaved persons lived or slept for significant periods, and the main house also housed enslaved persons (and in the postbellum period, Black workers), for example, the so-called mammy room in the basement.

As described in the introduction, I consider this range of spaces as a *continuum of coerced accommodations* composed of two clusters. The first cluster included unattached structures built exclusively or primarily for enslaved persons. At this site, this meant the north and south cabins and the remains of a third cabin, named the "Seed House" and also known as "Gabe Nargot's cabin." Two of the cabins are labeled at the site as "slave/tenant quarters," and they have been the focus of extensive archaeological research and physical restoration. The two cabins are advertised in promotional literature for the site, and some information about them is provided to site visitors. There are occasional exhibits inside the cabins.[2] There is conflicting information about whether the third cabin was a slave cabin or not, which I discuss in more detail later in the chapter.

The second cluster includes locations across the plantation where enslaved persons were regularly accommodated, and for which we have evidence or strong indications of this. In this second cluster were the main house, the cook's cabin, a carpenter's shop, the carriage house, the mule barn, and the corn crib. The main house is included here because it houses a so-called mammy room (also known as the "nanny's room") in the basement, which was occupied by Black women both during and after slavery. In this second cluster, only the so-called mammy room and cook's house are highlighted at the site as places where an enslaved person once lived.

Overall, I argue that the cabins and other spaces in which the enslaved slept or lived were relatively incorporated into heritage tourism at Oakland Plantation.

FOUNDING THE PLANTATION

The original name of what is now Oakland Plantation was "Bermuda Plantation,"[3] founded in 1789 by Jean Pierre Emmanuel Prud'homme, a second-generation Creole of French descent. Prud'homme and his wife Catherine Lambre established Bermuda Plantation on a land tract thirteen miles south of Natchitoches granted by Estevan Miro, governor-general of Louisiana. Part of this land tract eventually became the location of Oakland Plantation (Miller and Wood, 2000). The Prud'hommes drew heavily on the use of enslaved labor from the very start, which kept successive generations of the family among the wealthiest and most prominent citizens of Natchitoches for more than 200 years. During this lengthy period, a series of Prud'homme family members, primarily led by men, continued to run Bermuda Plantation until after the Civil War. The name Bermuda remained until the 1890s, when the plantation was divided in two. Half was renamed Oakland Plantation and the other half was named Atahoe.

The first crops grown at Bermuda were indigo and tobacco. The Prud'homme family was one of the first families to raise cotton successfully in the Louisiana colony. The plantation prospered during colonial days, and then grew considerably during the early nineteenth-century cotton boom (Haynie 2002, 15; Miller and Wood 2000, 17). There was an American ban on the international importation of enslaved persons from 1808 on, but the Prud'hommes continued to smuggle them into the territory (Miller and Wood 2000, 17). By the early 1800s, cotton was already becoming Bermuda's main cash crop. The Prud'hommes stayed at the forefront of the region agriculturally, experimenting with crops, equipment, and techniques at the same time as much of the antebellum South was moving toward a one-crop economy.

From the very start, enslaved labor on the plantation was central to fueling its expansion, producing profits and advancing the Prud'homme family's good fortunes. The 1810 census lists Jean Pierre Emmanuel, his wife Catherine, and three children under age ten, along with fifty-three enslaved persons. By 1820, he had seventy-four enslaved persons; by 1830, ninety-six; and by 1840, 104 enslaved persons (Miller and Wood 2000, 17). There is no evidence describing the accommodations occupied by the enslaved in these early days, although Malone is almost certainly correct when she suggests that they must have lived in humble dwellings (Malone 1999). Evidence from elsewhere in Louisiana and the South suggests that in these early periods, when farms and enslaved populations were small, whites and Blacks often lived and worked in the same spaces (Hall 1992; Kulikoff 1986; Blassingame 1972). As the farms expanded to become plantations, small cabins were built. In the absence of evidence to the contrary, we can assume it likely that the same pattern developed at Oakland Plantation.

PLANTATION GROWTH INTO THE ANTEBELLUM PERIOD

Bermuda continued its steady growth during the first half of the nineteenth century, although its fortunes corresponded, in terms of ebbs and flows, to the changing economic fortunes of the South more generally, and of Louisiana in particular. This included varying economic conditions in the 1830s and 1840s (Malone 1999). Phanor Prud'homme (1807–1865), the third son of Jean Pierre Emmanuel, took over plantation management around 1835 (Miller and Wood 2000, 17). By 1850, he had increased his human property to 124 enslaved persons and expanded the plantation to 1,800 acres. By the 1850s, things were looking up for the family. The plantation was producing significant profits to enrich the family. The older son went off to college in New Haven, and there was family consolidation at Bermuda. We are told in one report that "[t]he 1850s would be a decade of unprecedented prosperity for the Prud'hommes, if not one of unmitigated happiness" (HSR 2004, 20).

The 1860 census lists Phanor as having 3,400 acres and 145 enslaved persons in thirty dwellings (Miller and Wood 2000, 18). The next family member to take over was J. Alphonse Prud'homme, who attended the University of North Carolina at Chapel Hill, from 1858 to 1860, before succeeding his father, Phanor, as the plantation's supervisor. Slavery remained in practice at Bermuda Plantation until legal emancipation in 1865.

As early as 1837, Phanor Prud'homme I kept an account of corn that he sold to his enslaved workers, including "Lindor, Philippe, Gustin, Alexis, Jacot Zack, Malingo, Baptiste l'Anglais, Antoine, Gregoire, Charles, Alexandre, Belaire, Louis, Augustin" and others (see entries for March 6 and 14, and pages 1 and 7, month not stated, 1837. Prud'homme Journal for 1837, Vol. 2, UNC, cited in Malone 1999, n.p.).

In 1845, plantation records reveal that there were ninety-nine enslaved Africans working for the Prud'homme family, including: "Charles, coachman; Venus, cook; Hilaire, foreman; Bysainte, cow herder; Louis, cow herder; Phillipe, blacksmith; Solomon (Williams), blacksmith; Solomon (Wilson), carpenter; Lindor, weaver; Marie, house servant; Caroline, house servant; Martha Ann, washerwoman; Celeste, nurse; Nanette, hospital nurse and mid-wife; Alexis, shoemaker; Butler, brick mason" (Cane River Creole, National Park Service, U.S. Department of the Interior, n.d.).

Another document produced by NPS reports that "By 1853, 131 slaves were listed as plantation assets. Only thirty-seven people inventoried earlier appear on the 1853 listing. It is likely that the others were sold off or inherited as the plantation passed from one generation of the Prud'hommes to another" (Cane River Creole, NPS, US Department of the Interior, n.d.,3).

As the antebellum period continued:

Cotton picking records for 1860 have survived for Oakland Plantation. At Oakland, ninety slaves picked cotton during the last full week of August 1860. The top picker was Andrew, 24, who picked 335 pounds and averaged 248 for the week. With greater dexterity women were generally the equal of men in picking, and the second highest number of pounds on a single day, 330 pounds, was picked by Rosalie, 47, nearly twice the age of Andrew. Among the top pickers were four women over forty. (Malone 1999, n.p.)

One of the enslaved persons at the plantation was Solomon Williams, a skilled blacksmith. It is highly likely that he slept in the blacksmith shop, although we currently have no documentary evidence of this. He is briefly mentioned on the guided house tour as one of the key enslaved persons on the plantation, due to the importance of his profession.

The two slave cabins still extant at the site were built in the 1850s and 1860s. The "North Slave/Tenant Quarters (LCS No. 91638)" was built circa 1860 (Miller and Wood 2000, 26). The authors say, "Originally this one-room, dirt-floor structure with front and rear porches measured 31.7 by 24.4 by 18.2 feet. The rear porch has since been enclosed, and wooden floors added," (ibid.). The second slave cabin, the "South Slave/Tenant Quarters (LCS No. 91639)," was built in the 1850s or 1860s. It has been modified in the same way as the north cabin has, that is, the back porch was enclosed to create two rooms. Both cabins have "weatherboard and asphalt cover[ing] the walls" (ibid., 27).

Brief information about the enslaved workers is also recorded in the journal kept by overseer Seneca Pace in 1861, in which he describes some of the daily work routines, and we can get a sense of the ways in which labor was the primary driving force of activities at the plantation. Information from elsewhere suggests that the grandparents and, possibly, parents of Gabe

Nargot, the remains of whose cabin were at the site, were enslaved in the final decades of the antebellum period. However, clear documentary evidence of their experiences has yet to be discovered or revealed.

The kitchen, later known as "The cook's house (cottage) was built sometime between 1820 and 1870" and was "originally located behind the main house" (Miller and Wood 2000, 25). It was made of "bousillage construction" (ibid.). At the time of my research, no information was provided to tourists about the residents of the cook's house, though in all likelihood they were enslaved persons. It is also likely that they lived in the cook's house as well as working there. At the site during the research period, the cook's house was described as a slave cabin. The overseer's house was built for Seneca Pace in 1861, and he directed its construction (Miller and Wood 2000, 26). Seneca Pace was the overseer in the 1850s (ibid., 19).

The main house at Oakland Plantation was built between 1818 and 1821, and a number of Prud'homme family members lived in the house at different times (Big House, HSR 2004, 17). We do not know how many enslaved persons lived in the house, other than the so-called nanny or mammy. At the site, visitors were told that there is clearly evidence that other enslaved persons lived in the house, but that evidence has not yet been made available.

At the outbreak of the Civil War, the Prud'homme family—as powerful local master-enslavers, and in possession of more than 140 enslaved persons—supported the Confederacy in a number of ways. Phanor was among the wealthiest planters in Natchitoches as the Civil War approached. For example, in 1850, with only nine people reporting more than $20,000 of wealth, Phanor had $170,000 (Breedlove 1999, 39). Phanor possessed 145 enslaved persons in 1860, with only two other Natchitoches planters having more—Maria Bryan, who owned 171, and Ambroise Lecomte, who owned 234 (Eighth Census, 1860 slave schedules, on microfilm, 40).

Alphonse Prud'homme joined the Confederates in 1861, signing up with the Pelican Rangers, initially in Arkansas (HSR 2004). As discussed in chapter 1, he was one of many local white residents, rich and poor, who quickly joined the Confederacy. He was severely injured and became a prisoner of war, but he escaped. Because he was badly wounded, he was discharged from the military and returned to Bermuda Plantation. He later helped in recruiting men to the Confederate cause. Several other family members also fought for the Confederates, including Phanor's youngest son, Emmanuel (Big House, HSR 2004, 23–24).

Cotton planting at the plantation stopped after the April 1862 Union occupation of New Orleans, and of Baton Rouge shortly thereafter, due to difficulties in selling the product. In place of cotton, agricultural activities at the plantation turned to growing corn and other products, especially things that could supply the Confederate forces (ibid., 23).

The Prud'hommes experienced considerable financial losses during the Civil War. For example, 900 bales of cotton were burned at Bermuda (by the Confederates or "by Prud'homme himself") and the steam-powered gin was destroyed (Big House, HSR 2004, 26). The main house and its furniture remained intact, as did most of the plantation's outbuildings. These events had more adverse impacts on the plantation's Black inhabitants.

THE CIVIL WAR AND THE POSTBELLUM PERIOD

There were 145 enslaved persons housed in thirty dwellings at Bermuda Plantation in 1860, on the eve of the Civil War, and they did not remain passive (Miller and Wood 2000). Like elsewhere in the state and across the South, Black people found many ways to defend themselves and assert their rights, building on traditions, customs, and practices they had established for centuries (Glymph 2008; Dubois 1979; Levine 1977). Many men and women saw the opportunity for de facto freedom and took it. At Bermuda, for example, many left "with the Yankees in the spring of 1864" (Big House, HSR 2004). In 1865, Phanor indicated that all "the negroes" who did not leave with the Yankees—about thirty or so—were still with him and working on contract (Breedlove 1999, 104). Phanor negotiated contracts with those who remained. He died that October, and his son Alphonse took over.

When slavery was abolished, all enslaved persons at Bermuda Plantation were legally free and the financial value they represented to Phanor Prud'homme was gone. But while the Prud'hommes had lost their enslaved property, the enslaved were on the path to self-determination. Those that remained on the plantation after the war negotiated new contracts, either tenancy or sharecropping, and because they had so few resources (tenancy required renting the land), most became sharecroppers (Breedlove 1999, 45). Contracts were negotiated again in 1865, and then again in 1866, at which point the laborers demanded that they get Saturdays off work. Alphonse refused at first, but later conceded "Saturday PM" off (Big House, HSR 2004).

By 1866, the Prud'hommes were preoccupied with the plantation infrastructure, which included the outbuildings. They tore down a number of slave cabins and replaced them with new buildings, and they built a new kitchen (Big House, HSR 2004, 30). They were busy with plans to protect their wealth and heritage, maintain the plantation economically, and retain their role as the owners and managers. Their agricultural holdings remained the primary economic focus of the Prud'homme family, but they were also involved in other aspects of the economic development of the parish. This included efforts to develop the railway system, as well as to expand the range of merchandise offered at the plantation store, which was opened in 1873 (Big House, HSR 2004). The store was to be a mainstay of the plantation for many decades, fulfilling an economic function for the Prud'hommes, and also important social functions as a meeting place where plantation workers could interact socially. Workers were also required to purchase items there. The Prud'homme family was also involved with a range of financial institutions and was an original stockholder of the Bank of Natchitoches. In pursuing these economic activities, the family drew on all the advantages of race and class that it had long established in the parish and in their networks elsewhere in the region and the state (Haynie 2002).

Like others dependent on agriculture, the Prud'hommes faced many challenges during this period, including the infestation of the boll weevil throughout the South—overall, cotton farming was dramatically and negatively affected. At Bermuda Plantation, as elsewhere in Natchitoches, paternalism with all its racist elements prevailed (Dollar 1998; Breedlove 1988). Farming at the Bermuda Plantation continued under these new conditions. But the Prud'homme family remained the most powerful actors in these negotiations and Black laborers remained the main source of labor (Haynie 2002). For example, in 1865, in response to the view that the enslaved were now free, Pierre Prud'homme responded:

> That is very good in theory, and those who do not know the negroes take pride in that, for they do not know that the negro understands liberty only as a means of not working and of pillaging everything that they find . . . I still have all my blacks with me, they work as in the past with the exception of two or three whom I have decided to send away. (cited in Estes, 1969, 6)

Many of Bermuda's legally freed workers remained at or near the plantation, at first because they were ordered to do so by the Union commander at Natchitoches (HSR 2004, 27; Breedlove 1999, 15). In time, though, they worked the fields under Freedmen's Bureau labor contracts, then as sharecroppers or tenant farmers (Dollar 1998). Some, like Bermuda's longtime blacksmith, Solomon Williams, negotiated separate bargains for higher pay and a different work schedule (Big House, HSR 2004). A plantation commissary replaced the issuing of rations with a central location to buy supplies on credit against a year's harvest. In the 1890s, the two Prud'homme brothers partitioned the plantation, renaming the portion on the right bank "Oakland," while the portion on the left bank was renamed "Atahoe" (Big House, HSR 2004, 31).

And thus, at Bermuda there was set in place, by the late 1860s, "an imperfect system of tenancy and sharecropping (which) had become the arrangement of choice between planter and worker and began to bring some semblance of order to their relationship" (Big House, HSR 2004, 29).

Blacks at Bermuda continued to live in the same buildings that had been slave quarters. As the Oakland Plantation site map stated, "After the Civil War, sharecropper and tenant farmer families continued to live in these quarters as late as the 1970s." And a Black woman remained as "nanny" or "mammy" in the main house. Prud'homme family members and family members and descendants of Black enslaved laborers occupied and farmed Oakland Plantation until late in the twentieth century, continuing a relationship with the site that had spanned three centuries (Crespi 2004; Haynie 2002).

THE TWENTIETH CENTURY

Cotton prices rose at the start of the twentieth century, and there was a brief period of some success for plantations, including the Prud'hommes' (HSR 2004, 35). World War I saw increased cotton prices, but they crashed in 1919. Technological improvement in the early 1900s led to telephone service being introduced in the Cane River area in 1906, and the main house at Oakland Plantation received acetylene-gas lighting (Big House, HSR 2004, 35). The Prud'hommes then experienced a "precipitous decline in fortunes" (Malone 1999, 145–46, cited in Big House, HSR 2004, 38). To broaden their economic base, they added sheep and goat raising to their economic activities. The stock market crash of 1929 harmed them greatly, but they continued to farm cotton. By the end of World War II, the countryside was abandoned by large numbers of agricultural workers, including significant departures from Oakland, as mechanization kicked in. As the twentieth century continued to unfold, more and more machinery was introduced to the plantation.

The changing economic and political conditions at Oakland Plantation clearly and directly affected the plantation's Black residents. Economic misfortunes disproportionately impacted them, as did the growing use of agricultural machinery. Work requirements on the plantation severely restricted opportunities for education, even at the basic level. Black workers at Oakland Plantation continued to function as a subordinate and cheap labor pool. As time passed, large numbers of Black people who worked as laborers left the plantation "for better jobs and less discrimination in the North" (Big House, HSR 2004, 37). Extensive departures occurred around the time of World War I. The period around World War II saw an increased number of departures, along with a dramatic increase in industrialization "as tenancy and sharecropping gave way to large-scale, mechanized agricultural operations" (Big House, HSR 2004, 39).

Of course, many Black people remained at Oakland Plantation. We know the names of some of the families, some of their daily activities, the kinds of jobs they did, and their living standards. We also know about cultural patterns, including how they identified themselves (in racial or ethnic terms) and their religious beliefs. We also have many photographs of people at the Oakland Plantation over the decades of the mid-twentieth century, in the Cammie Henry Center and elsewhere (Teal 2008). Bobby DeBlieux also shared with me a number of images of Black people living in the cabins around Natchitoches, including some at Oakland Plantation. Some of these were of the children and grandchildren of Clementine Hunter. These sources provide us with an extensive amount of information, and they demonstrate some of the ways in which Black residents at the plantation attempted to make the most of their situation—economically and socially—throughout the Jim Crow period.

By the 1960s, cotton agriculture at Oakland Plantation had become primarily mechanized, "which virtually eliminated the need for tenants and other cheap labor on the South's cotton plantations" (Big House, HSR 2004, 40). During this lengthy period, the cabins continued to be occupied by tenant farmers and sharecroppers, all of whom were Black or of mixed racial origins (Crespi 2004). A number of improvements to the cabins were made by the residents. For example, many of the cabins that had originally been constructed for two families were remodeled for one family. These changes generally provided more room and space to families. By this time, local Black people were calling the cabins "the quarters," a name the Black community used for the entire period the cabins were occupied (Crespi 2004; Malone 1999).

As their business fortunes waxed and waned over the decades, the Prud'hommes improved buildings or moved them around the plantation. For example, they moved the cook's house from behind the Big House and they restored four cabins and furnished them so that they could be rented to fishermen along Cane River Lake (Big House, HSR 2004, 39).

A research project at Oakland Plantation carried out by a Louisiana State University student reported in the 1960s that "Peter Phanor's son, James Alphonse, currently occupies the plantation which still derives a portion of its livelihood from cotton. There are 400 acres left of the original tract. One of the original slaves lived on the plot until 1942 and his descendants remained until 1962" (Estes 1969, 5).

Estes also reported on one of the cabins on the site:

> It is most fortunate that this study could be conducted at this time, for I was able to record photographically the single remaining slave cabin on the plantation, which will in all probability deteriorate completely in a year or so. It is currently being used as a pigpen. It is of bousillage construction with vertical posts and lateral corner bracing. Its state of being allows details of this type of construction to be seen clearly. (Estes 1969, 4)

Estes provided several photographs of this very dilapidated "single remaining slave cabin," but he was mistaken about it being the last one. In his map/drawing of the site, the cabin is located just past the overseers' cabin. The cabin he mentioned is in fact Gabe Nargot's, now in ruins. There were two other slave cabins on the site at the time, also in very dilapidated condition. They were identified by the NPS, rescued, and restored. Estes must have overlooked them, possibly because they had sharecroppers living in them at the time and he presumed they were sharecropper cabins. The fact that Gabe Nargot's cabin was being used as a pigpen reflected pragmatic needs.

HERITAGE TOURISM BEGINS

As agricultural work at Oakland Plantation became increasingly mechanized, as its labor force departed, and as many of the buildings deteriorated during the middle years of the twentieth century, a different trend in the town of Natchitoches prevented Oakland Plantation from disappearing altogether. As we saw in chapter 1, several aspects of this trend had begun immediately after the end of the Civil War and had begun to gain greater steam in the early decades of the twentieth century. The main thrust of this trend involved efforts to celebrate the finer aspects of southern history, and the promotion of heritage restoration and tourism.

The Prud'hommes were involved in this pattern—in particular, Lucile Prud'homme, who was actively involved with the women who founded the APHN. For example, Lucile opened up Oakland Plantation for tours, made changes to the building, and created a museum in the basement. She and the women of Natchitoches were later joined in their efforts by Bobby

DeBlieux, a key figure in the Natchitoches preservation movement (HSR 2004, 42; DeBlieux 1993, 1986). DeBlieux saw Oakland Plantation as one of the most important sites for attracting tourists. DeBlieux's involvement was critical to the rapid expansion of heritage tourism in the parish. He was an indefatigable promoter of building preservation and heritage tourism, and he established and cultivated political and other connections across the state and the nation, including in Washington, DC. It was DeBlieux who encouraged the Prud'homme family to sell the site to the National Park Service (interview with DeBlieux, 2007).

The Prud'homme family was initially reluctant to sell their cherished home, but harsh economic realities led them to change their view. By the last quarter of the twentieth century, it was clear to them that opportunities for success through agriculture were dramatically reduced. Not only had most of the laborers departed, but many family members had also moved on to greener pastures. Yet the family still had its memories, and the NPS was now presenting an opportunity to institutionalize those memories. As one family member later noted, the idea of "tales of how the plantation was when (her grandfather) was a boy motivated the family more towards the dream of restoring the plantation to its once grand splendor" (cited in Big House, HSR 2004, 42). Similar views were expressed by the owners of Magnolia Plantation, including Betty Hertzog (see details in chapter 3). If it had not been for the intervention of the NPS, it is highly likely that representations of Oakland Plantation history at the site in the twenty-first century would have been far more nostalgic, conventional, and distorted than became the case. In 1997, the family sold the plantation to the National Park Service, and they vacated the plantation in June 1998 (Big House, HSR 2004, 42).

HERITAGE TOURISM IN THE TWENTY-FIRST CENTURY

A wide array of buildings could be seen at Oakland Plantation, many of which dated to the first half of the nineteenth century. Among them were the main house, the plantation store and post office, a doctor's house, an overseer's house, a roofed log corn crib, a carriage house, two pigeonniers, a mule barn that was originally a smokehouse, a carpenter's shop, a cook's house, two slave cabins, and the remains of a third slave cabin. There was also the Live Oak Allée, a "shaded avenue of live oak trees planted circa 1825," which is a popular attraction (Oakland Plantation site map, n.d.). When visitors entered the site, an Oakland Plantation site map was provided to assist with the self-guided tour. The map provided an introduction to the past owners

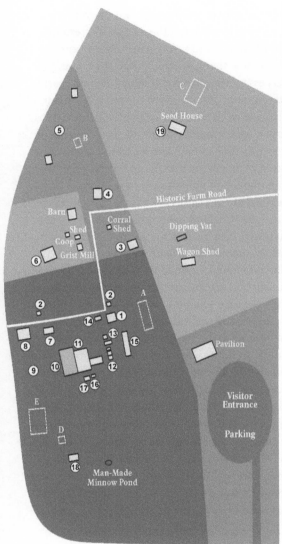

Oakland Plantation Site Map Key

1) Mule Barn
2) Pigeonnier
3) Square Corn Crib and Cistern
4) Overseer's House
5) Slave/Tenant Quarters and Ruins
6) Doctor's House (Park Administration)
7) Carriage House
8) Store and Post Office
9) Live Oak Allée
10) Bottle Garden
11) Main House
12) Wash House
13) Poultry Sheds
14) Carpenter Shop
15) Tractor Shed
16) Privy
17) Turkey Shed
18) Cook's House
19) Seed House (Park Administration)

Ruins
A) 1960s Cotton Picker Shed
B) Gabe Nargot's Cabin
C) Cotton Gin Ruins
D) Blacksmith Shop
E) Grass Tennis Courts

Map of Oakland Plantation. © National Park Service.

and the workers at the site, and listed eighteen locations, with brief details about each. Site management and staff indicated to me that the majority of visitors visited the main house and the plantation store, although there was also some interest in the various outbuildings, including the slave cabins. School groups often visited and depending on circumstances, toured the grounds or visited just the main house.

When my research began in 2007, there was limited and uneven visitor access to the slave cabins (as well as to the other outbuildings). For example, the cook's house was open, but the north and south slave cabins were usually locked. Visitors could ask to view them, at which time they would be unlocked by the staff. As with access to the other outbuildings, this was partly a matter of limited staffing and resources. By the end of my research, in 2010, the cook's house typically remained open, and one of the two slave cabins was regularly unlocked and open with a small exhibit on slavery inside it. This was despite the fact that by this time, there were increased constraints on the staff and dwindling resources due to the broader economic crisis that began in 2008 and had a strong impact on Louisiana, as elsewhere.

Many of the buildings at Oakland are of considerable historic importance. For example, one report notes that the "Oakland main house is one of the best examples of a French colonial raised cottage. It is the second largest house of its type in Natchitoches Parish, Louisiana" (Miller and Wood 2000, 21). The plantation store dates to the immediate postbellum period, and the carriage house to the 1820s. The north and south slave cabins date to the 1850s.

Tours were infrequent when the site was first opened in large part, it seemed, due to ongoing work and limited staffing. In 2001, Oakland Plantation increased the frequency of its tours and offered several forty-five-minute tours each day. Because the park facilities were still under construction, tours at other times were available on a limited basis, with a twenty-four-hour advance reservation necessary. The park superintendent at the time (2001) said that Oakland had established the new hours to accommodate the increasing number of tourists interested in the site. Visitors were told to come to the "Big House" five minutes before the tour was to start. The site also offered a small exhibit entitled "Memories Saved, Memories Shared," which featured photographs and quotes about Cane River residents. Several other regular, intermittent, and periodic tours and events have been held at the site.

The Oakland Plantation website in fall 2007 highlighted the cultural aspects of Oakland:

A cultural chorus of voices accompanies the echo of French colonial style that rings throughout the Cane River plantations. Skillfully crafted ironwork lingers on both Magnolia and Oakland as lasting evidence of the African hand in the area's development. Oakland survives as one of the last vestiges of the original Spanish land grant from which it was carved, while archaeological excavations continue to produce artifacts, which imply a historic American Indian presence on both sites. The Cane River community has evolved under the influences of the French, African, Haitian, Spanish, and American Indian cultures and Cane River Creole National Historical Park reflects those influences.

and

The Cane River meanders alongside both plantations, and has provided transport, sustenance, and entertainment for their inhabitants for many generations. Numerous live oaks gracefully enhance the entrance to Oakland Plantation, while Magnolia Plantation is dotted with the fragrant trees for which it was named. The natural landscapes of the sites are in harmony with those created by early agrarian settlers. Today, tempered growth maintains the intimacy of these fragile, embraceable landscapes. These elements work together to create the distinctive environment of Cane River Creole National Historical Park.

The site made clear efforts to describe the range of residents on the plantation. For example, the site map highlighted "Workers of African Descent":

The skills and strengths of enslaved African Americans are evident in the buildings they constructed at Oakland Plantation (originally called Bermuda). The proficiency of enslaved blacksmiths such as Solomon Williams, for example, can be seen in iron latches and hinges, in numerous grave crosses from the cemetery, and in a collection of skillfully made well-drilling tools found on Oakland Plantation.

and

Descendants of many enslaved workers remained at Oakland as tenant farmers and sharecroppers. These farmers sought to glean a small living as well as a bit of freedom from their labors. The vibrant African American communities in the Natchitoches region today trace two hundred years of cultural history to this fertile land surrounding the Cane River.

There were a number of African Americans associated with the site—as workers or volunteers—at the start of the twenty-first century who had family members who had previously lived on the plantation and in the cabins. Some had family members going back several generations. One, Leslie Vercher, worked in various capacities at the site. There were others who lived in the vicinity of the plantation and were involved in various temporary activities.

Typically, upon arrival at the plantation, visitors would see the welcome pavilion, close to the parking lot. Various types of information were posted there, including a site map, site leaflets, and tourist leaflets for other sites in Natchitoches, the vicinity, and the state. There were various signs and leaflets with practical information—about the heat in summer, the uneven terrain, and the need to carry drinking water and maybe a raincoat. There was also a restroom. Signs at the pavilion directed visitors to the plantation store, which doubled as another welcome office, and was usually the departure point for the guided tour of the main house. When resources permitted, there was a staff member or volunteer located at the pavilion to welcome visitors.

During the period of my research this site saw a number of significant changes, some of which represented improvements, from the point of view of representations of slavery and the slave cabins. For example, in fall 2007, both cabins were locked, and access was possible only with the assistance of a staff member, and there was no exhibit or other information inside the cabin. At that time, Peggy Scherbaum, the chief of interpretation for the Cane River National Historical Park, had already made substantial plans for an April 2008 conference on representing slavery at plantation heritage sites across the South.[4] By spring 2008, one cabin was regularly open and a small exhibit on slavery was on display inside it.

The Buildings and Twenty-First-Century Slave Cabins

As at most southern plantations, enslaved people typically slept in a range of buildings at Oakland Plantation in what I call a *continuum of coerced accommodations* in two clusters. The first cluster at Oakland—the unattached structures built exclusively or primarily for enslaved persons to live in—included the north and south slave cabins and Gabe Nargot's cabin. However, while it is clear that this cabin was in fact used as a slave cabin, there is ambiguity over whether Gabe Nargot was actually enslaved. The site lists it as a slave cabin, as does at least one report.[5] It seems clear that his grandparents, and possibly his parents, were enslaved, and may have lived in this cabin. The same report goes on to state that Gabe Nargot was born after 1865 (Miller and Keel 1999).

The second cluster included structures where we have evidence that enslaved persons commonly lived there, including the cook's cabin and the main house, where there is a so-called mammy room. It also included other structures or buildings where there was no available evidence but still a strong likelihood that enslaved or formerly enslaved persons lived in them at some time. This included the wash house, carpenter's shop, carriage house, mule barn, and the two pigeonniers.

I continue now with details from the cell phone tour, as it represented an innovation and provides a good indication of the kinds of information likely to be heard at the site. This description is then followed by brief details about each of the key buildings at the site.

The Cell Phone Tour

The goal was to provide an accessible tour to the many visitors to the site, according to Nathan and Tarona, the park interpreters responsible for the tour.[6] Visitors were provided with a one-page leaflet/map entitled "Cane River Creole. Oakland Plantation Cell Phone Tour Map." This contained a map of the site, a numbered list of the various structures at the site, which were also stopping places on the tour, and the tour's cell phone number, along with a phone number for contacting a park ranger, if necessary. There were also numbers to call in case of emergencies, including one for the Natchitoches Parish Sheriff's Office. The tour lasted sixty to ninety minutes. Visitors called the phone number provided and were then walked through a series of stopping places, with a short descriptive summary provided at each location. The cell phone tour actually covered both Oakland and Magnolia plantations, with stops 1 to 10 at Oakland, continuing with stops 11 to 17 at Magnolia. Many descriptive statements were made on the cell phone tour, some of which were written by the park interpreters, and others of which were quotations taken from research documents written about the site.

The map listed all the key buildings, including "Pavilion," "Main House," "Mule Barn," "Pigeonnier," "Carpenter Shop," "Corn Crib," "Doctor's Cottage," "Overseer's House," "Slave/Tennant [sic] Quarters," "Store and Post Office," "Cook's House," and "Backyard Main House."

The first stop was the "Pavilion," where an introduction to the CRNHP was provided, along with brief details on the history of Oakland Plantation and its owners and workers, including their multicultural backgrounds, which were a "combination of colonial French, Spanish, African, or Native American descent." It noted that "Oakland Plantation was a thriving agricultural community for nearly 200 years. The workforce was originally comprised of enslaved laborers. Following emancipation, sharecroppers and tenant famers worked the fields." The narration continued with a description of the range of jobs available at the plantation, including "doctors, blacksmiths, carpenters, laundresses, and store clerks." It described how to follow the tour,

advised visitors to be safe as they traveled the grounds, and invited visitors
to provide feedback by dialing a phone number. And it informed visitors
that "started by Jean Pierre Emamanuel [*sic*] Prud'homme in 1785, Oakland
would remain in the Prud'homme family for the next two centuries. During
that time span the family would endure the Civil War, outbreaks of the boll
weevil, and the Great Depression."

The second stop was the "Mule Barn, Pigeonnier, and Carpenter Shop."
About the pigeonniers, "the Prud'homme family housed pigeons in these
buildings, which they would harvest for pigeon pie or squab on toast." Basic
information was provided about how the mule barn began as a smokehouse and was later converted after the original mule barn on the site was
"destroyed in a lightning storm." The carpenter's shop was described as being
made of "hand-hewn cypress logs" and "covered with a coat of lime wash
paint," with a description of lime wash.

Stop 3 was the "Corn Crib," which was built "between 1820 and 1830"
as "a storage place for corn grown on the plantation." The description added
that "[c]orn was an essential part of the diet of the enslaved worker, and
also used as feed for livestock." A brick cistern to the left of the corn crib
was also described.

Stop 4 was the "Doctor's Cottage," where the narration began: "For much
of its history, Oakland Plantation was a thriving, self-sufficient farm community. Everything the Prud'homme family and the laborers needed was
here on the plantation, including their own doctor. Various doctors would
occupy this building throughout its history." It added that

> [s]lave-owners were responsible for the medical treatment of their
> enslaved laborers. Quite often doctors would make rounds to area
> plantations treating the ill. In some cases, like Oakland, a doctor
> resided on the property. The ailments of the enslaved were numerous.
> Due to their strenuous work schedule and environment, along with a
> poor diet, the enslaved fell victim to a variety of illnesses.

And finally, "[a]fter a succession of doctors, the doctor's cottage became home
to various members of the Prud'homme family." By 2007, it had become the
administration building for the park.

Stop 5 was the "Overseer's House." The overseer is described as "the manager of the farm," who was responsible for making sure that "cotton was
planted, chopped, picked, ginned, and pressed." He was also responsible
for "delegating labor to repair buildings, mend fences, and tend to the livestock." We were told that the first overseer to occupy this home was Seneca

Pace and that "he kept a journal of his activities at Oakland" that provides information on the "record of the planting cycle and other numerous labor activities." He frequently wrote about the weather in this journal. It was also pointed out that the building was the home of the Metoyer family in the "first half of the twentieth century," during which time "Leon Metoyer lived here with his parents, wife and three children" and that he was "the yardman at Oakland" and "tended to the animals and the yard in front of the main house." It finished with the information that "Leon's children are still alive and often participate in special events at Oakland, telling visitors about their childhood growing up on Cane River."

Stop 6 was the "Slave/Tennant [sic] Quarters." Visitors stopped at one cabin and on the cellphone tour this was called the "Slave/Tennant [sic] Cabin." The narration at this stop began: "These buildings were originally the homes of slaves, but for most of their existence they were the homes of tenant farmers or sharecroppers. Many of those families and individuals were former slaves or descendants of former slaves, who continued to toil in the fields where their ancestors had labored."

It then described tenant farmers and sharecroppers, "who did not own their own farms, and in order to work the land they had to turn over a share of the crop to the landowner" and added that "[t]hese people would shop for goods at the plantation store on a credit system. When the crop came in, they had to settle their debt with the landowner and the plantation store, and whatever was left over was their net profit." However, "[i]f it was a bad growing season, or if the boll weevil invaded the crop, the sharecroppers might be in debt at the end of the year. It was extremely difficult to get ahead under this labor system, so many farm workers from the south began migrating to large northern cities to find better jobs." And finally, "by the 1950s the small numbers of sharecroppers that were still here were permanently displaced by the modern tractor."

Stop 7 was the "Store and Post Office." Visitors were told that this was built after the Civil War ended "and quickly became a focal point of the community." The tour narration quoted historian Anne Malone as saying "the postbellum rural merchant was all things to his community. . . . His store was the hub of the local universe. It was the marketplace, banking and credit source, recreational center, public forum, and news exchange." It added that the store "also served as a post office on and off during its existence." We were then told that "the plantation store could also prove to be a financial burden to the sharecroppers. Quite often sharecroppers could not get out from under the mountain of debt that they accumulated at the stores" and "[h]istorian Carol Breedlove believes the Prud'hommes were kinder to their patrons then [*sic*] many of their contemporaries. She noted, 'Perhaps the Prud'hommes could have done more, or been more generous. On the other hand, they could certainly, in their environment and historical period, have done less, been less supportive and more selfish." The store "closed for good" in 1982, "as the numbers of sharecroppers dwindled."

Stop 8 was the "Main House" which, visitors were told, "stands as an excellent example of French Creole architecture that utilizes old world and new world concepts mixed with regional techniques." The details highlighted the history and architecture of the main house, informing us that "[a]s Europeans began settling along the Gulf Coast and Mississippi Valley they incorporated old world architectural styles to suit their new climate." It described the pitched roof "characteristic in French structures from Normandy to Quebec" and other "characteristics brought to North America from the West Indian Creoles including the elevated first floor, spacious porch, and multiple double doors." It added that such styles were also functional, for example, helping "to cool the house during the humid summer months." And it added, "One regional component of the main house and other structures along Cane River is bousillage. Bousillage is mud from the river mixed with moss or straw creating a brick like substance which is prevalent in the interior walls of the main house." It also described the oak trees leading to the main house—and that "[i]t was thought that the Oak Alley helped cool the home by acting as a funnel for breezes off Can [*sic*] River."

Stop 9 was the "Cook's House" where we were told that the building used to be located closer to the main house and "served as the cook's house." During the Depression, the house was moved to its current location and used as "a cabin for recreational fishermen." Finally, "[t]his building today stands as a great example of the family's ability to successfully adapt to and eventually overcome a difficult economic situation."

Stop 10, the final stop, was the "Backyard Main House." At this location, there were several small outbuildings including a "Setting Pen, Fattening Pen, [and] Wash House." Details were provided about the role of these buildings in maintaining the "self-sufficiency" of the plantation: the setting pen was used "to house nesting chickens," the fattening pen "was for chickens they planned to eat," and "[t]he wash house was where the laundry was done." The narration cited John Michael Vlach's book *Back of the Big House* to describe some of the advantages of raising chickens in terms of "meat and eggs," the low levels of maintenance they required, and that they "could be killed at short notice, thus reducing the risk of spoilage." And finally: "Laundry was originally done by enslaved workers, and then by paid domestics. Louisiana lore contends that on laundry day, people would eat red beans and rice, since that meal required little attention, giving folks time to concentrate on doing the laundry." The tour then ended.

Overall, the cellphone tour provided basic details about the history of the plantation, the numerous buildings on it, the range of people living there, and some of the activities that took place over time. It mentioned slavery, the Civil War, the transition from slavery to freedom, and the increasing role of mechanization at the plantation. The difficulties and struggles that enslaved workers and later legally free workers faced are described. But only the planters and their family are named, and the overall framing is about the whites, and their struggles, energy, and perseverance in the face of obstacles. This framing continued during the house tour.

The Plantation Store and Post Office

Preliminary information about the plantation store and post office was provided on the site map: "Store and Post Office—Opened after the Civil War, sharecroppers and tenant farmers continued buying their supplies for family and farming at this store until 1983." An assessment published in 2004 reported the following:

> Prud'homme's Store is a one-story, wood-framed structure set on brick piers, measuring approximately 41'-5" by 57'-5" and containing just over 2,000 square feet of floor space, which includes the front porch. The structure consists of the original end-gabled building (c.1873) plus a series of additions that brought the structure to its present form and configuration by about 1910. Not used as a store for nearly twenty years, the building remains in relatively sound condition, in spite of significant deterioration of the front and back porches and of porticos of the additions. (Prud'homme's Store, HSR 2004, 3)

Since that time, significant improvements and restorations have been made to the plantation store. The plantation store and post office were typically open for visitors. This building functioned as a welcome center and point of departure for house tours, and thus every visitor to the site had to go there. It also had some office space used by the park rangers.

The store began operating in the early 1870s and continued through 1982 (Prud'homme's Store, HSR 2004, 2). During this time, it had a wide range of items for sale and was more like a department store. It also acted as a

Plantation Store and Office at Oakland Plantation.

social center for the inhabitants of the plantation (Malone 1999). Many of
the records collected during its long period of operation—on purchases and
other transactions, for example—are currently housed in the NPS facility
in Natchitoches.

The store was a large white building with a rusted and corrugated iron
roof. Visitors approached it from the front and climbed a few steps or entered
by way of the ramp available for disabled access. There was a front porch and
several signs with tourist information on the front. To the right of the porch
was a large wooden barrel. A US flag was hoisted to the right, and a slate
sign on the floor of the outside porch level welcomed visitors—"Welcome
to Oakland Plantation." Another sign related "Bermuda Store, 1868." There
was an extensive array of oak trees standing off to the left of the building.
A poster standing on the porch related "Guided Hour Tours of Main House
begin here at: 10:00, 11:00, 1:00 & 2:00." This tour frequency occurred during
summer hours and was the case during my visit in August 2010. The poster
had a color photograph of the main house on it. In the small room to the
left, there was an array of leaflets and information about the site and other
sites in the vicinity and across Louisiana.

There were several rooms inside the store, but only two seemed to be open
to the public. The first room, as one entered the store, was small, and at the

side was another room that appeared to be an office. In this first room there was a big plantation bell, and several other items, as well as a computer on a table with a chair, for doing a virtual tour of Oakland Plantation. There were copies of various reports, including some of the historic structure reports for Oakland Plantation and Magnolia Plantation, which visitors might browse through. Copies of some of them were kept in a storeroom and were available upon request by visitors.

The second, much larger room was the main room, and it also contained an assortment of items. It was a large room with a long counter and various pieces of furniture. The room housed an exhibit that included a telephone and other items. It had a very overcrowded appearance with pieces of furniture all around, placed close to one another; there was a set of shelves that looked like a bookcase on the wall with various items on the shelves; a big fan on the floor; and various pieces of slate with information on them. There was a stepladder leaning against one of the shelves, and what looked like a weighing machine.

On the counter was a series of black and white photos that looked like "before and after" photographs of the various buildings on the site, including the plantation store and the slave cabins. Some of the buildings were in very dilapidated condition in the "before" pictures, and then looked great after being restored. There was no information provided about what was in the photographs. There were several leaflets providing information on various farming processes like cotton processing, and also on bousillage.

There was an exhibit inside the store in 2008. Much of the same exhibit was there in 2010, but there were a few additional items that provided more information about the history of the plantation. There was no significant change between these two dates. The several slate panels had titles like "Preserving the Store," "limewashing," "bousillage," "hand picked cotton," "machine harvested cotton," "Civil War," "tobacco," and "indigo." There were various and sundry items around the room, for example, bales of cotton, scales, and various pieces of furniture. There was a great deal of literature on Oakland Plantation and other sites, including Magnolia Plantation.

I did not see any images or mention of Black people in the main signs or in any of the images in the store. But there were descriptions and details of slavery in some of the NPS leaflets available there. Overall, my impression was of a store created to have the appearance of existing around the 1960s, just as the site indicated. I think this was successful.

Basic images, artifacts, and information about slavery and/or tenant workers were clearly documented in the exhibit and various items in the store.

But again, almost none of the information personalized Black people, and there was almost no mention of Black women.

The Main House

The main house was variously referred to as "the main house" (for example, on the site map and during the house tours), or the "Big House" (for example, in the Historic Structure Reports).[7] The main house got more attention than any other building on the plantation, as did the elite white residents who lived in it. It was the only location at Oakland that offered a guided tour. Tickets for the tour were purchased in the plantation store and post office, from which visitors were escorted to the front garden of the house. The house tour began in the garden and was led by a park ranger. After this tour concluded, visitors had the option of self-guided tours—with a map—of other buildings and structures on the plantation, or the cell phone tour. I did several house tours in fall 2007; several house tours in spring 2008; and a house tour in 2010. I also took multiple self-guided tours.

The site map informed visitors that "[t]he Prud'hommes' house is an excellent example of a raised Creole cottage. The brick piers allow air to move freely around the structure." The house was built between 1817 and 1821 and was continuously occupied by members of the Prud'homme family for seven

The Main House at Oakland Plantation.

generations before being sold, as part of the site, to NPS. I describe one tour here—led by a white park ranger, aged about fifty or so, who had a southern accent. She talked like she had been at the site for many years. She was confident and relaxed.

We were told that what was unique about this plantation is that nine or ten generations of one family had lived in and owned the house, and that the site had the largest number of buildings—twenty-seven—and was the most complete plantation in the United States. As we walked to the house the ranger said that there were two pigeonniers on the site and that, although they were close by, in the past they would have been placed at opposite ends of the plantation for symmetry and balance. She said that pigeons were kept for three reasons: 1) to deliver messages; 2) to race—"My pigeon can go faster than yours! Want to race?" type of thing; and 3) for food. Squab is baby pigeon that cannot fly yet. And it would be served on toast.

As we walked towards the main house, we passed a large metal bowl— the kind used for boiling sugar—that is commonly seen on plantations across southern Louisiana. The ranger said that sugar cane was grown on the plantation for domestic use and to feed people on the plantation but was never grown there commercially. She mentioned that such food was for the "enslaved labor" and then for what she called the "enslaved laborers."

The park ranger informed us that the plantation was still undergoing development and restoration: "We are still finding out new things about what happened here. And we are still making changes." She mentioned that lots of new things were being discovered about the basement to the house. As we got to the main house, she said that the basement was not open to the public and continued:

> We are working on it and discovering things. We are finding out that far more people lived under the house than we previously thought. We knew that mammy was here because mammy had a room, and she had a trap door to get into the house. She also used it to get up to the house to do laundry and to take care of the kids. But it is now clear that other people lived there as well. And let's face it, it was convenient because if they wanted assistance they would just stomp on the floor.

At this point, she stomped on the floor and several of the visitors laughed. So, in addition to the so-called mammy, there were other workers whom it was convenient to have in the basement. She added that the staff at the site were also very "overstretched" with multiple tours and nonstop visitors, even over the winter. We went next to the "bottle garden," which she said contained over 2,500 bottles. Visitors were not allowed in the garden because of the value and delicacy of the bottles. She added, "They don't want us to know how much they are worth." And, "Maybe they don't want us to take any," she joked. She pointed out that in the past, the garden would not have had grass in between the flowers, as it does now—it would have been dirt and the dirt would have been swept, not raked, as the grass is done nowadays.

We went up to the porch and the ranger described the "stranger's room," which had an outside door. Strangers who were traveling would be allowed to sleep in the room and would not have to pay. Any news they brought to the house—from, say, New Orleans, Baton Rouge, Alexandria, or other places—would be regarded as payment. Stranger rooms had an outside door only, designed for the safety of the house residents. And they had outside access only. We were told that the porch retained its original cypress floor. The park ranger added, "If you want anything made in Louisiana you make it of cypress—it lasts forever and ever!"

We entered the house, proceeded through all the rooms, and exited at the back. The tour was typical of many I had been on—details of the decorative elegance, family origins and history, curious elements, and idiosyncrasies of several objects. Some of the personal interests of the ranger were evident as well, for example, her favorite items or her particular way of looking at the house. She told us that most of the house was built between 1817 and 1821, with some additions made immediately in 1821 when the family came back from Europe and some of their new furniture could not fit into the house. We were told details of the nineteenth-century policy of families having to pay taxes on doors, thus there were windows you could walk in and out of. We were also reminded that taxes were paid on chimneys: "This chimney has four fireplaces, two on the first floor and two in the basement. This tells us that people must have lived in the basement."

The park ranger described several of the portraits, including one of Ambroise Lecomte, whose daughter married a Prud'homme. The daughter brought the portrait to the house with her so that people would know that he was her father. This was because Ambroise was much richer than the Prud'hommes and had more plantations. She told us more of the family history. She described the portrait of a woman in "mourning" dress and told us that she herself was a student working on the history of "mourning" dresses. The next room was the children's room, which contained two beds, with lots of decorations at their tops.

She then informed us that the plantation era really ended in the 1960s, which is when most labor stopped being done. We entered the master bedroom, which we were told was added on in 1822. All the furniture in the house was basically what was there in the 1960s. "We have photographs of it," the ranger commented, and also "people's memories" of what it was like then. She pointed to the corner of the room and said that that was where there used to be a "trap door" for mammy, but that the trap door had been covered up by the National Park Service. Now it had a rocking chair next to it and it is next to a chimney, so that it was not possible to see the trap door. The trap door, said the tour guide, is where mammy came up to tend to the baby. The people in the room would just stomp on the floor and she would come up. She probably took the baby down through the trap door with her, the park ranger joked, "that is just what we need, so we can get a good night's sleep!" She then told us that there was lots of recycling done on the site. For example, the armoire was raised onto wood blocks as the family members got taller so that it would still be of use.

Next stop was the dining room, which contained books in French from the 1800s and a punkah (which is a West Indian word, she said), which operated as a large fan above the table. "They would have an eleven-year-old boy pull it," she said. "Why eleven?" she asked rhetorically, "Well, ten was too young. And by twelve they would be out working in the labor force. So, eleven was a good age. And the work they did pulling this, whether they did good work or bad work, would help determine what kind of work they did afterwards."

She said that there was a photo of "Miss Lucille" in the white case at the back, but did not tell us who Miss Lucille was, and no one asked. She said that this was how the room looked in the 1960s. The house had a telephone as early as 1909. She pointed to a cotton basket, "which is two hundred years old" and was made by "enslaved labor." It was called a cotton basket, but it was used to carry many different things. She described several other items, for example, the "his and hers" set and the moustache bar, which was used by the overseers. She added that "the overseer was the middleman between the planters and the slaves." She then said that Uncle Buddy's room was in the store (but she did not tell us who Uncle Buddy was). She continued, "They put my office in there. He was a guy who had very bad hygiene. I don't know what it means that they put my office in there," she joked.

We went through a long corridor that seemed to run almost the entire width of the house. The park ranger pointed to a trap door and said that this was another trap door that went down to the room adjacent to the wine cellar. The next room, we were told, was a bedroom. It had a narrow door to the gallery, which used to be a porch. This was called a gentleman's door, because it was narrow. Women with wide dresses could not get through it. Gentlemen went through it and smoked, drank, played cards, and so on. A door was added to this room to get into the stranger's room, but the door was not there in the old days. There was an exhibit of newspapers in this room, but they were not mentioned by the park ranger. We entered the stranger's room, and we were reminded that it did not, in the past, have a door to the main house.

Then the park ranger looked very serious and said:

> I've told you about the family history and now I must tell you about two enslaved persons. One is Solomon Wilson, and the other is Solomon Williams. Solomon Wilson was a master carpenter and did all the craft work at the house. Solomon Williams was a master blacksmith, and he did all the important blacksmith work. Their work was very important to the house. And they also kept up on the technology of their trades. Solomon Williams made a drill bit, about four-foot-long, and it was inspired by an African design. It was later copied. He made a prototype drill bit. It is now called a "Hughes drill," as in Howard Hughes. But it was Solomon who invented it.

The park ranger then began a reflection on the house:

> We were here long before Eli Whitney invented the gin, long before the constitution of the United States, and we were here long before cotton was king. We did indigo—which is a dye, deep blue dye. It is from indigo that the phrase "blue collar worker" comes. We are the longest permanent settlement in Louisiana. New Orleans was wiped out and it was rebuilt. But we are a permanent settlement.

She then mentioned that there was an attic. "We don't think anyone lived up there. We think it was used for storage."

We entered the next room—a kitchen, which had the look of the 1950s and 1960s, and the park ranger said that this was her favorite room. This kitchen was inside the house—built at a time when the family was no longer afraid of fire, because in earlier periods kitchens used to be outside because of the fire hazard. She added that lots of things, such as goods and tools, were made on the plantation itself, and that a lot of recycling took place also.

We went across an enclosed walkway to another kitchen. It was cold, not climate controlled. This is the "above the ground kitchen," said the park ranger. She then described it. It was only attached to the house by the walkway. She described the plug that had an extra switch to disconnect it. She described how, in her younger days, families would never leave plugs connected to the socket. They would unplug them from the socket because they were afraid that they would explode. "This plug here is a double protection." We proceeded outside to the back gallery. The park ranger mentioned that there was discussion of making the house a self-guided tour. As we went down the stairs, she pointed out Solomon Wilson's handiwork—the log beam joint. She praised his handiwork. It is precise, solid, and unmovable.

Then she pointed towards under the house—where the oven was—and gave a few details. She walked over and rubbed something, and said the red dust came off: "This is what Indians would make war paint with!" I assume that was meant to be a joke, but I wasn't sure! Then she told us to look through the wood pieces, like a window, and we could see the mammy's room. We could also see the staircase and the handrail that mammy used to go up and down.

The Slave/Tenant Quarters and Gabe Nargot's Cabin

A professional assessment of the north and south cabins places their construction between 1850 and 1860 (Miller and Wood 2000, 74), and Gabe Nargot's cabin was built in the 1850s. None of these buildings are in their original locations, all having been moved around the site for several purposes. And none of them are in their original condition, all of them deteriorated substantially over the years, and then the NPS, once it acquired the site, researched and very substantially restored them. It is clear that the NPS has saved these cabins from extinction. Some initial information about the slave cabins was provided on the Oakland Plantation site map, where we are told: "Slave/Tenant Quarters and Ruins—These structures are remnants of a larger community, which extended for a quarter-mile southward along the river. After the Civil War, sharecropper and tenant farmer families continued to live in these quarters as late as the 1970s."

When the NPS took control of the site in the 1990s, the three slave cabins were in very serious disrepair. One cabin (that of Gabe Nargot) was already in ruins and by the time of research was all but gone, except for four small brick corners and a chimney. The NPS invested considerable resources into researching, restoring, and maintaining the other two cabins. This process was still in progress, and information about the cabins was still being acquired, with changes continuing to be made to them. While limited information about the cabins was being presented to site visitors, far more information about the cabins could be obtained from the research reports commissioned by the NPS (Miri 1998a, b). This information is primarily historical, but there is also architectural information and details about the materials and maintenance of the cabins.

On first impression, the two cabins appeared similar. They seemed to be about the same size, shared a similar shape and color, and had a similar number of rooms. They were made of a combination of bousillage and wood. But first impressions are deceiving, as several staff members pointed out to me during my visits, and the cabins are very different in terms of both exteriors and interiors. When I first visited in fall 2007, neither cabin was regularly open to visitors, nor did they have any significant items inside. Nor at that time was any descriptive information about the cabins posted outside or inside, except for a small slate sign that said "Slave/Tenant Quarters." I was provided with access to one of them and looked inside. By spring 2008, the north cabin was open and in it was mounted a small exhibit on slavery and tenant life, including photographs and text. This small exhibit had been expanded a little by the time I returned in 2010. Brief information about the cabins was provided in the cell phone tour, also introduced in 2010.

"North Slave/Tenant Quarters (LCS No. 91638)." Built circa 1860. "Originally this one-room, dirt-floor structure with front and rear porches measured 31.7 by 24.4 by 18.2 feet. The rear porch has since been enclosed, and wooden floors added" (Miller and Wood 2000, 26). This is the cabin nearest to the office.

"South Slave/Tenant Quarters (LCS No. 91639)." This cabin was built in the 1850s or 1860s. It has been modified in the same way as the north cabin,

The North Slave/Tenant Quarters at Oakland Plantation.

The South Slave/Tenant Quarters at Oakland Plantation.

for example, the back porch was enclosed to create two rooms. In both this and the north cabin, "weatherboard and asphalt cover the walls" (Miller and Wood 2000, 27). More description of this cabin can be found in the architectural reports (Miri 1998a, b).

The exhibit inside the north cabin provided basic information about slavery and the cabins. Most of the information was general, taken from Library of Congress files and several other sources, with a main focus on conditions in Louisiana. None of the information in the exhibit—neither photos nor descriptions—seemed to be directly from Oakland Plantation itself. The cabin inside looked dusty and old-fashioned. The walls were mainly bare, the ceiling also. There were very faded copies of newspapers on some of the walls—I had been told using newspapers for wallpaper was a common practice of tenants in the mid-twentieth century. This was also described in some of the reports on the site (Crespi 1999). The overall impression conveyed was one of inequality, deprivation, and poverty, especially after I had just completed a tour of the luxurious main house.

The small exhibit, organized on several makeshift tables, included signs and placards; a variety of photographs, mainly black and white; several musical instruments, including drums; and a few other items. The slate panels included "CODE NOIR," "SLAVERY," "PRESERVING THE CABINS," "AGRI-CULTURE," "MUSIC," and "TENANT LIFE." Alongside several of the panels were one-page NPS leaflets with details of various aspects of the lives of the enslaved, including information about Creole culture and cotton picking and processing. Several of the photographs were of cabins in the past, when they were in a highly dilapidated state, and at present, after they had been successfully restored. A notice informed visitors that "the black and white photos are from the Library of Congress" and "depict scenes from plantations across the United States, predominantly from Louisiana." In these black and white photos were images of Black men, women, and children working in the fields, including several of Black children in cotton fields.

One of the photos was of a Black woman with a child, who appeared to be of African descent, but was clearly mixed, maybe Creole. There was also a photo of a Black woman apparently teaching a young girl at a blackboard. Several photos conveyed the very degraded conditions inside the cabins, which also appeared to be sparsely furnished and to have very rough interiors.

Gabe Nargot's cabin was listed as a "seed house" on the Oakland Plantation site map, where it indicated that "Gabe Nargot was a gin engineer, whose African-born grandmother had been enslaved at Oakland. Gabe Nargot was the last person living at Oakland who had been enslaved there, and the ruins (B) of his cabin are located in the area of the slave/tenant quarters." Miller and Keel (1999, n.p.) identify the remains of a fourth slave cabin on the site as Gabe Nargot's cabin:

> In 1860 there were 145 slaves living at Oakland in 30 houses. Only 3 of these cabins are still standing. One, the cook's cabin, was moved north of the big house and converted into a fishing cabin. The other two cabins are located south of the big house, near the overseer's house, cotton gin, and seed house. The cabins were constructed of bousillage and wood lathe on raised brick piers. Those near the cotton gin have been covered with wood siding. A fourth exists as a ruin. Family tradition, site maps, and local oral history claimed the cabin had been of poteaux-en-terre (post in the ground) and bousillage construction. Furthermore, the cabin was the residence of Mr. Gabe Nargot, the last surviving slave of the plantation.

Gijtano (2007) suggests that the cabin was built prior to the 1850s. All that was left of Gabe Nargot's cabin was what looked like several corners made of brick, and the remains of a chimney/fireplace. There was a small signpost there, and a huge tree with massive branches that overshadowed the ruins. While it was still not clear to me that Gabe Nargot had ever been enslaved, it still seemed that the building certainly functioned at one time as a slave cabin.

Gabe Nargot's Cabin at Oakland Plantation.

The Cook's House

This building was variously called the "cook's house" (site map) and the "cook's cabin" (on sign at pavilion in 2010). The cook's house had also been substantially restored and was available for self-guided tours by visitors to the site. The architects Miller and Wood commented that "[t]he cook's house (cottage) was built sometime between 1820 and 1870. Originally located behind the main house, it was moved in the twentieth century and used as a fishing cabin" (Miller and Wood 2000, 25). Their report continued that the cabin was an "excellent example of bousillage construction" and had a shed roof gallery on three sides (ibid.). They then added, "The cook's house needs immediate stabilization, preservation, and repair" (ibid.). The NPS responded right away, and substantial repairs and restoration were made; after that, the cook's cabin was in excellent condition.

The Oakland plantation site map described the cook's house as follows:

1. Cook's House—Creole structures were commonly moved from one location to another. The cook's house, once located behind the main house, was moved to its present site by P. Phanor's Prud'homme II in the 1930s and its appearance modified as seen today. Here it was used as a "fishing camp" which was rented out to various families who

The Cook's Cabin at Oakland Plantation.

came to Cane River to fish. "Grampa" also rented wooden boats and sold bait to the fishermen. Minnows were raised for fishing bait in the small pond behind the cook's house.

One report on the cook's house indicated that the cook was an enslaved person who lived there. The cook would almost certainly have been a woman, a Black woman, though no further information is provided at the site or in other documents. Kitchens like this, in which enslaved women lived, are documented elsewhere in Louisiana and across the South (Modlin et al. 2018; Eichstedt and Small 2002). However, because the report on the cook's house was only able to date the cabin to sometime during the lengthy period between 1820 and 1870, we do not know with certainty that the cook's house existed before the legal abolition of slavery in the 1860s. And thus, we do not have proof that it ever functioned as a slave cabin. However, it is a fair assumption that with no evidence to the contrary, whoever worked in the cabin in the 1870s or beyond was probably born enslaved.

When visitors arrived at the cook's house there was a slate sign that read "Cook's Cabin. C. 1821." The cook's cabin had a distinctive appearance, in part because it had a strange corridor going around the entire building. This is described in one report: "Has a shed roof gallery on three sides" (Miller and Wood 2000, 25). The cabin was almost entirely empty, with no descriptive information about it or its history. In the interior of one of the rooms, visitors could see the bousillage walls. In one room, there was a wooden-type box in the middle of the room, about three feet high, with two undated photos of what the cabin looked like before and after its restoration. The photos conveyed very vividly that before restoration it had been in very bad shape. After restoration, it had significantly improved, although the roof was still rusty. Further restoration had clearly taken place since that time. One room contained the remains of a bed-spring and some wooden slats leaning up against the wall. There was also a trash can in the room and some other wooden debris leaning against a wall. While this building was not presented at the site as a slave cabin, there was evidence that suggested that it functioned as a place where an enslaved person slept and may have originally been built as a slave cabin (Miller and Keel 1999, n.p.).

The "Nanny's Room" or "Mammy Room" in the Main House

Several times during the tour of the main house, visitors were told that a living space existed in the basement of the main house that was typically occupied by a Black woman who looked after the family's children. Information about which people filled this role at different times is based on family oral tradition and is limited and somewhat uneven. No names, personal information, or details were presented at the site, nor was it clear whether a person occupied this role prior to the Civil War. My interpretation is that someone did occupy this role prior to the Civil War and that it was also occupied after the Civil War, though not necessarily by the same person. All evidence suggests it would have been filled by an enslaved woman through the 1860s, and later a legally free Black woman.

It is clear that at this site this woman was sometimes called a "nanny" and sometimes a "mammy," although "mammy" seemed to be the name most commonly used.[8] As I mentioned earlier, the so-called mammy room was first mentioned on the guided tour before visitors entered the house. We were told about a trap door in the floor and that the "mammy" came up and down to do the laundry and to get the kids. We were also told that there is increasing evidence that there were people other than the main family living in the house—people who did work in the house—and that it was convenient for the family to have them living in the house. As noted earlier, a joke was made about how we all need this kind of help in dealing with kids.

Although it was not related during the tour, there was information about this room available from various other sources. The main source is the Big House Historic Structure Report (2004). It stated:

Mammy's room (101). Located on the southwest side of the house, this room is thought to have been used as a bedroom for the Prud'hommes' black "mammy" in the nineteenth century. Charged with care of the children, this servant was typically the only slave who actually lived in the house with the family. The only basement room used as living space; this room is one of two rooms that composed the original basement story of the house. A wooden staircase in the northeast corner of the room rises to the main floor; and, although it has been thought that the staircase rose to the master bedroom (202), it was actually connected to the southeast bedroom (205), which would have been used as a nursery or children's bedroom. The stairs opened through a trap door in a small closet in the northeast corner of the master bedroom (202). The staircase remains in place but access to the main floor of the house was eliminated by construction of the present, somewhat larger closet (204) in that location in 1953. (Big House, HSR 2004, 82)

Other Structures (Wash House, Carpenter's Shop, Carriage House, Mule Barn, Pigeonniers, and Overseer's House)

There were several other buildings at Oakland Plantation that might at one time have housed enslaved persons, though I could find no definitive proof. I suggest that we should consider them quite likely to have been residences for enslaved people because substantial evidence from across the state and across the South indicates that such buildings fulfilled that function.[9]

In referring to the wash house, the 2010 Oakland Plantation site map tells us the following: "Wash House—The many outbuildings at Oakland illustrate the relative autonomy of a 'plantation.' Martha Ann, an enslaved laundress, worked in the wash house in the 1850s. In the 1940s, Martha Helaire earned $4 per month working here as laundress."

This is another instance in which visitors can hear something about the role and experiences of Black women on the plantation, the first instance being in the so-called mammy room in the main house.

With regard to the carpenter shop, the site map informs visitors that "[s]killed workers built and repaired plantation structures from this workspace."

With regard to the carriage house, the site map told us that "[i]n recent years this structure was used as a car garage and a farm workshop, but the carriage house dates back to 1820. In its earlier years, the east bay was used as a horse stall. The overseer had the horse saddled each day and tied to the chain so that it was available for riding and checking the fields." Given that

The Overseer's House at Oakland Plantation. © Library of Congress, Prints & Photographs Division, Historic American Buildings Survey, HABS LA,35-BERM,2-Q-.

this building dates back to the 1820s, it is highly likely that it was worked in by enslaved men, and quite possible that they lived in the space or above it. Similar habitations of enslaved laborers, typically men, in carriage houses are documented elsewhere in the South, for example at Joseph Manigault House in Charleston, South Carolina (see also Follett 2005a; Rehder 1999; MacDonald 1993; Wade 1967). There were two pigeonniers and a mule barn that probably served as sleeping quarters for the enslaved as well, probably men.

Finally, there was also an "overseer's house" on the plantation, which was far bigger than the slave/tenant cabins. It was built for Seneca Pace in 1861, and he directed its construction (Miller and Wood 2000, 6). Miller and Wood say that Seneca Pace was overseer (ibid., 19). His race is not mentioned, so he must have been white.[10] The site map informs visitors: "An overseer was responsible for management of the plantation's laborers, stock, land, and tolls. This residence was constructed by enslaved labor in 1861 for an overseer named Seneca Pace. Pace kept a daily journal of work and weather at Oakland." During all my visits to the site, the overseer's house was locked up. Each time I peered through the windows, all I could see were some miscellaneous items stored in the building.

. . .

In this chapter, I have argued that at Oakland Plantation slavery and the slave cabins were relatively incorporated into the main representations of heritage tourism.[11] I have demonstrated that slavery received relatively significant attention as did the ways in which the majority of inhabitants (primarily Blacks and other people of color, including "mixed-race") interacted with the powerful whites that owned and managed the plantation (and the working-class whites that worked there too). Information was provided on the plantation website, in promotional literature, in various locations at the site and during the house, cell phone, and self-guided tours. Brief details were provided on how the cabins functioned as central components of the plantation under slavery, and there were opportunities for visitors to obtain further details. Tour guides were also available to respond to questions on these topics from visitors. In all these media, most attention was devoted to the elite white residents conveyed through articulation of the distinctive ethnic identity of French Creoles and their descendants, vis-à-vis Anglos, for example, with regard to ancestry, family names, and cultural practices such as language, religion, architecture, and food. It was also conveyed via details of the multitier racial system, especially the role of legally free people of color. We heard little or nothing about enslaved people of mixed origins. And overall, we heard very few Black voices, and the ones we heard were largely stereotypical, especially in the tour of the main house.

It would be inaccurate to say that slavery and the slave cabins were fully incorporated into the representations at the site because they remained in a very clear second place to the nature and quality of information and detail about elite whites and their accommodations. This was reflected in the overall framing of the site's story, the details provided about the lives of different inhabitants, and the amount of attention devoted to different buildings. For example, the only guided tour was devoted to the main house and its elite white residents, most of whom were personalized and individualized. Information about and access to the cabins was uneven and inconsistent. Typically, visitors heard very little that personalized or individualized the enslaved or other Black residents of the site (except for passing reference to Solomon Wilson and Solomon Williams) and we heard very few Black voices.

Limited attention was paid to the slave cabins or to the other places in which the enslaved lived or slept, though they were briefly mentioned. While cabins were not generally open to visitors, early on in my research one of them was opened, and had a small exhibit installed, with further additions and openings made over the course of my fieldwork. Still, the information about the cabins was limited, perfunctory, and far from creative, and the exhibits were old-fashioned and staid. There was no detailed information individualizing and humanizing the enslaved, illuminating their lives, and their culture, nor were there details about the cabins, despite the existence of extensive research that could provide this kind of information. This stood in stark contrast to the information provided about elite whites at the site. Black people remained abstract, undifferentiated, and anonymous, while white people were concrete, individualized, and personalized.

The fact that there was limited information on slavery and cabins should take into account an important observation by several staff—who pointed out that the cabins functioned for far longer periods as tenants' cabins than as slave cabins, and therefore it made sense that less attention should be devoted to slavery. They also pointed out that far less primary information about the lives of the enslaved was available, and that any that may have existed, for example, in archives, could not be accessed because of limited resources.

There was some attention paid to women and it was clear that gender shaped the organization of heritage tourism at the site, including far more attention to men than women—most obviously to the white residents. For example, in the main house, the rooms and spaces in the rooms were arranged by gender and this was conveyed explicitly to visitors. The men were presented as the driving force in the plantation's establishment, growth, and success; they were the leaders, hard workers, and innovators; they built and expanded the plantations; and it is men that struggled in hard times to preserve family, culture, and traditions. It was clear that the role of overseer was always fulfilled by a (white) man and that white men went to fight for the Confederacy. It is clear that it was the (Black) men who were responsible for maintaining the cotton machines. When white wives were mentioned, they were typically in secondary roles, primarily domestic and child-rearing, although in the few instances they were mentioned, they were still individualized and humanized.

The group most neglected was Black women. The portrayal of the so-called mammy was highly problematic. Given that the majority of visitors to the site only visited the main house, this was the main and possibly the only image and information they received about Black women at the site—servile, caring for white women, and lacking agency. This is a highly stereotypical representation for which the guide admitted there was no concrete evidence.

It was clear that the park superintendent had made significant efforts to represent slavery and the slave cabins in a more substantial way than existed at other sites and to make sure that attention was paid to the majority of residents at the site—Black people—and to the majority of buildings, sites of work, or accommodations for Black people. The superintendent took pride in the efforts devoted to promoting representation of as wide a range as possible of buildings and structures on the site, including the cabins, rather than just the main house. Several significant changes were implemented to achieve these goals, including relocating some parking to the back of the main house to provide a different entrance to the site and making sure that period dress (such as hoop skirts) and a "Gone with the Wind" approach (also known as "Moonlight and Magnolias") were avoided (Gates 2002). Leaflets and documents at the site used language like "enslaved" rather than "slave," and raised questions about inequality and struggle. Similar language was sometimes used by site interpreters. Staff were trained to offer interpretations of the entire site, including the cabins. Substantial work was also invested into maintaining the buildings.

This was clearly an ongoing process, and during my research, the site introduced significant new information, new elements, and a range of different exhibits. Staff at the site also cultivated links with docents and curators at other sites, and with scholars working in the field, as for example, at the conference that took place in April 2008. Substantial archaeological research was also carried out on multiple buildings at the site, including the main house, overseer's cabin, and the twenty-first-century antebellum slave cabins. Several reports on the cabins based on archaeological and archival research were published that provided rich descriptions of the material construction of the cabins, and brief historical overviews of physical and structural changes. There were also some brief details on the lives of their inhabitants. The fact that the reports existed at all—and that the research upon which they are based was funded—testifies to the importance attached to them.[12] It was clear that the impact of state involvement—in the form of the National Park Service—had been instrumental in these efforts.

Six factors explain the overall situation at the site (which are mentioned here and elaborated upon in the concluding chapter). First was the obeisance to a narrative of southern gentility, comprising elite white lifestyles, paternalism, and romance. It reflected the continued privileging of elite white people and the high culture, architecture, and furnishings regarded as achievements of southern white society. A second factor was staff beliefs and experiences of visitor priorities, with the majority of visitors—overwhelmingly white—coming to see the main house and the elite families that occupied it. Resource constraints were a third factor and certainly made it difficult to carry out research on the histories of Black people or mount more creative or elaborate exhibitions. A fourth factor was the lack of sustained and broad involvement of Black people at the site, including professionals with experience in organizations and institutions working on public history. Fifth, entrenched racial inequality and institutional racism, past and present, were major reasons Black people were not more involved in the sites. They had other priorities at all times during and beyond Jim Crow segregation and after the heritage sites were established. This included struggles to survive and succeed. Racist hostility throughout the South had also led them to create their own memorials in their homes, churches, and communities. And finally, the fact that it was owned by the state—in the form of NPS—meant that some resources were available—including those that enabled the site to be purchased and to get up and running.

Chapter Three

MAGNOLIA PLANTATION

The second site in Natchitoches that belonged to the National Park Service as part of the Cane River National Historical Park was Magnolia Plantation Complex, located about ten miles from Oakland Plantation and managed and maintained by the head office of the park, located at Oakland Plantation. This site did not include the main house, nor the cook's cabin, both of which were on private property adjacent to the plantation. The main house was occupied by Betty Hertzog, one of the family members who was still in residence during the main phases of my research. Although the main house was private, it was sometimes open to the public at the owner's discretion.

Because the NPS owned and managed both sites, this site shared many similarities with Oakland Plantation in the themes that it presented, including the history of colonization, frontier influences, French Creole culture and architecture, cotton agriculture, slavery and tenancy labor systems, changing technologies, and evolving social practices over two hundred years. It aspired to cover all aspects of the plantation history, the impressive mix of original buildings, and the range of plantation inhabitants, elite and poor, Black, white and mixed origins, both male and female. This was reflected in opportunities for visiting many buildings on the plantation, and in the information provided about many types of plantation inhabitants. Magnolia also focused on the period around the 1960s. Like Oakland Plantation, Magnolia had remained in the hands of the same family for multiple generations. The Prud'homme family owned Oakland Plantation, while the Hertzog family owned Magnolia Plantation. As will be further described, the families were closely intertwined with a long history of personal, familial, and professional relationships.[1]

Magnolia Plantation offered several opportunities for self-guided or guided tours of various outbuildings, including a plantation store, the "slave hospital/overseer's house," the blacksmith shop, and the gin barn. A distinctive feature of the plantation was the eight brick slave cabins arranged in a so-called grid format. Few cabins in Natchitoches, Louisiana, or indeed the

South were constructed with brick (Follett 2005; Vlach 1993, 1991; Taylor 1974). Brick cabins typically existed where brick was made on the plantation and was thus cheap and accessible, as was the case at Magnolia Plantation.[2] The same is typically true of stone cabins (Vlach 1993; McDaniel 1982).

Like all plantations across the South, Magnolia Plantation had its own distinctive features. These included its unique range of buildings, family histories, the experiences of the enslaved, and the specific factors that led to its incorporation into the heritage tourism industry.

Like Oakland, Magnolia Plantation had a *continuum of coerced accommodations* occupied by the enslaved, in two clusters. The first cluster included eight twenty-first-century antebellum brick slave cabins, specifically seven double pen cabins and one single pen cabin. The second cluster included several other locations at the site in which enslaved people used to sleep or live, including the blacksmith shop, the slave hospital/overseer's house, and the gin barn. The plantation main house is also relevant, but it is not addressed here because it was not part of the heritage site.

The Magnolia Plantation website in February 2009 described the cabins as "eight duplex-style quarters." All were original to the site and were in their original position and configuration. This location originally had a total of twenty-four quarters in the antebellum period (Keel 1999, 10). Other evidence suggests there were more cabins elsewhere at this location (Hahn and Wells 1991, 1). Originally called a "slave village," they were known during my research as "slave/tenant cabins" because after slavery ended, the former enslaved persons that remained on the site, and their descendants, resided there as tenant farmers or laborers through the third quarter of the twentieth century. Most of the people who lived in the cabins in the mid-twentieth century or later preferred to call them "the quarters" (Crespi 2004). Considerable details exist about their situation thanks to research carried out in the last few decades (Crespi 2004; Malone 1996).

The site's plantation store, built in the postbellum period, had functioned as a major social nucleus. The site also had a slave hospital/overseer's house. It was originally built in the 1840s as a slave hospital. After slavery ended, it later became an overseer's house (Overseer's House, HSR 2004, 11). Magnolia Plantation also had several other structures in which it is likely that enslaved persons lived for significant periods, including a blacksmith shop and a gin barn. There are no remains of the kitchen that was on the site. And then there is the main house, privately owned and not part of the site during the research period, but which almost certainly housed enslaved workers (and perhaps Black workers in the postbellum period). The main house was built, postbellum, with bricks from some of the slave cabins. I discuss this in more detail later in the chapter.

The site scheduled only a few guided tours of the buildings, typically on the weekends, more often in the summer, although park rangers sometimes provided an improvised tour if the site was not busy. I benefited from these improvised tours several times. Visitors could take a self-guided tour, and a map of the plantation was available for that at the plantation store. The map included an overview of the history of the site, a list of the main buildings, and brief details about each, including the slave cabins. It was clear from the beginning of my research that the site had significant resource issues because it had fewer opening times and/or staff available on site than did Oakland Plantation. A cell phone tour was introduced in 2010, which enabled visitors to complete a self-guided tour by phoning into a provided number and following the narration.

Overall, I argue that, as at Oakland Plantation, the cabins and other spaces in which the enslaved slept or lived at Magnolia were relatively incorporated into heritage tourism. In part, this is because both sites were owned and operated by the National Park Service.

THE ESTABLISHMENT OF MAGNOLIA PLANTATION

Magnolia Plantation traces its origins to 1753 when Jean Baptiste Lecomte acquired the land upon which it was to grow (Hahn and Wells 1991, 29). Under his ownership, the plantation was established, began cultivation, and achieved initial successes. A portion of the land constituting Magnolia Plantation has remained in ownership and management of the family ever since (Keel 1999). The first crop at the site was tobacco, and enslaved African Americans were forced to cultivate it. When Lecomte died, the plantation passed into the hands of his son, Ambroise Lecomte I, and then his grandson, Ambroise Lecomte II. The transfer through the family over generations saw the expansion of the plantation's holdings (Hahn and Wells 1991, 29). In his lifetime, Ambroise I saw a major shift in crops from tobacco to cotton. Profits from cotton peaked at 33.9 cents per pound in 1817 and were higher than those from tobacco planting. Many other plantations made a similar shift (Keel 1999, 18).

Strategic purchases of land fed Lecomte's success, and the continued use of enslaved labor ensured that the land was profitable. For example, Ambroise I took advantage of the Panic of 1819 and bought "several tracts of land on the left bank of the Red (Cane) River from neighbors and relatives who needed cash" (Keel 1999, 18). The family continued to buy more land in the years that followed, through to the 1830s.

Ambroise Lecomte II and his wife, Julia Buard, established Magnolia Plantation around 1830. As one report notes, "All the land acquired between 1824 and 1835 and the left bank property from the original Lecomte land grant became part of Magnolia Plantation" (Keel 1999, 19). Some hard economic times for all planters followed, but the Lecomtes weathered the storms, and by 1849, cotton profits were back. During this period, Lecomte also shifted the focus of his agricultural pursuits—from several food crops and small-scale tobacco exports to large-scale cotton production. The shift was largely shaped by the changing profitability of cotton, which was directly shaped by Whitney's cotton gin. The family built the main house several decades after the end of the Civil War.

The Lecomtes bought Barthelemy Plantation in 1833, which included four arpents (an arpent is about one acre) on the left bank of the Cane River. Through the 1830s, the family continued to make purchases of land on both sides of the river. After Julia Buard died in 1845, Ambroise II married Lise Victorie Desiree Sompayrac in 1846 and moved his family to a townhouse in Natchitoches. At that time, "[d]ay to day operations of Magnolia Plantation and Shallow Lake Plantations was left in the hands of overseers" (Keel 1999, 19). Julia's sister-in-law, Suzette Hertzog Buard, and her children remained at Magnolia Plantation along with Suzette's brother Matthew Hertzog.

As with Oakland, enslaved Blacks did the bulk of the heavy work. Their numbers were small at the start, but more and more were acquired by the family to expand their properties and increase their profits. As with Oakland Plantation, we have very little information on the cabins and accommodation occupied by the enslaved in their early period. Most of the available information about the cabins during slavery is for the 1840s and 1850s.

MAGNOLIA PLANTATION IN THE ANTEBELLUM PERIOD

Changes in family composition—through marriage, childbirth, and death—continued to be the basis for the maintenance and growth of the plantation and the Lecomte family's fortunes throughout the antebellum period. For example, in 1852, Atala (daughter of Ambroise II and Julia) married Matthew Hertzog. Matthew was the son of Jean Hertzog and Marianne Prud'homme, neighbors of the Lecomtes. The decades following this merger and partnership of Lecomte and Hertzog were the most prosperous for the owners of Magnolia Plantation.

By 1860, Ambroise Lecomte II produced more cotton and owned more enslaved persons than anyone in the parish, with a total of 235 enslaved persons in his ownership (Keel 1999, 19). At this time, he owned three plantations—Magnolia, Shallow Lake, and Vienna (Hahn and Wells 1991, 33). His properties came to a total of 5,395 acres. The workforce of enslaved laborers owned by the Lecomtes had already cleared almost half of these acres and their labors were producing huge cotton crops. The enslaved persons lived in seventy cabins (Brown 2006, 28). In 1860 the Lecomte-Hertzog holding, including Magnolia Plantation and other properties, was worth $25,100 and by 1870 it was worth $76,700 (Keel 1999, 20).

We don't know the exact number of enslaved persons living at Magnolia Plantation itself at this time because the census includes "resident slaves" from several other Lecomte properties (Keel 1999, 19). Inventories from 1840 to 1860 contain some information about who worked in specific areas of the plantation. Offering an assessment of the plantation for that period, Keel suggests: "The slave community at Magnolia Plantation experienced a certain amount of stability. During the lean years, many planters had been forced to sell their slaves, but not Lecomte. He stopped buying enslaved persons and concentrated on holding the ones he already owned."

Information from a variety of sources provides basic details about the enslaved population at the plantation. For example, there is evidence of the names of several of the Magnolia Plantation blacksmiths during the antebellum period—all of whom were enslaved African Americans (or possibly Creoles). "It is known from Ambroise Lecomte's ledgers that there were at least two blacksmiths on his properties: Charles, aged 23 years (date of record unknown) and located at Magnolia; and Daniel, aged 43 years (1852) and located on the Shallow Lake Plantation" (Brown 2006, 36–40, cited in St. Clair 2008, 4). The report adds, "There is also a bill of sale that lists Lecomte as the agent for Louis Buard in the purchase of a blacksmith named Saturday, aged 24 (1833)" (St. Clair 2008, 3). No other details are given about the blacksmiths in these reports.

When Laura Lecomte Hertzog, wife of Henry Hertzog, died in 1857, she left a will (in French) and among the various clauses is one indicating that an enslaved woman, Priscilla age eighteen, should be sold, "she having had tapeworm and becoming barren" (cited in Hunter 2005, 20). There is also some evidence for how enslaved persons were treated at Magnolia Plantation. For example, one author maintains that "[l]ittle documentary evidence to indicate abuse or neglect of the slaves has survived. Indirect information

indicates that punishment included being locked in stocks or temporarily
losing privileges" (Keel 1999, 19).

Another author describes the whipping of an enslaved person who had
broken into one of the houses, saying that the overseer did not whip the
slave who broke into the house "as much as he deserved" (cited in Keel 1999,
19). Keel asserts that "Magnolia's slaves had better housing and diet than did
other slaves in the area. Despite the reliance on a one-crop economy, records
indicate that the slaves enjoyed a relatively balanced diet. Rations consisted
of corn meal (processed at Magnolia), pork, and molasses. Beef, flour, rice,
macaroni, and oysters occasionally supplemented their diet" (Keel 1999,
19). Apparently, the enslaved enjoyed lots of other good things too, including medicine (ibid.). To an uncritical reader, this may sound fine. But then
Keel adds

> The mortality rate among slaves (and whites, as well) was high.
> Droughts, floods, hurricanes, and tornados all had an impact on the
> plantation population. Yellow fever and cholera were endemic during
> the 1830s, 1840s, and 1850s. Slaves were often buried at the Shallow
> Lake Cemetery. However, according to descendants of Magnolia's
> slaves, later burials were in the "people's graveyard" east of the slave
> quarters. (Keel 1999, 20)

Things were not so fine after all. But with the idea of "balance" clearly in mind,
Keel reminds us that things were not so fine for the whites either.

Magnolia's eight duplex-style quarters were built as part of a "rare masonry
slave village" (Magnolia Plantation website, fall 2007). The cabins were initially built in the 1840s to house two enslaved families each. Keel reports:
"Archaeological evidence suggests that the slave village was laid out in a grid
pattern, four cabins across and six down for a total of twenty-four cabins.
They were formally oriented in the cardinal directions. This so-called slave
village was reportedly the finest in the parish" (Keel 1999, 10). During slavery,
the cabins were occupied by "the plantation's artisans and skilled labor force,
along with others who worked in the plantation complex" (Yocum 1996, 7).
Magnolia Plantation at its peak in 1860 had more than 260 enslaved persons
and seventy cabins (Hahn and Wells 1991, 30).

The precise date of construction of the blacksmith shop is unknown,
but documentary evidence and the fact that it was built in part with
bousillage, suggests a high likelihood it was built prior to the ownership of the site by Lecomte (St. Clair 2008, 4). Similarly, we have limited

information on the cook's cabin, but again, all evidence indicates it is an antebellum structure.

THE CIVIL WAR AND POSTBELLUM PERIOD

Being the largest owners of enslaved persons in the parish and having a substantial amount of wealth and property, all of it acquired via the exploitation of enslaved labor, it is little surprise that the owners of Magnolia Plantation supported the Confederacy (Keel 1999, 20). A number of the male family members joined the Confederate army, and several of them were killed in the conflict. The main house at Magnolia Plantation was burned by Federal troops in April 1864 during the Red River campaign, and only the brick foundations and portions of exterior walls survived (ibid.).

Despite the devastation caused by the Civil War, the elite white owners at Magnolia Plantation still retained relative power and influence as well as extensive connections across the city, parish, and state. Between 1861 and 1914, agricultural production at Magnolia Plantation varied. The powerful Creole families continued their long-established tradition of family consolidation and expansion through marriage, amassing greater wealth, and generally keeping it within the family. For example, in 1892, Ambrose J. Hertzog married Sarah (Sally) Hunter and they had "five surviving children" (Keel 1999, 21). Later on, the Hertzog brothers bought Ferry Plantation from the Derbanne family, north of Magnolia (Hunter 2005, 12).

When Ambroise II died in 1883, his estate was assessed at $134,000 (Keel 1999, 20). Atala inherited Magnolia Plantation, but portions of the estate were sold. Matthew and Atala moved into the rebuilt main house at Magnolia. Atala died in 1897. Matthew died in 1903. They had two children, Ambrose J. Hertzog and Frances "Fanny" Hertzog Chopin. The plantation and other property were divided between the two, but no inventory was carried out because the estate was not in probate. Fanny inherited the area occupied by the gin and quarters, which she sold to her brother to keep the work area complete.

The family's wealth and property were also reflected in holdings in town. The family had a dwelling house on the corner of Front and Church, which was known as the Lecomte townhouse. It stood until the early twentieth century. The present-day Nakatosh Hotel was constructed on the site (Hunter 2005).

The Magnolia Plantation store, built by the Hertzogs after the Civil War, was also developed into a prosperous business. The store "stocked medicine,

food, clothing, and plantation supplies" (Keel 1999, 20). The Hertzogs sometimes provided entertainment for the whole community. It operated throughout the twentieth century "not only as a plantation commissary but as a
general merchandise store and social center for the community of Rivière
aux Cannes" (ibid.). The store was "a public space" that "served as an economic and social magnet for men, women, and children of all ethnicities,"
although "[w]orking men might have been the primary users, making purchases, as well as lounging on the porch and its bench" (Crespi 2004, 36).
The store was in decline in the late 1960s and early 1970s, due to diminishing
population and increased costs, and it closed "after Mr. Matt's death in 1973"
(ibid., 37).

After the original plantation house that was built in 1850 was burned
down by Union troops during the Civil War, a reconstruction of the original
was built in 1897. As one report tells us: "Reconstruction of the 'Big House'
began in the mid to late 1890s. Bricks were used from the original house
and also from the brick quarters, some of which, perhaps already damaged
by various forces, including the passage of time, were demolished for the
purpose. Columns, mantelpieces and the like, were ordered from catalogs"
(Hunter 2005, 35).

After the war had ended, many of Magnolia Plantation's former enslaved
persons remained on the plantation to work as legally freed people—they
were contracted as gang laborers and later as day laborers or sharecropper tenants. The sharecroppers "worked on designated farms of forty
acres on Magnolia land utilized mule power" (Keel 1999, 20). It was also a
requirement that they own a cow and mule, and that they grow their own
vegetable crops.

After the Civil War four plantation owners in Natchitoches were ready
to provide education for those who had been enslaved. Hertzog was one of
them. In a report at the time, a letter from Hertzog indicates he was ready
to start a school and that "[t]he schoolhouse will be in one of the (quarters),
His colored people are making the benches. There will be 80 children in the
school from 2 plantations" (Dollar 1998, 18).

In the aftermath of the Civil War, fraternal organizations and freedmen's
churches helped hold the community together. One African Methodist Epis-
copal Church, Saint James, stood on Magnolia itself until the 1960s, performing burials just across the river at St. Andrew's Baptist Church. The influence
of the plantation continued to be significant, and not just as an employer.
Baseball diamonds and bush racetracks at Magnolia and other area plantations were common ground for local groups, as was the plantation store.

The cabins continued to be occupied and most of the former slaves remained in them, now as tenant farmers. Some modifications were made to the cabins to improve them for the residents.

THE TWENTIETH CENTURY

The owners of Magnolia Plantation shared similar economic fortunes with their fellow elite whites in Natchitoches after the Civil War and into the twentieth century. They did not achieve as much as they wanted to economically, but they certainly achieved more than most others. Agriculture remained the center of their activities, with planting and farming at the center of agriculture. Profits suffered blows from infestations, occasional storms, and from out-migration. On the other hand, they enjoyed the benefits of increased mechanization and lower labor costs. While the "way of life" was certainly changing, economics remained the driving force of the plantation, and the family adapted to the changing circumstances with relative success.

The Great Depression of 1929 created an "era of difficulty" for Magnolia, but "despite the hardships, the family kept tenants and workers employed" (Keel 1999, 21). Good management and the federal government's New Deal program helped. The tenants were not charged rent in the 1930s, but they had to own a milk cow and mule and provide for their own family's needs in garden patch allotted to them (Hahn and Wells 1991, 35).

World War II led to high prices and fueled production. Some men were drafted; others left for war factory jobs. Mechanization and new fertilizers and herbicides were used. Cotton crops were replaced by other lucrative crops such as soybeans and peanuts, and beef production increased (Keel 1999, 21). The plantation continued as a working plantation through the twentieth century, and, as at Oakland Plantation, saw its population of workers dwindle as the economy faced harsh conditions, mechanization increased, and residents migrated to other jobs.

Many of the cabins continued to exist, with modifications, as the twentieth century unfolded. For example, after bricks had been taken from the cabins to rebuild the main house, by the 1920s, wood-frame additions had been added to the backsides of the remaining quarters (Yocum 1996, 7). Other cabins were relocated on the plantation, for example, to serve as fishing cabins. White cement-based masonry paint was applied to the exterior brickwork of the cabins sometime after the 1920s, as evidenced by a 1920s-era photo (Yocum 1996, 7). The interior doorways connecting the two rooms appear to date to the twentieth century (ibid.).

Population census records and ledgers indicate that several generations of families worked at Magnolia at this time. Some eventually moved out of the tenancy and purchased their own land elsewhere. Between 1914 and 1945, twenty-five to fifty families lived and worked on Magnolia and other Hertzog properties. Some lived in the eight extant cabins and the cook's house. Other tenant families occupied farms located along the river road fronting Magnolia. "Cooks, yardmen and overseer's [sic] lived on the plantation as well" (Keel 1999, 20).

By 1939, "only 50 tenant families lived on the plantation, seven families in the old slave quarters, and the others in newly constructed frame houses" (Hahn and Wells 1991, 35). In 1939, a tornado severely damaged the Cottage Buard, the eight remaining cabins, and the gin barn. The cottage was damaged beyond repair, but the cabins and the gin barn were salvaged (Keel 1999, 21). The tornado destroyed the east half of one of the slave cabins, and this half is still missing. Metal roofs replaced wood shingles, probably at about the same time (Yocum 1996, 8). Additional fences and outbuildings were constructed, moved, or taken down as needed in this period (Keel 1999, 21).

We are informed that around this time, "One brick cabin had a raised plank porch braced by sturdy log posts. A bench was situated on the porch and two rain barrels were located at its edge. The roof was covered by wooden shingles, and a fence separated the porch from that of the neighboring cabin. Yard vegetation was spare, which probably indicates a swept yard. By the mid-twentieth century, frame and sheathed rooms with shed roofs had been added to the cabins (figure 3)" (Keel 1999, 21).

Between 1945 and 1960, the gradual economic demise of Magnolia Plantation changed the landscape: "Barns disappeared, tenant houses were torn down, shares were absorbed into large fields and tractor sheds replaced mule lots. Although most of the sharecropping families had departed by 1950, those involved in day labor continued to live at Magnolia into the 1970s" (Keel 1999, 21). One report pointed out that with regard to the brick cabins, "Tenant farmers occupied them from abolition until the late 1960s. Tenant farmers, the sharecroppers, had lived north of the main house, beyond the NPS holding" (Crespi 2004, 6). This was confirmed by Betty Hertzog, who indicated to me that the day laborers at that time lived in one set of buildings, and other workers in another set of buildings.

A detailed study of the area undertaken by Muriel Crespi in 1996 offers information about the experiences and perspectives of the Black residents of the cabins and neighboring areas (Crespi 2004). One of the important issues to emerge from this study concerns the attachment and social significance given to the cabins by the residents, especially as compared with outsiders. Many Blacks preferred to call them "the quarters" rather than slave quarters (Crespi 2004). To the residents, it was a place for family, for social solidarity, and for safety, steeped in tradition. Some of the families had been residents there going back generations, even to the antebellum period. It was an important social location to the residents, rather than a place to be evaluated simply in terms of its physical appearance or cost (especially in comparison to other buildings). In a video interview, historian Rolonda Teal conveyed how the importance attached to such cabins goes back to the period of enslavement. Speaking about the role that the slave cabins and tenant's quarters at Magnolia Plantation would play in heritage tourism she offered the following:

> Many of the interpretive aspects of this plantation haven't completely been decided. One interpretation could be to show some of the activities that took place within the cabin. For example, at night when people came in from the fields, what happened in those cabins? Well, we know that this is where the quilting might have taken place because they needed covers in the winter. This is where the cooking took place because there was no designated cook for the entire plantation. So that gives a sense of how the space was used other than a space to sleep in.

The final residents of the cabins, described as "three elderly people," left at the end of the 1960s (Hahn and Wells 1991, 36). A Lecomte family descendant, writing not long after the start of the twenty-first century, waxed nostalgic:

> In the half-century plus since my first visit to Magnolia much has changed. The fields that were once tended by workers are now cultivated and harvested by machines. Many of the home sites for those workers can only be detected through subtle hints in the vegetation: a grove of trees, the bloom of a paper white narcissus or spider lily. A few wooden cabins remain all but obscured by vines and undergrowth. (Hunter 2005)

HERITAGE TOURISM TAKES HOLD

As the century unfolded, the challenges facing Magnolia Plantation were increasingly clear—economic fortunes continued to decline, labor continued to leave, and things were looking shaky. It was on the slippery slope to oblivion. Most of the workers had departed. Family members had also moved on—some to professional opportunities elsewhere in the state. By the 1960s, there was an increasing fear of the plantation falling into complete disrepair, and of the possibility of vandalism. It was this combination of factors that led family members to sell it to the National Park Service.

Again, it was former mayor and community heritage activist Bobby De-Blieux that intervened to save Magnolia Plantation. DeBlieux had already established a track record of involvement in the promotion of heritage tourism and was by then the mayor of Natchitoches. As with Oakland Plantation, he saw the opportunity for incorporating Magnolia into the parish's heritage tourism drive. He had been a long-term resident of the parish. He knew many of the family members who had lived at the plantation, and they knew him and his commitment to preserving and restoring the cultural heritage of the parish. In this context he took action—and Magnolia Plantation was saved.

DeBlieux was a founding member and prominent player in the organization Museum Contents, Inc., which was able to acquire most of the buildings at Magnolia Plantation.[3] At that time, the cabins were in a bad state of repair and at least six required extensive restoration (author interview, spring 2008). As a result of this intervention, "extensive repair and restoration was carried out in 1991 on 7 of the 8 quarters, i.e., not building 07, by Museum Contents Inc., and salvaged brick was used to construct brickwork gable (possibly incorrectly) on four of the quarters" (Yocum 1996, 8). Magnolia Plantation opened to tourists in the 1990s as part of the Cane River National Historical Park.

HERITAGE TOURISM IN THE TWENTY-FIRST CENTURY

Magnolia Plantation has a number of interesting buildings, a broad range of activities, and an impressive series of themes useful for heritage tourism. The buildings at the site during the period of research included a plantation store, a blacksmith shop, the slave hospital/overseer's house, eight brick slave cabins, and a gin barn. They were all located within several hundred yards of one another and were easily accessible on a flat piece of land. Because it was part of the Cane River Creole National Historical Park site, heritage tourism at this site highlighted similar themes to those at Oakland Plantation, including the history of colonization, various frontier influences, aspects of French Creole architecture, cotton agriculture, and slavery and tenancy labor systems, as well as changing technologies and evolving social practices over several hundred years. For example, information about the construction and history of several buildings was a key theme at the site, with a focus on the distinctive Creole architecture, including bousillage. Most of this information was provided in leaflets, a site map, and in plaques and information posters on walls. The details and information given about these buildings was uneven. Most details were provided about the plantation store, the slave hospital/overseer's house, and the blacksmith shop. There was also significant information about the gin barn. Information on the slave cabins was much more limited.

Unlike the other two sites in this study, Magnolia Plantation had no permanent staff on site, in large part because of limited finances. Instead, the NPS staff based at Oakland Plantation visited the site during set times and by request. As a result, there were fewer scheduled activities at the site and no regular guided tours (except in peak periods, for example, in the summer and in December during the Festival of Lights). In spring 2008, the guided tour occurred twice a day on the weekends at 11:00 a.m. and 3:00 p.m. In August 2010, there were also several tours per week. By 2010, the site had introduced a self-guided audio tour, which visitors could follow by making a call to a phone number with their cell phone. The visitor was then directed to a series of stops throughout the site, with details provided at each stop. The cell phone tour included a stop at the slave cabins.

Typically, when visitors arrived at the site, there were no staff there. Signs in the parking lot directed them to the plantation store, which was less than a couple of hundred yards away. A range of maps and descriptions of self-guided tours of the various buildings, including the slave cabins, could be found at the plantation store. They included the plantation store itself, which visitors could enter and tour. There was also an extensive collection of leaflets with information about the buildings at the site, and various agricultural processes such as cotton ginning, along with details on slavery more generally and on other tourist sites of interest in Natchitoches and across the state. At the back of the store was a staff office for NPS interpreters when they were at the site.

The site saw a number of significant changes during the research period, many of them improvements from the point of view of representations of slavery and the slave cabins. For example, the slave hospital/overseer's house initially had no exhibits in it, the plantation store had basic information and limited leaflets, one of the cabins was open but it was completely empty inside, and the blacksmith shop was closed and locked. By fall 2010, there was an exhibit and multiple pieces of information about agriculture, farming, and slavery on display in the slave hospital/overseer's house. There were several exhibits on slavery and a variety of other topics. There were more leaflets provided at the plantation store. And the one slave cabin that was open now had an exhibit on slavery mounted inside it. Over the period of my research several more archaeological excavations had been undertaken and the preliminary results from them published (Brown 2008a, b). Which reminds us, as mentioned in the introduction, that all three of these plantations are "works in progress" that continually change, with new knowledge produced; they frequently see improvements in representations of slavery based on new research findings and discoveries.

The Buildings and Twenty-First-Century Slave Cabins

The buildings at Magnolia Plantation included a range of spaces in which enslaved people typically slept. Once again, as outlined in previous chapters, it is useful to think of the dwellings and spaces for enslaved persons at this site in two clusters, an approach that highlights some of the ways in which enslaved people were housed in a *continuum of accommodation*, involving a wide and tightly interconnected web of social relations between the enslaved and the elite whites at the plantation. The first cluster included the purpose-built slave cabins that were built exclusively or primarily for enslaved persons to live in. At Magnolia this primarily meant the eight brick cabins. The second cluster included structures in which enslaved persons commonly lived (or were expected to live), and buildings with a high likelihood that the enslaved, or formerly enslaved persons, lived in them at some time. This included the blacksmith shop, the gin barn, the main house, and the cook's cabin. While the main house and cook's cabin were not located on the site, as both were private property, both could be seen from the Magnolia Plantation, and both were mentioned on the cell phone tour. The cook's cabin typically could not be visited, but sometimes the main house was made available by the owner for public visits. The slave hospital/overseer's house, which was used for an important and significant period of time as a "slave hospital," clearly had enslaved persons living in it at least for a period of time in the history of the site.

Visitors had two or three options for visiting the site. They could do a self-guided tour, the cell phone tour, or a guided tour. I describe the cell phone tour, introduced at the same time at both Magnolia and Oakland, as it represents an innovation and provides a good indication of the kinds of information likely to be heard at the site. I follow this summary with details about each of the buildings at the site.

The Cell Phone Tour

The cell phone tour at Magnolia Plantation was introduced in 2010, along with the cell phone tour at Oakland. As mentioned in chapter 3, the tour

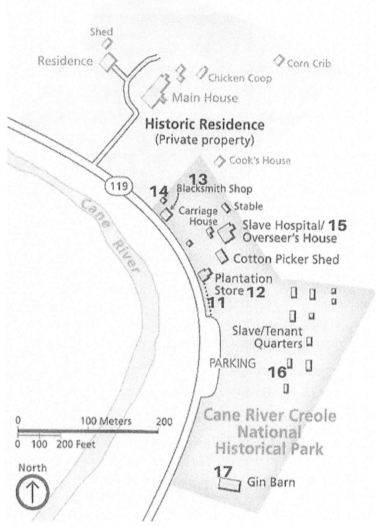

Shed

Residence

Corn Crib

Chicken Coop

Main House

Historic Residence
(Private property)

Cook's House

119

13

14 Blacksmith Shop

Carriage Stable
House

Slave Hospital/ **15**
Overseer's House

Cotton Picker Shed

Plantation
Store **12**

11

Slave/Tenant
Quarters

PARKING **16**

Cane River

0   100 Meters   200

0   100   200 Feet

North

Cane River Creole
National
Historical Park

17 Gin Barn

Map of Magnolia Plantation. © National Park Service.

actually covered both plantations and technically began at Oakland Plantation with stops 1 through 10. The Magnolia Plantation tour began at stop
11 and continued to stop 17. The goal of the tours was to provide easily accessible information with basic details about a range of buildings, and some
background history, to site visitors. This was all the more necessary at Magnolia because it had no staff on site.[4] The tour lasted sixty to ninety minutes,

and entails calling the provided phone number. Visitors were then walked through a series of stops, with a short descriptive narration provided at each location. Many descriptive statements were made on the cell phone tour, some of which were written by the park interpreters, and others of which were quotations taken from research documents written about the site. In particular it drew extensively on the Crespi report (Crespi 2004).

The goals of the tour were outlined in the document prepared by its creators: "Visitors will gain an understanding of the different types of people and buildings that inhabited the plantation and the various roles that these people and structures played in the community's survival and success" (Magnolia Tour Outline). Visitors were provided with a one-page leaflet/map entitled "Cane River Creole. Magnolia Plantation Cell Phone Tour," which had a map of the site, a numbered list of the various structures, which were also stopping places on the tour, and the phone number to call for the tour, along with a phone number for contacting a park ranger, if necessary.

The map listed all the key buildings: "Blacksmith Shop," "Slave Hospital/ Overseer's House," "Cotton Picker Shed," "Plantation Store," "Slave/Tenant Quarters," and the "Gin Barn." It had a highlighted "Tour Stops Key" that listed the places visited on the tour, specifically, the "Magnolia Introduction at the Store," the Plantation Store, Blacksmith Shop, Pigeonnier, Private Property: Main House and Cook's Cabin, the Slave Hospital/Overseer's House, the Slave/Tenant Quarters, and the Gin Barn.

At the first stop (11), the introductory narrative provided background details about the site, describing that it is part of the Cane River Creole National Historical Park, and that Magnolia Plantation was added to the National Register of Historic Places in 1979. It continued with details about the Lecomte family's arrival at Cane River in the 1750s, and how the family established and extended the plantation, growing crops and expanding it until it "became one of the largest and most successful French-Creole cotton plantations, consisting of over six thousand acres of land." The links between the Lecomtes and the Hertzogs were mentioned.

There is an original "Corn Crib" on the plantation that was described as "a storage place for corn grown on the Plantation." But this structure is now on private grounds and cannot be visited as part of the public site. Stop 13 was the "Blacksmith Shop": one of most important buildings, a "French-Creole style building [that] has walls constructed of a wooden frame with bousillage infill." Bousillage was then described. The narration continued, "If you look carefully, you can find finger mark indentations left by the people who smoothed the bousillage mixture into place." It also described various tasks carried out by blacksmiths. At Stop 14—the "Main House/Cook's

Cabin"—the tour indicated that "if you stand near the pigeonnier, you can see the plantation's main house on the other side of the fence. It is private property and not part of the park." The main house here was built in the 1890s. This stop mentioned the cook's cabin, which was also located on private property, which "served as the Cook's house and the kitchen for the Main House." It was noted that it was always built away from the main house due to fire.

Stop 15 was the "Slave Hospital/Overseer's House," a building that dated to the 1840s, and "was first used as a Slave Hospital." When the main house was destroyed in 1864, it became "the residence for the plantation owners" and later on a residence for the overseers. Quoting information from the Oakland Plantation cell phone tour, the narration commented that "[s]lave owners were responsible for the medical treatment of their enslaved laborers," and added that the "enslaved laborers fell victim to a variety of illnesses because of their strenuous work schedule and environment" and "poor diet." It continued, "The young were especially prone to illness and death at an early age because of a lack of prenatal care." And it added that the house later became the home of overseers and detailed that "[f]requently, plantation overseers were white men. At Magnolia, however, overseers in the postbellum period were often local Creoles." The job of overseer was then described.

Stop 16 was the "Slave/Tenant Cabins." The tour indicated that "originally, seventy cabins stood here in the Quarters. Twenty-four of the seventy cabins were made out of brick; the rest were made out of timber. Each cabin contained two rooms with back-to-back fireplaces that shared the same chimney. These seventy cabins housed the plantation's 275 enslaved laborers, with families living in each cabin. Now only eight brick cabins remain."

After the abolition of slavery, these cabins became home to both tenant farmers and sharecroppers, and many of the families who lived here "were former slaves, or descendants of former slaves, who continued to toil in the same fields where their ancestors labored" (Oakland Plantation cell phone tour). And then it added: "The terms tenant farmer and sharecropper are sometimes used interchangeably. A tenant farmer lives and farms on land owned by someone else. A sharecropper, however, does not live on the land that is farmed."

Further details were provided about aspects of tenant farming, the difficulties the farmer faced, and how such difficulties, along with how infestation of crops by the boll weevil, led to significant migration to northern cities. So, by the 1950s, "the few remaining sharecroppers that were still here were permanently displaced by the modern tractor." This stop concluded, "In 1969, the last family moved out of the Tenant Cabins."

Stop 17, the final stop, was the Gin/Press Barn, which highlighted the wood-screw press and its uniqueness, stating, "It is believed to be the only known press of this type still in existence in its original location in the United States." Turning to the labor process, it indicated that "[c]otton was hand-picked and cleaned by enslaved laborers, and the cleaned cotton lint was placed into the top box" of the wood-screw press. It then gave details of the double-box steam press and mentioned the influence of mechanization: "Laborers no longer had to painstakingly clean, or gin, the cotton because the ginning equipment now did this. However, working the machinery was dangerous. If workers were not careful, they could lose limbs or even lives." The tour ended with an "exit message" concluding the tour and providing information on how visitors could go on to visit Oakland Plantation. It also provided a website for more information on the Cane River Creole National Historical Park, and details about the book *Magnolia Plantation: A Family Farm* by Henley Alexander Hunter.

Overall, the tour provided basic information about slavery, and the transition from slavery to freedom and from laborers to mechanization. It had some basic details about the enslaved and their struggles. However, it failed to provide individual details about enslaved people, did not humanize them, nor draw out their experiences, and we learned only the names of the plantation owners.

The Plantation Store

Most visitors arrived at the site by car or bus. Signs in the parking lot directed them to the plantation store, which was quite close by and was typically the first building that visitors entered. It served as the welcome center for visitors and also as the staff office when National Park Service staff was on site. It could also be visited. It had a main room, presented as the store main room, and contained a range of items.

As described earlier, the plantation store is a big white building built by the Hertzogs after the Civil War. It is made of wood and has a red roof. Throughout the twentieth century, it played various roles, including a store with merchandise of various kinds, and also a community social center. Due to the changing fortunes and organization of the plantation—including mechanization and population loss—the store had declined considerably by the 1960s and was closed in 1973. Over the front door of the store are the words "Magnolia Plantation, 1835," and "cotton" and "cattle." There was a sign standing on the floor in front of the main entrance to the store that said, "Cane River Creole National Historical Park" and "Welcome to Magnolia

Magnolia Plantation Store.

Plantation" and listed the buildings then open "for self-guided tour." The last time I visited this included the "Gin House," "Overseer's House," "Blacksmith Shop," and "Slave/Tenant House." The signage also said, "Take a map and please watch your step."

A plate on the ground had the words "VISITOR INFORMATION IN NORTH FOYER." To the right of the front was a set of open doors to an extension wing (the north foyer), in which the site maps and a wide range of leaflets were located. There was a Magnolia Plantation site map on the wall facing you as you entered. There were leaflets about the Cane River National Heritage Area, a range of attractions in the area, and other attractions in the state.

For example, there were several black and white leaflets for "Cane River Creole," including one describing the history of cotton and cotton cultivation in the United States. Another leaflet described "Cane River Creole" and "The Earth of Fire: War Comes to Cane River" with details of Maj. Gen. Nathaniel Prentiss Banks's "Red River Campaign" in 1864. There was one defining and describing bousillage, the building material made of mud, "cured Spanish moss, lime, straw, and dried grasses" and used by Creoles in Natchitoches and throughout the state. Another leaflet described "Agricultural Changes" in the Natchitoches area, from the early years (eighteenth century) through the period of "King Cotton," Reconstruction, and on into the twentieth century and "mechanization." There was an NPS black and white leaflet detailing "slavery": its history, slavery in Louisiana, "the life of a slave," and "slavery at Oakland Plantation." It set slavery in the United States and Louisiana in the context of slavery before and after the antebellum period, including slavery in the modern world, thus universalizing slavery. It stated, "Although outlawed today, slavery is still practiced in parts of the world. Indeed, the number of people enslaved today is higher now than at any time in history. The percentage of the world's population enslaved is at an all-time low, however" ("Cane River Creole. Slavery," NPS leaflet, n.d.). There were also leaflets describing various pieces of machinery, for example, "the cotton screw press" and "the double box steam press," as well as the "ginning process." There were examples of each of these presses in the gin barn. There were also leaflets on the Badin-Roque House in Natchitoches; the Mansfield State Historic Site, located close to Natchitoches; on Louisiana's National Parks, Associated Jazz Commission, and National Heritage Area; and one entitled "Celebrate Black History in Your National Parks."

A quick glimpse at the guest register, also in the foyer, indicated visitors from Louisiana, Texas, Arkansas, Oklahoma, California, Mississippi, Missouri, Massachusetts, and Maine.

In terms of details about slavery and slave cabins at the plantation, probably the most important among these leaflets was the Magnolia Plantation site map, which I picked up at the plantation store during one of my early visits. It was already several years old, yet it provided the best first information on the site, slavery, and the cabins for visitors. It had a map of the site with all the buildings listed on the map. It had a several paragraph overview of the history of the site, focusing on the Lecomte family and their relations with the Hertzog family, but also mentioned the use of enslaved labor and then tenant labor, and the African American community. It also mentioned African American resilience "in spite of difficulties." The map also provided short descriptions of each of the main structures. It was the first substantive information visitors would get about slavery. That is, if they read it.

On the site map, the "Plantation Store" (1) was described first. We were told it was "probably constructed circa 1873" as "the center of the labor systems that arose after the Civil War." The store "carried a number of household items such as medicines, candles, kerosene, clothing, and small tools. The store became a gathering place for the former slaves and others in the community." It was a place where music and other gatherings took place. Second is the "Blacksmith Shop" (2), which "was one of the most important buildings on the plantation and would have been one of the first buildings constructed," probably before Lecomte bought the site in 1824. It is a "poteaux-sur-sol style building that is a Creole form of architecture" and it "contains hewn wood, hand-wrought nails."

Next described was the "Pigeonnier" (3), dating to 1840 to 1855. Pigeonniers were common to plantations and were "an elegant part of the Creole landscape and served to emphasize the wealth and importance of the owner." They were also put to practical use to house pigeons. Young pigeons—a delicacy "called squab"—were served as food, and pigeon droppings were used as fertilizer.

Next was the "Slave Hospital/Overseer's House" (4), which was originally built as a slave hospital, but since then "has been used for various functions," including when it served as the "home for Atala and Matthew Hertzog for thirty years, while they were rebuilding the Main House" after it had been destroyed by Union soldiers during the Civil War. Subsequently, it was also used as an overseer's house. "Overseers," we are told, "were usually white men who were paid an annual salary and provided with a house and a domestic worker. In this area however, overseers in the postbellum period were often local Creoles."

Next described were the "Slave/Tenant Cabins" (5): "eight unusual brick cabins are all that remain of the 70 cabins that once housed the plantation's 275 enslaved workers." We were told that "of the original cabins, 24 were brick, and the rest were timber construction." We were told that "[f]amily tradition holds that most of the cabins were torn down after the Civil War and that many bricks from them were used to rebuild the Main House in the 1890s." Finally, "Originally, these cabins would each have held two families or groups of enslaved workers. After emancipation, a door was cut between the two rooms in the cabins and each cabin held only one family of tenant workers."

Last, there was a description of the "Gin/Press Barn" (6), which housed ginning and processing equipment, a wooden screw-type cotton press, and a double cotton gin and hydraulic press, the latter from the late 1800s. Some of this equipment "was used as early as 1835, some of which was in use as late as 1939." The press dates to 1835 and was originally mule powered. The press process was briefly described, and we were told that bales of cotton "weighing between 400 and 500 pounds" were produced.

Further information about the history of the store could be found by visitors who enter the building. The main room of the store was a museum itself and held an array of artifacts and images, old and new. In the main room was a long counter, lots of shelves, mostly empty, various items such as lamps, old books, signs from the early or mid-twentieth century, empty coke bottles, an old typewriter, a barrel, and various agricultural tools, some of which were hanging from the ceiling. There were a couple of wooden rocking chairs next to one another, with a small table in between them. Another older set of rocking chairs had a chess set on a table between them. There were also more tourist leaflets for the site, region, and state, most of which conveyed information for the period of the mid-twentieth century.

On one of the shelves, there was a reproduction of a handwritten letter by W. B. Eddins to Mr. A Lecomte, dated March 26, 1851, that related "the death of one our Negroes. Dannial the Black Smith from Armsteads side" who "had been eating something that he should not have eat [sic]" namely "ashes plentifully." He was given medical attention but died. Another letter reproduced from W. B. Eddins detailed how "we lost a negro, the child of Lucette. It had been sick for some length of time—and as I thought was getting well—at least the morning before it died it appeared prist and playfull." This letter was dated May 9, 1851.

Another sign—typed—described "calling the press," which was the practice of "workers" singing songs so as to maintain a regular pace, thus avoiding accidents such as being caught in the press, and also to keep morale up. This also led to an increase in production. The sign had no date. There were a number of photos, some black and white, some color, on the shelves on one of the walls, with examples of various processes, plus photos of Magnolia Plantation store and Oakland Plantation store, no dates, with details of their acquisition by National Park Service. Overall, the appearance and information began to convey what the store might have been like in the mid-twentieth century, absent, of course, of the people and the racial hierarchy in any substantive way.

A staff office at the back of the building contained various office and administrative items and a photo of one of the slave/tenant houses. It was used by NPS interpreters when they were on site.

The Slave Hospital/Overseer's House

The slave hospital/overseer's house was located a short walking distance behind the plantation store. The house had a slate sign posted on the wall, which could be seen as you approached it. With no air conditioning, this building was extremely warm. The main room had a ceiling fan but was still very warm, such that the sweat dropped from my brow as I walked from room to room. There were nine rooms in the main portion of the house and one room in each of the wing additions. I toured all of the rooms that were accessible and open. A couple of the rooms had mounted exhibits with detailed information about the history of the plantation, agricultural techniques and farming, and the lives of enslaved persons, written on panels

The Slave Hospital/Overseer's House at Magnolia Plantation. © Library of Congress, Prints & Photographs Division, Historic American Buildings Survey, HABS LA,35-NATCH.V,2-C-.

and accompanied by photos. A couple of rooms just had basic furniture and no details or text.

In the main room was a large informational panel standing on the mantel above the white fireplace. It had multiple texts and color photos and was entitled "Managing the Historic Advertisements & Retail Display Collection from the Oakland and Magnolia Plantation Stores. F. C. Brown and Dustin Fuqua." Various texts described issues like exhibits, storage, reproduction, and cataloguing of artifacts. There were photographs of the two plantations and some brief mention of their history, especially emphasizing that they were owned by the same families for more than two hundred years.

There was an exhibition in the room to the right of the main room. The information panel was entitled "Notable Agricultural Events Since the Civil War." It mentioned how the Civil War "signals the end of slavery and the rise of sharecropping and tenant farming." It had details about various Prud'homme family members, and a black and white photo of Jacques Alphonse Prud'homme in military uniform. It provided brief details of Reconstruction, the Depression, and a text about the 1867 struggle between Jacques Alphonse Prud'homme and his Black workers over their labor contract. The struggle resulted in a compromise—the workers wanted Saturday off work, and he conceded to let them have half of Saturday off.

There were also several summary texts about the site's history, its acquisition by the National Park Service, the struggles of agriculture, the boll weevil, Hertzog, mechanization, and some black and white photos of buildings, including cabins. And there were several photos of workers in the fields—mainly Black men. In another room was the exhibit "Artifact Recovery and Field Processing Techniques. W. Ryan Smith & Dustin Fuqua," which provided descriptions of the various aspects of these processes, along with some photos. A fifth room was empty. Next was the kitchen, mainly empty, except for a few basic pieces of furniture.

In the back unit was the slave hospital! Here visitors came face to face with two doors, and during each of my visits from 2007 to 2010, both were locked. There was no signposting or information about what might be inside. At the extension wing at the back, a slate sign said, "Slave Hospital." This gave the impression that the back was the hospital, and the front was the overseer's cabin. But this was unclear, as the Historic Structure Report on the overseer's house suggests the whole front building was the slave hospital (Overseer's House, HSR 2004).

The building conveyed significant and real information about slavery and its legacies at the plantation. It provided details, information, and images of the range of people that lived on the plantation, and significant messages about the role and contribution of the enslaved. However, once again, only the elite whites were named and humanized, and thus the information on Blacks was limited; on Black women it was negligible.

The Brick Slave Cabins

There were eight well-preserved and well-restored brick slave cabins at Magnolia Plantation. Substantial money had been spent to preserve and restore them, and significant maintenance was continually carried out on them. Seven of the cabins were double pen cabins and one was a single pen cabin. The single pen used to be a double pen but one half of it was destroyed in a tornado that hit the site in 1939, as mentioned earlier.

These cabins were particularly striking for at least three reasons. First, they were made of brick, which is extremely unusual. Second, they were still arranged in a grid formation to form a so-called slave street; and third, they were still situated in their original antebellum location. These last two points are especially important because they are uncommon in the state and the South.[5] At the other sites described in this book—and indeed at a very large number of plantation heritage sites across Louisiana and across the South—most of the extant twenty-first-century slave cabins have been

The Brick Slave Cabins at Magnolia Plantation.

relocated, usually several times around the site in which they were located. Indeed, some of them have been moved across sites.[6] In addition, the "slave street" conveys a clearer sense of the original layout and conditions of such cabins, though it did not even begin to approach anything like a "realistic representation" because of very real physical and social transformations of the grounds, the region, and social relations since the antebellum period.

The plantation website stated: "Magnolia's eight duplex-style quarters are the remnants of a rare masonry slave village. The cabins were initially built in the 1840s to house two slave families each. In the twentieth century, the two rooms were linked to form a single family tenant house and furnished with electricity" (January 29, 2011).

The cabins were very clearly presented at the site as slave cabins. That is, they were described, interpreted, and presented as slave cabins. Information about them was available on the website, in promotional literature, and in discussions and presentations made about the site by NPS interpreters. And there was information provided about slavery, and details about slavery and the cabins at this site in the cell phone tour, which was useful especially in the absence of on-site staff. This included information about the lives of enslaved people, their working conditions and various forms of resistance to slavery.

One of the eight cabins was usually open to visitors, and in 2010, it had an exhibit inside it. The other seven were usually closed and locked. They were located in a large, wide field alongside the parking lot. On the many visits I made to the site, the field was overgrown with grass but the sections of grass around each of the cabins were well maintained. There were plants and bushes located between some of the cabins. As you approached, there was a sign warning that the site was being monitored against theft of cultural resources. Several huge trees stood amid the cabins, and some cast shadows on them in the bright daylight sun. Several of the cabins had fading white-wash on the exterior walls, and red brick showing through it. Some have clearly deteriorating exterior walls, and the red brick seemed to be dissolving, as if by water. The cabins had two doors on the exteriors, each of which was slightly raised from the ground. One of the cabins had a fire extinguisher attached to the external side of one of the doors. One cabin appeared to be in a worse state of repair than all the others and was propped up by a set of three long wooden sticks at least twelve to fifteen feet long, which held up a wooden frame attached to the cabin wall, in order to offer it physical support and possibly prevent it from collapsing.

Obviously, the most important cabin was the open cabin because it was the only one that visitors could enter. As one approached the cabin that was accessible, one door was open. The roof did not appear to be made of tin like the others. It hung over the front portion of the cabin and had four square wooden poles holding it up. A washing tub (it seemed) hung on a hook on the outside wall. Inside the cabin were two rooms. The first room had a clean wooden floor, and several chairs about the room. The walls looked like they had been whitewashed, and the whitewash was fading in many areas, so that the red brick beneath it could be clearly seen. The windows in this room had wooden shutters on them, closed, presumably to keep the heat out. The room was dark as one entered, but the lights automatically came on, with a series of lights attached to the ceiling. Some of the wooden rafters on the ceiling were loose, revealing sunlight above. There was a chimney and fireplace, clean and apparently relatively new. The first room hosted a small exhibit, laid out on several tables, with texts and panels. The second room, accessible via a small door (less than five feet seven inches high) was empty.

One table of the exhibit comprised two panels. One panel was entitled "AGRICULTURE" and the other "TENANT LIFE." The first held seven black and white photos; the second, thirteen photos. On the agriculture panel were seven black and white photos of the gin process and hoeing in the field, as well as Black people picking cotton, riding a horse-driven plow, and sitting on a wagon. The second panel on tenant life also had several photos, one of a Black child in a classroom with someone who appeared to be a teacher, one of a Black woman washing clothes, another of a slave cabin, a Black man with a baby, and a couple more of Black children. One photo of a Black woman holding a child on her lap, was in color. One photo showed a Black child holding an even younger Black child, sitting in front of a fireplace, in what seemed like very dilapidated conditions, presumably inside one of the tenant cabins. There was no date.

One of the signs/texts stated, "The images on these displays are from the Library of Congress prints and photographs collection. They depict scenes from plantations across the United States, predominantly Louisiana."

In the far corner was another exhibit entitled "MAGNOLIA QUARTERS," which had three panels with various texts and photos, some black and white and some in color. One panel was titled at the top "Slave Resistance. The Struggle for Identity and Independence"; another had the title "Dehumanization of Slaves" and described "humiliation" and other issues of exploitation. There was a drawing of the British slave ship the *Brookes* from the New York Historical Society that described "how slaves were packed in the cargo hold." The image of this ship was one of the most widely circulated images of slave ships in museums and exhibits across the United States and Europe (Finley 2018). There was also a panel on slave auctions.

Other panels had headings like "passive resistance," "active resistance," including running away, and then "violent resistance," with brief details of the January 1811 slave revolt in Louisiana, which was reported here as "one of the most successful slave revolts in the United States." Also, there was a picture "with an artist's interpretation" of the slave rebellion in "French Caribbean island of Santo Domigan" [sic].

Other items in the exhibit included a list of some of the laws on slavery in Louisiana, and black and white photos of the slave/tenant cabins before renovation. There was also a reproduction of a letter from W. B. Eddins, the plantation overseer in 1851–52, saying that the slaves were complaining of sickness. A note at the bottom, presumably written by NPS staff comments, "Were the slaves complaining of illness really sick? Could they have been attempting to spend the day at the hospital instead of working?" One of the panels used the word "enslaved" rather than "slave," reflecting current academic and museum usage.

This small exhibit provided some concrete details and direct confrontation with the harsh realities of enslavement for Black people. What it lacked in creativity—it is plain and basic in its message—it made up for in its range of basic images and the scope of the text, presenting Black men, women, and children as human beings struggling for dignity and self-esteem, and for freedom, in a harsh world. But there was little or nothing to individualize or humanize the enslaved, or the plantation workers in the long period of Jim Crow after slavery ended.

The Blacksmith Shop

The blacksmith shop at the Magnolia Plantation was located close by and just to the side of the plantation store. It was a significant structure and attracted a number of visitors. Information about the blacksmith shop and about past blacksmiths was mainly available on the website and from the plantation site map. There was little to no information about them provided at the structure itself.

The website informed visitors: "The blacksmith shop, workspace of enslaved workers, first Daniel and then Charles, would typically have been one of the structures in place to provide the developing plantation with wheels, tools, and nails" (accessed January 29, 2011). At plantation heritage sites across the South, we are often told that blacksmiths are among the most important workers on the plantation because they erected the first buildings, and they made it possible for many other workers to do their jobs, for example, by providing equipment, tools, and repairs. The blacksmith shop would typically be one of the first buildings constructed. Blacksmiths on slave plantations were very commonly of African American or African descent (Vlach 1993). There were, of course, many white men who worked as blacksmiths. There was limited information about the blacksmith shop at Magnolia Plantation, with no reliable evidence on its exact date of construction, nor precise details of the changes made to the building over time. Nor was there any precise evidence on who the blacksmiths were in the shop over time—during or after slavery. Two specific blacksmiths were mentioned, Daniel and Charles, but we got no further details about them.

However, archaeological excavations of the blacksmith shop in the early 2000s have produced significant new evidence and insights (St. Clair 2008). These excavations were ongoing in 2010 and promised to add significant archaeological evidence, along with oral histories, to the limited documentary evidence that existed about the blacksmith shop. These investigations seek to examine questions such as whether it served at some time as a residence for African American workers. In particular, archaeologists "investigate a workplace for ritual behavioral signatures" and seek to combine "historical documentary research, oral histories, and archaeological investigation to present a study of the cultural expressions of the lives and craft of plantation blacksmiths of the Cane River area, primarily on the Magnolia and Oakland Plantations" (St. Clair 2008, 1). They also examine "the transmission of

African cultural practices to African American artisans" and "the dual role of the African blacksmith as Spiritual practitioner" as well as blacksmith (ibid., 3).

For site visitors, the Magnolia Plantation site map provided the first introduction to the shop. It was also mentioned on the website. The blacksmith shop was open in 2010 to visitors, who could enter and look around. However, what visitors saw was a representation of what it looked like in the recent past. There were no signs posted or written details, and no images of any of the past blacksmiths.

Separate documentary sources provide evidence and the names of several of the Magnolia Plantation blacksmiths during the antebellum period—all of whom were enslaved African Americans (or possibly Creoles). As mentioned earlier, Ambroise Lecomte's ledgers indicate that there were at least two blacksmiths on his properties: Charles and Daniel (Brown 2006, 36–40, cited in St. Clair 2008, 4), and "[t]here is also a bill of sale that lists Lecomte as the agent for Louis Buard in the purchase of a blacksmith named Saturday" (St. Clair 2008, 3). No other details are mentioned about these blacksmiths in these reports.

Other Structures: Gin Barn, Main House, Cook's Cabin

The gin barn at Magnolia Plantation is a large and impressive structure, with a range of machinery inside it. It attracts a significant number of visitors. It houses a gin and a rare wooden screw cotton press. The eleven-by-thirty-foot cotton press still stands in its original location and was used until the late nineteenth century, when the plantation converted to steam. A comprehensive evaluation of the history and possible future uses of the gin barn reported: "With two stories and a roof ridge nearly 32' above the ground, the structure dominates the landscape at the southern end of Magnolia Plantation and is the first structure that many visitors see upon arrival" (Gin Barn, HSR 2004, 63). It certainly was the first building I saw, especially when approaching the plantation from the freeway coming from the south, rather than on the highway from Oakland Plantation. It stands alone, a long distance from all the other buildings. The HSR adds that "the park's GMP [General Management Plan] calls for it to be one of the focal points for exhibit and interpretation" at the site (Gin Barn, HSR 2004, 73).

The barn is situated near the southern boundary of the site, about 225 feet east of Highway 119, and is "a two-story, wood-framed, end-gabled building with a metal roof and set on low brick piers. The building is rectangular, measuring approximately 89 feet east to west and approximately 38 feet north to south, plus arcades 9'–8" wide that run down both sides of the structure" (Gin Barn, HSR 2004, 39).

The gin barn and equipment are impressive. The HSR reports that "[t]he building itself is most significant for having been originally constructed to house both gin and cotton press under the same roof, an important advance in the operation of plantation gins in the third quarter of the nineteenth century" (Gin Barn, HSR 2004, 2). It adds that "the wood-screw cotton press is one of the park's most-important artifacts [sic]" (ibid.).

In 2011, the information available in the gin barn and related exhibits was almost exclusively focused on the equipment in the barn. This is also the case with the HSR, which is preoccupied with the equipment, but makes a case for more attention to be paid to the building itself, in terms of both preservation and exhibit. When visitors come to the site, there is almost no mention at all of people, although the Gin Barn HSR reminds us that mention of plantation residents is expected by the General Management Plan.

The best available evidence suggests that the gin barn dates to the third quarter of the nineteenth century, a previous gin barn on the site that dates to 1835 having been accounted for (Gin Barn, HSR 2004, 2, 28). It was built shortly before or shortly after the Civil War. As cotton was the major crop at the plantation, the gin barn, and the gin it housed, played crucial roles. In that regard, it would have been run and maintained by enslaved labor through the antebellum period, and primarily by Black workers after that time.

Apparently little documentary evidence exists for the antebellum cotton gin and press at Magnolia Plantation except a brief mention of an individual tragedy, a notation in Magnolia records that "Little Ned" died September 29, 1856, "burnt in the press" (Gin Barn, HSR 2004, 17). He was an enslaved worker. It is not clear how he died from burning, says the Gin Barn HSR, because it's not clear what burned him. The notation about "Little Ned" implies that his burning was due to steam, and that the gin and presses were running by steam. The Gin Barn HSR says this is still not clear, because the engine and boiler would have been outside the building. But it seems likely to me—he was burned with steam, not fire. The engine house was destroyed in a 1939 tornado, and the gin barn incurred "significant damage" (Gin Barn, HSR 2004, 23).

. . .

In this chapter, I have argued that in heritage tourism at Magnolia Plantation, slavery and the slave cabins were relatively incorporated into the main representations at the site. I revealed some of the ways in which slavery received relatively significant attention, as did the majority of inhabitants (primarily Blacks and other people of color, including "mixed-race") and how they interacted with the powerful whites who owned and managed the plantation (and the working-class whites that also worked there). As at Oakland Plantation, information at Magnolia was provided on the plantation website, in promotional literature, in several locations across the site (including some temporary exhibits), and during the cell phone and self-guided tours. Some information was provided on how the cabins functioned as central components of the plantation under slavery and there were opportunities for visitors to obtain further details. Occasionally, especially during the summer, tour guides were available to answer visitor questions. In all these media, most attention was devoted to the distinctive ethnic identity of elite white residents who were French Creoles, and to their descendants, and contrasted with the experiences of elite white Anglos. This included key attributes like ancestry and family names, and cultural practices such as language, religion, architecture, and food. Once again, details of the multitier racial system that prevailed in the region historically, and the existence of legally free people of color, were highlighted. And once again, very little was said about enslaved people of mixed origins, and very few Black voices were heard, except for stereotypical voices.

Although Magnolia Plantation shared much in common with Oakland—in large part because they were both part of Cane River Creole National Historical Park—there were three dimensions to Magnolia that made it significantly different from Oakland. First, there was no main house at the site; second, there was no kitchen; and third, there were no permanent staff on site. This meant that there were fewer opportunities for site tour guides to provide information about the plantation, and fewer spaces in which to represent anyone—white, Black, or of mixed origins—who lived on the site historically. The absence of a main house and kitchen is highly relevant because those are the structures that the vast majority of visitors to heritage sites of this kind come to see and where they spend most of their time, often on a guided tour. At most of these sites, more information about Black people was typically provided when touring the main house and mentioning or visiting the kitchen. With these two buildings missing, visitors saw fewer images—and heard far less information—about white and Black women in domestic roles, and thus fewer images of women overall (as compared, for example, with Oakland Plantation). However, significant attention was given to the lives of Black people in the blacksmith shop, including as a result of the archaeological studies undertaken on it (St. Clair 2008; Brown 2006). As a result of these differences, I found the site inferior to Oakland Plantation.

Just as at Oakland, it is inaccurate to conclude that slavery and the slave cabins were fully incorporated into representations at Magnolia. Here too, they remained in a clear second place to the nature and quality of information about elite white lives on the plantation, and to the accommodations and buildings lived and worked in by elite whites. There was far less information provided at Magnolia than at Oakland, but the information provided displayed the same deficiencies as Oakland because it followed a very similar narrative framing of southern gentility.

Similarly, far less attention was paid at Magnolia than at Oakland to the slave cabins and to the other places in which the enslaved lived or slept, though they are briefly mentioned on the website and in promotional literature at the site. Without a main house or kitchen on the site, we could not hear if any enslaved persons lived in spaces in either structure. Most of the eight slave cabins were not generally open to visitors, although one was open early on in my research and had a small exhibit installed in it. This exhibit was improved with further additions over the course of my fieldwork. But again, like Oakland, the exhibits were old-fashioned and staid, information was limited, perfunctory, and lacked creativity. Again, no detailed information individualized and humanized the enslaved, or illuminated their lives and their culture. This is again despite the existence of extensive research that could provide this kind of information. This stood in stark contrast to the stories that bring the elite whites at the site to life. Black people remained abstract, undifferentiated, and anonymous, while white people were concrete, individualized, and personalized. Again, this conveyed what was valued at the sites, and who were regarded as the most important residents.

The lack of information on slavery and cabins, or the lives of the enslaved, should take into account the observation by several staff at Oakland that the cabins functioned as tenants' cabins for a longer time than they did as slave cabins. To several staff, it seemed more appropriate to spend less time on slavery and more on post-slavery.

At Magnolia, insights into the gender and the racial division of labor were evident but were far more implied than described. Early in the research period, most information and images about whites were provided on the website and by leaflets in the main store, with very little on Black people. Later on, a bit more perfunctory information was provided as the exhibits in the one open cabin were improved. And again, like Oakland, Black women received the least attention of all groups, though I consider it a blessing that there were no details about a so-called mammy provided at the site.

The efforts made by the park superintendent at Oakland to increase attention to slavery and slave cabins there, and to the lives of the enslaved, were also relevant at Magnolia, though she had far fewer resources and far less material to assist her in these efforts. That meant that fewer changes were evident compared with Oakland. Perhaps the biggest improvement was the implementation of the cell phone tour. This tour provided some brief information to the visitors about the cabins, which was helpful especially since there were usually no staff present. Some further information about slavery (and to a lesser extent, about the cabins) was also made available in the exhibit in the slave hospital/overseer's house that had been installed by the time of my visit in August 2010.

The site benefited from archaeological investigations, especially at the blacksmith shop, and from discussions with scholars, curators, and others at the 2008 conference, and the exhibit in one of the cabins was significantly improved over what existed before. Similar language—"enslaved" rather than "slave" was used too. And substantial work was also invested into maintaining the buildings, especially the blacksmith shop.

The same six factors that explained heritage tourism at Oakland provide insights into the situation at Magnolia. First, was a narrative created under the thrall of southern gentility, including elite white lifestyles, paternalism, and romance. Once again, this narrative foregrounded the cultural practices of elite white people and the architecture, furnishings, and gardens that graced their houses. Staff opinions and beliefs about visitor priorities was the second factor. Third was the limited resources available to staff to carry out the kind of research that would enable them to provide more detailed histories and/or creative exhibitions on Black people. A fourth factor was the limited or negligible involvement of Black people, especially professionals from community and other organizations or institutions run by Black people. Fifth, widespread and long-standing racial inequality and institutional racism, past and present, discouraged Black people's involvement in the sites. In a context of Jim Crow segregation and widespread racism, they had different priorities than those organizing this kind of heritage experience. And finally, state ownership of the site—in the form of NPS—provided the original funding to purchase and maintain the site. These six factors were of course directly shaped by the lack of a main house, a kitchen, and a permanent staff presence at the site, which meant that fewer visitors came to the site, and they received far less information than at Oakland.

Chapter Four

MELROSE PLANTATION

Coin Coin, Cammie, and Clementine

Melrose Plantation (originally called Yucca Plantation) was the most popular of all the heritage plantation sites in the Natchitoches region. This popularity derived from the fascinating array of owners, residents, and stories at the plantation, in particular the lives of three women: Marie Thérèse Coin Coin, Cammie Henry, and Clementine Hunter. Marie Thérèse Coin Coin was the so-called matriarch of the legally free family of color that established the plantation. Her many children and grandchildren—mainly led by men—became the Metoyers, a legally free family of color, that by the mid-nineteenth century, owned more enslaved persons than any other legally free people of color in the entire antebellum South. They became rich, powerful, and celebrated figures in Natchitoches Parish (Mills 1977).[1]

Cammie Henry was the innovative, determined, and eccentric owner of Melrose who established a writer's and artist's colony there in the 1920s, which attracted many prominent southern (white) writers. It also attracted François Mignon—writer, columnist, gardener, and close confidante of Cammie Henry. He was resident at Melrose for forty years, and although born in the United States, he tricked everyone into believing he was from France.[2] Clementine Hunter was also a long-time resident of Melrose. She became a renowned folk artist, who rose to produce magnificent art. Born in Natchitoches in 1896/97, the grandchild of enslaved persons, she had worked most of her life in the fields and kitchens at Melrose.

Stories about these individuals, families, friends, and associates were enriched by portraits, paintings, and images, heavily saturated with information about Spanish and French culture, Catholicism, music, and the occasional dash of voodoo, and made a savory stew served up daily to the thousands of tourists that visited the site each year. The fact that some of the stories were told by the several descendants of the Metoyer family who worked as site interpreters only made them richer. As the old adage goes, if none of these characters had existed, they would have needed to be invented just for the amazement and fascination they have brought to subsequent generations. Melrose heritage tourism was inherently intriguing, and as a proxy for broader social relations—those constituted through race, gender, and economic stratification—at the site itself and elsewhere in Louisiana and the South, it also offered compelling insights.

Melrose Plantation was a not-for-profit site, owned and operated as a heritage tourism site since 1986, by the Association for the Preservation of Historic Natchitoches (APHN). The plantation itself dates to 1796, when the plot of land on which it was built was purchased by Marie Thérèse Coin Coin's son Louis Metoyer (Mills 1977). Heritage tourism was organized around several major themes. First, it was the home of the largest and most (in)famous families of legally free people of color across the South who owned enslaved persons—the so-called Cane River Creoles. In antebellum America, people of color who owned enslaved persons were a rare occurrence, and it is even rarer to find heritage sites dedicated to them in the twenty-first-century South. This family is the fulcrum of presentations at the site (with a focus on the eighteenth and nineteenth centuries).[3] The second theme is the site as the home and vocation of Cammie Garett Henry and the writer's and artist's colony that she created in the 1920s and 1930s. The third is as the home and creative space of Clementine Hunter, one of the South's most celebrated folk artists. In elaborating these central themes, a wide range of people and events are touched upon, including slavery, legally free people of color and the enslaved, Civil War and independence, women's rights, literature and poetry, and art and architecture. In this regard, the site covered lengthy historical periods (from the 1700s through the 1980s) and a wide range of topics.

APHN secured ownership of Melrose Plantation by donation from the company that was its previous owner and secured substantial funds for its restoration and the purchase of artifacts and furniture inside the plantation. Several buildings were restored, and a history of the plantation was written. This led to the site being designated a National Historic Landmark in 1974 (HSR, August 2005, appendix). During my research, Melrose still operated as a working plantation of more than 1,600 acres.[4] Tourist visits were organized around a guided tour with two parts; one part covered the Main House, and a second part covered the various outbuildings.

In this chapter, as with the two previous chapters, I describe the *continuum of coerced accommodation* occupied by the enslaved at the site in two clusters. In the first cluster, were five twenty-first-century antebellum slave cabins that were separate, purpose-built structures, each of which was occupied on a consistent basis by enslaved persons in the nineteenth century.[5] These were the bindery/gift shop, the weaving house, the Ghana House, the female writer's cabin, and Yucca House. In the second cluster, were spaces in the main house, the kitchen ruins, the African House, the barn, and the Clementine Hunter cabin. There was no evidence that Hunter's cabin was ever used as a cabin for the enslaved, but it was clearly closely linked to slavery, as will be described later in the chapter.

None of the first cluster of cabins at the site were original to the plantation. All were moved from other local properties in the mid-twentieth century by Cammie Henry (Cammie Henry Diary 1934).[6] She brought them to Melrose to provide temporary housing for her guest writers from the 1920s to 1940s (Moore 1984). She also used the cabins for weaving and for binding her scrapbooks. Since then, all the cabins have been moved around the site multiple times for purposes of tourism and convenience, and all have been substantially restored.[7] The main house and kitchen ruins are original to the plantation.

I argue that heritage tourism at Melrose engaged in the symbolic annihilation of slavery and the slave cabins, because slavery was marginalized, the cabins were not described as slave cabins but as cabins occupied by white writers in the 1930s, and little or nothing was said about the fact that there were many other spaces in which the enslaved slept or lived.

MARIE THÉRÈSE COIN COIN AND THE ORIGINS OF YUCCA PLANTATION

It all began with Marie Thérèse Coin Coin, born enslaved and taken as a de facto wife by a local white Frenchman. She eventually secured her legal freedom and started the agricultural holding that developed into a large plantation. She also secured legal freedom for her enslaved children and helped them to acquire land and purchase enslaved persons, and thus created the foundation for their remarkable success as plantation owners. At least that is what some of the early research informs us (Mills 1977). Closer inspection reveals, however, that key elements of the story lack concrete evidence and some facts are at variance with existing evidence. We do know that the Metoyers were one family of a group called the "Cane River Creoles," a group of mixed African and European origins, who became owners of multiple plantations and multiple enslaved persons in the Natchitoches region. The Cane River Creoles constituted a "third racial class in Louisiana" whose members believed themselves to be "a race apart from blacks" (Mills 1977, xiv).

As a result of intermarriage, by the Civil War, there were families with at least seventeen different surnames in the Isle Brevelle community (Mills 1977, 102). Isle Brevelle is not technically an island; rather, "it is a narrow strip of land some thirty miles in length with three- to four-mile breadth, delineated by a waterway that splits, meanders, and joins again" (Mills 1977, 50). Many of the Cane River Creoles supported the Confederacy (Mills 1977). Coin Coin's family—the Metoyers—became the richest and most powerful group in this community, although there were other legally free people of color in the parish who enjoyed similar types of preferential treatment, especially vis-à-vis Blacks in the region, the state, and across the South (Schweninger 1990; Mills 1977).

Despite the power of her legacy, and the frequency with which it is retold in promotional literature and tours at the site, the facts of Marie Thérèse Coin Coin's ethnicity and birthplace are highly disputed. Some claim Coin Coin was born in Africa, others that she was born in the United States; some say she was "pure African," others that she was mixed. Recent scholars convey that the ancestry of Marie Thérèse Coin Coin "remains to be satisfactorily resolved" (MacDonald et al. 2006a, 126). For example, Mills maintains that Marie Thérèse Coin Coin was the second daughter of Francois and Francoise; that she was "fluent in an African dialect" and was "well trained by her parents in the native use and application of medicinal herbs and roots" (Mills 1977, 3–4). He adds that no accounts exist of her "personal characteristics" (ibid., 11). Later scholars have suggested that many of Mills' arguments are "based on rather shaky archival evidence" (Macdonald et al. 2006b, 128).

Mills writes that Coin Coin was born enslaved in 1742, the property of Sieur Louis Juchereau de St. Denis, who was one of the founders of what became Natchitoches. In 1714, he founded the military post and colonial settlement in the area now called northwest Louisiana. His family were "the largest slave owners in the colony" (MacDonald et al. 2006a, 126). St. Denis died not long after Coin Coin was born, and she worked mainly for his daughter. After growing up in the household, Coin Coin was then leased out by St. Denis's daughter, to a young French soldier named Claude Thomas Pierre Metoyer, and she was eventually sold to him in 1758. By 1810, Metoyer was the largest slaveholder in the parish with 103 enslaved men, women, and children among his property (Mills 1977, 27). While she was in his possession, and under his control, Metoyer and Coin Coin entered into a long-term liaison that produced ten children. Seven of the children survived to adulthood, and all the surviving children were of "mixed blood" (Mills 1977, 19). All were fathered by Metoyer, it seems. Metoyer eventually legally freed Marie Thérèse when he decided to marry a (white) Frenchwoman in 1786.

All of Coin Coin's children were also legally freed, paid for by her as result of her hard work. Metoyer gave Marie Thérèse a yearly allowance and a parcel of land at Cedar Bend, upon which the Maison de Marie Thérèse still stands (MacDonald et al. 2006a).

Between 1794 and 1803, Coin Coin and her sons acquired several land grants and developed their agricultural holdings, and by 1793 she had established "an efficient plantation operation on her small tract" and sought to expand her holdings (Mills 1977, 32). In 1815, Coin Coin and her sons inherited property from Claude Thomas Pierre Metoyer, and they amassed other land and bought enslaved persons. Coin Coin settled in a cabin on the sixty-eight acres given to her by Metoyer and began tobacco cultivation (Mills 1977, 28). She also trapped wild bears and marketed their grease for export to Europe (ibid., 30). Family tradition says she also cultivated indigo, and possibly also manufactured medicine (ibid., 30, 31). She received a land grant from the Spanish king, and she began a *vacherie* (cow grazing).

Coin Coin's story is told with great emphasis on her as a highly exceptional and remarkable woman. Some scholars attribute Coin Coin's success to her individual agency. For example, Mills says:

> With loyalty, determination, foresight, ingenuity, and a considerable degree of business acumen, this exceptional black woman and the children she produced overcame the stigma of slavery that had been branded upon them by birth. By engineering their own fate, she and her remarkable family were to become the respected and renowned proprietors of an imposing and, ultimately, legendary plantation operation. (Mills 1977, 6)

But other scholars highlight the institutional context and propose that it was not simply individual agency that led to her success. They point to, for example, the help she received from Metoyer as a white man with power; the fact that the "Spanish authorities had some interest in propagating a third social class of colonists"; and because there were, in the community, other white fathers of "mixed-race" children who saw "race mixture" as beneficial for their offspring (Habs 2001; Mills 1977, 5). In attaining her success, it is clear that she received substantial assistance from the white community, as did so many other successful legally free people of color in the colonial and antebellum period of the South (Leslie 1995; Alexander 1991; Schweninger 1990; Johnson and Roark 1984; Mills 1977, 49).

By old age Coin Coin had brought fourteen children into the world (Mills 1977, 34). By 1816, she owned twelve slaves and local tradition says Marie

Thérèse Coin Coin treated her slaves "kindly" (Mills 1977, 44–45). The date of her death in not known for sure, but records suggest that it was probably between April 1816 and December 1817 (ibid., 48). She divided her estate among her children.

EARLY DAYS AT YUCCA

Yucca Plantation was one of a series of land tracts acquired by Marie Thérèse Coin Coin and her family. The land plot upon which Yucca was located was bought by Louis Metoyer, Marie Thérèse Coin Coin's second son, in 1796 (Macdonald et al. 2006a, 129). Her first son, Augustin, was also central to these developments. Augustin was born enslaved and secured his legal freedom in August 1792 (Mills 1977, 41). Augustin—known in oral and family tradition as "Grand-pere Augustin"—became the community patriarch, and he helped the family and community achieve security, peace, and refuge against the Americans who were increasingly taking over the state (Mills 1977, xxix). He remains a central figure in the history of the site. There is a huge portrait of him that hung in the local church, which then was moved to Melrose, where it is now on display in the main house.

Yucca Plantation began small and was developed into a significant plantation that was worked at its peak by sixty-five enslaved persons (Mills 1977). Yucca House, tradition claims, was built by Marie Thérèse Coin Coin. It is a "maison de poteaux en terre" (ibid., 69). An authority on houses in Louisiana dates its construction between 1796 and 1800 (ibid., 67). Louis Metoyer was deeded the property in 1796, and Yucca House was probably built around 1796. It is believed to be Louis Metoyer's first main house (Macdonald et al. 2006a, 138). Yucca remained the largest domicile on the plantation until 1833, when Louis Metoyer built the main house that eventually became known as Melrose. Significantly, it was built by someone who had been born enslaved, and whose mother had also been born enslaved. Like so many plantation main houses across the South, Yucca House almost certainly had enslaved persons living in it. Louis and Augustin developed the property further and expanded its holdings and the enslaved population that they owned. Louis Metoyer saw his family make its greatest progress; so too did Melrose see its most rapid gains (Mills and Mills 1973, 48).

Metoyer's property had been located upriver, but the children of Marie Thérèse Coin Coin settled down river. Augustin led the Metoyers to Isle Brevelle, to buying land and plantations and expanding their holdings (Mills 1977, 50). Augustin, "living frugally in a small cabin that he erected hastily on his plantation," acquired more land (ibid., 64). Augustin bought at least another twenty-two enslaved persons between 1810 and 1817. Natural increase added another nineteen to this number (ibid., 67).

According to the census of 1810 for the Territory of Orleans, Augustin had seventeen enslaved persons (Mills 1977). At the time, the census listed 259 households, of whom only 166 owned at least one enslaved person. There were thirteen legally free Blacks or legally free people of color listed as heads of households, of whom only four owned enslaved persons, with an average of two each (Mills 1977). By the time Coin Coin died, she and her family had acquired between 11,000 and 12,000 acres of land and at least ninety-nine enslaved persons (Mills 1977, 67).

METOYERS RULE AS MASTER-ENSLAVERS

As early as "the end of the Louisiana colonial era, Marie Thérèse and her children were the proprietors of some 6,400 acres of land. The Metoyer domain consisted of some 13,000 acres that stretched farther south than Gorum and farther north than Grand Encore, a span of some thirty miles. The Metoyers married whites, cousins within the family, or other legally free people of color, and they sought partners from across the entire state (Schweninger 1990; Mills 1977, 78). In this way, they increased their holdings and status (Mills 1977, xxvii). Gender shaped these patterns. For example, women married men from New Orleans, because legally free women of color in New Orleans did not marry legally free men of color, because they typically became concubines to white men (Mills 1977, 79; see also Dominguez 1986).

The peak period of Metoyer affluence was between 1830 and 1840. At that time, at least four of the families had 1,000 acres or more; and three had between 500 and 1,000 acres (Mills, 1977, 111). Thus:

> Melrose was to remain the central plantation of the Metoyer colony on Isle Brevelle for three decades after the death of Marie Thérèse. In those three decades the Metoyers of Melrose and surrounding plantations literally worked their way into the highest levels of Southern planters. Large stately homes graced their plantations, appointed with simple but elegant furnishings. Sterling silver, organs, pianos, racehorses, and other such badges of a Southern planter's wealth were all included among the Metoyer property inventories of this period. (Mills and Mills 1973, 47)

SLAVERY AND THE ENSLAVED AT YUCCA

By 1810, the census indicates that there were fifteen enslaved persons at Yucca Plantation. This number increased to twenty-three in 1820, and to fifty-four in 1830, during the final years of the life of Louis Metoyer. The enslaved population peaked in 1838 when there were sixty-five enslaved individuals and then began falling, so that by 1843 there were only thirty-three enslaved persons owned by Theophile, Louis's grandson (Macdonald et al. 2006a, 129). The enslaved at Yucca traced their origins to various sources, and there was "a greater mix of birthplaces and ethnic origins at this property" as compared with Marie Thérèse Coin Coin's plantation (Mills 1977, 129). There were some from Tennessee (in 1811), some from Africa (in 1816), and others from Louisiana (MacDonald et al. 2006a, 130).

The 1838 succession file of Jean-Baptiste Louis Metoyer inventories all of his property and records "65 slaves" present at the site (MacDonald et al. 2006a, 130). These enslaved people had various owners—some owned by Jean-Baptiste and his wife; others owned by his father's widow, others by his son. Among them were Charlotte, "a 30-year-old of the Caukau nation (presumably Kaka from the area of Modern Nigeria)"; Marie, "a 20-year-old from the Congo nation"; another called Marianne, in the inventory, age sixty (ibid.). A series of invoices accompany the inventory and lists the activities of the slaves, indicating that they did more than field work; for example, they ran errands of various kinds: "Zenon hired out in September 1838" (ibid.); "October, goods ordered from town were collected by Cesaire, Hilaire and Marie" (ibid., 131); also, an enslaved blacksmith, Frederick, was "valued at $1,400" (ibid.).

It is estimated that with sixty-five enslaved persons at Yucca "during its 1830s peak" there would have been ten or more slave dwellings (Macdonald et al. 2006a, 137).

The Metoyer clan in the Cane River Colony owned more enslaved persons on average than the whites. The 1830 Census provides an overview. The Metoyer colony—including the Metoyers and allied families—as a whole owned 287 enslaved persons (up from 58 in 1810). There were ninety-nine people of color in the Metoyer households, with an average of 2.3 enslaved persons for each man, woman, and child. In contrast, there were 3,801 whites in the parish, with ownership of 3,266 enslaved persons, or 0.9 enslaved persons per white. Legally free people of color not in the colony had 0.2 enslaved persons each (Mills 1977, 108). So, the Metoyers owned more enslaved persons than any other legally free people of color. The total of 5,667 acres of improved land "owned by the Metoyers and allied families in 1850 were tilled by 436 slaves" (Mills 1977, 111). As other scholars have pointed out, legally free people of color in the lower South, especially Louisiana, on average, owned more enslaved property than did their counterparts in the upper South (Schweninger 1990; Berlin 1984).

Augustin became the wealthiest man in the Cane River colony, with an estate of $140,958 in 1860 (Mills 1977). He was not the richest man of color in Louisiana, but this community of color was richer than any other community of color, and there were no other such communities that "boasted as many prosperous men and women or which retained such a degree of wealth for so long a period of time" (Schweninger 1990; Mills 1977, 139). However, by this time, the Metoyer family lost Yucca, and their fortunes were soon to change dramatically.

As prominent planters in the area, the Metoyers benefited from the more flexible racial hierarchy that prevailed in Natchitoches, the "three-tier racial caste" itself the result of French cultural inheritance, the generosity of some elite white men towards their "mixed-race children," and the remoteness of the parish from Anglo America and its rigid binary racial hierarchy.

As is common in many writings (and in many heritage sites) across Natchitoches, Louisiana, and the South, the Metoyers are described as "good slave owners" (see Eichstedt and Small 2002, 161, for examples). Mills reports, "As a rule it appears that the slaves belonging to the Cane River Creoles of color were treated as well, if not better, than those of the average white planter," and "[g]enerally speaking, slave housing on the Isle exhibited a better standard than either the parish or the national average" (Mills 1977, 120). On several Cane River plantations, a cabin larger than the others was set aside as the slave hospital. For example, on Louis Metoyer's plantation, their old home was used as a hospital for the enslaved after they built a larger one (ibid., 121). Also, Jerome Sarpy, tradition relates, insisted upon excellent housing conditions for his bondsmen; cabins not only had to be kept clean but were whitewashed twice a year, inside and out" (ibid., 120). But note too that "[t]he housing which was provided for the Cane River slaves was rudimentary, as was most slave housing, and seems to have been typical of that of the late antebellum period, as described by Fogel and Engerman" (ibid.).

THE METOYERS LOSE YUCCA

In the later decades of the antebellum period, and those following the Civil War, the Metoyers and related families suffered substantial losses. Anglo-Americans had moved into the state, and they did not accept or condone the special status afforded people of color—as distinct from Black people generally—in Natchitoches or Louisiana generally (Malone 1992; Mills 1977). Yucca Plantation passed into white hands in 1847, when it was purchased by Henry and Hypolite Hertzog for $8,340. It had been valued nine years earlier at $40,000 (Mills and Mills 1973, 51). The Metoyers lost other holdings after the Civil War.

The Hertzogs continued to farm cotton on Yucca, and by 1850, there were fifty-one enslaved persons on the plantation (Macdonald et al. 2006a). It remained in their hands for three decades. Oral tradition holds that the Hertzog brothers used Yucca as a hospital prior to the Civil War (HSR, August 2005, 14). It is clear that enslaved persons continued to live at Yucca under the Hertzog ownership, though there was no detailed information about all of them. We do have details of several formerly enslaved persons who continued to live on the plantation—and who lived in Yucca House itself—after the Civil War and were still there when Cammie Henry arrived in 1899. Some lived at Melrose well into the early decades of the twentieth century. One of these was "Uncle Israel." He was raised on Yucca, and in the 1850s, was owned by Hypolite Hertzog. He was born "on Numa Lambre place" (a plantation) "which joined old Kilgore originally [the] Achille Prud'homme place" (Mills 1977, 86). He lived at Melrose the remainder of his life, dying there in 1923. A second enslaved person owned by Hypolite Hertzog was "Aunt Jane Suddatt, who was born in North Carolina" (HSR, August 2005, 14). Jane was brought to Louisiana from North Carolina "when a grown girl" and sold in New Orleans off the "old slave dock" at the St. Louis Hotel. She was bought by Hypolite Hertzog and owned by him until freed. She also remained at Yucca after the Civil War. She died July 12, 1921.

THE CIVIL WAR AND ITS AFTERMATH

During slavery, Metoyer success was based on the paternalism and tolerance of the whites in power, on their light skin, and on the colony being far from centers of white power, especially Anglo power. The increased presence of Anglo-Americans led to a rapid and decisive decline in the fortunes and privilege of the Metoyers and of the people of color in the parish. Many like the "Verdun and Metoyer families in Louisiana, subsisted on small plots of their once-great plantations" (Schweninger 1990, 48). As the white population of Louisiana increased, so did the white population in Natchitoches. Due to its isolation, its relatively small community, and the social relations long established between prominent people of color and whites with power, the elimination of social distinctions did not happen as quickly in Natchitoches as it did elsewhere in the state. The parish was also less affected, in practice, by the severity and extent of sweeping changes that occurred elsewhere in the state, especially in New Orleans. Nevertheless, says Mills, the Metoyer colony suffered terribly.

Legally free people of color lost the privileges they had enjoyed, and the distinctions from Blacks and "the people of Brevelle were now hopelessly submerged in the new mass of black freedmen" (Mills 1977, 246). Some were able to keep hold of their land, but many lost land. Among those who were able to keep their land, many saw a precipitous decline in their fortunes and standards of living. "Those members of the colony who managed to hold their land but could not afford the upkeep on their large houses moved into the cabins formerly occupied by those they had enslaved" (Mills 1977, 247). The "mansion houses" were torn down, and the bricks and lumber sold for whatever they would bring. Some family members moved away altogether.

YUCCA PLANTATION BECOMES MELROSE PLANTATION

Francis Roman Cauranneau bought Yucca from the Hertzogs in 1881 and later sold it to Joseph Henry (MacDonald and Morgan 2006, 129; Mills and Mills 1973, 51). Henry was born in Ireland and immigrated to the United States, where he became the owner of several plantations in Louisiana during the antebellum period. He served in the Confederacy (HSR, August 2005, 14). He changed the name of Yucca to Melrose "in honor of Sir Walter Scott's burial place, Melrose Abby" (Mills and Mills 1977, 51). After Henry bought it, no whites lived at Melrose for several years, but at least several Black people, former enslaved persons, continued to live there. For example, Uncle Israel and his wife, Aunt Jane, continued to live there after the Civil War ended, and were living in Yucca House when Cammie Henry moved to the plantation with her husband in the 1890s (HSR, August 2005, 16). It is more than likely that there were other Black people living there, too.

When Joseph Henry died in the 1890s, his widow sold the property to his son, John Hampton Henry (McNaughton, HSR 2005, 15). John Hampton Henry was born in Natchitoches in 1862, studied in Virginia, and graduated from St. Louis University (Mills and Mills 1977, 15). In 1889, he and his father opened a store in Derry, Natchitoches (ibid.).

Carmelite (Cammie) Garnett Henry was born in 1871 on Scattery Plantation in Ascension Parish, in southern Louisiana. Her family owned several plantations, and as a young person, she developed deep interests in many aspects of southern history, gardening, plants, and architecture. She was fascinated with southern and local history; she was an avid reader from early childhood and spent long periods as a youth reading and writing her reflections. She moved from southern Louisiana to Natchitoches to attend Natchitoches Normal School in the 1890s. John Henry met Cammie at Natchitoches Normal School and they married in 1894. She moved for a short while to a local house, before relocating to Melrose in 1899.[8] After arriving at Melrose, she set about restoring the plantation—which had remained unoccupied for several years—and recording its history. She also recorded the history of the parish, indeed of the region and the South. During her lifetime, she amassed more than 300 scrapbooks of photographs and news clippings, and a range of other objects and heirlooms. She restored and transformed the plantation from a dilapidated structure with overgrown gardens into a vibrant household. She collected extensive information on historic buildings, including plantations, churches, and private residences, and sought to preserve the architecture and culture of a civilization that she believed was passing rapidly away. "With abundant energy and a healthy appreciation of history, 'Miss Cammie' labored to restore 'Melrose' and its auxiliary buildings and to preserve the tradition which the plantation's first owners had begun" (Mills and Mills 1973, 51). Of course, she did not do this without the labor of many Black women and men at the plantation.

Cammie Henry acquired former slave cabins from nearby plantations to preserve them and transform them into accommodation for her writers. According to Thorn (1990/1991), Cammie "began to search out log cabins from the surrounding countryside, transporting them to the Melrose compound to serve as various workshop and guest rooms" (19). Two of these cabins were reserved for her "special interests" of "book binding and weaving" (ibid.). Thus, "she renovated a cabin which dated from the 1820s and designated it as a bindery" (ibid.). Another cabin acquired by Cammie was filled with "ancient looms" and "with one old loom that a field hand, Henry Hertzog, found in the attic of the old barn and then restored" (ibid., xxx).

Another friend remembers her bringing to the site the cabin that was to become the Ghana House. "She restored another outbuilding, Ghana House, which she had moved from the cotton fields onto the grounds near the so-called 'Big House.' It was to become another studio for the writers and artists who would begin to frequent Melrose" (Moore 1984, 12). She also refurbished Yucca House for the writers. Later on, Cammie's son, J. H. Henry, bought the "Old Chelette Place" in 1934, from which he gave two cabins to his mother, which she relocated to Melrose.

During this time, Cammie continued weaving and collecting Louisiana documents, books, and other items. She became friends with many local people, including several local women writers. She visited many buildings across the region and read and heard about the Cane River Creoles. She entertained visitors and guests from across the state, and beyond. After her husband died in 1918, she encouraged more writers and artists to visit. She was probably lonely and almost certainly obsessive. The majority of her friendships were with white people, not untypical in the segregated South. During the entire time she spent at Melrose, many Black people were also resident at Melrose or in its vicinity, with men working in trades, women in domestic labor, and both men and women in the fields. This included Uncle Israel and Aunt Jane. It also included Clementine Hunter (and her parents), who arrived at Melrose Plantation around the year 1900, when Clementine was thirteen or fourteen years old.

CAMMIE HENRY'S WRITER'S COLONY

After her husband's death, Cammie Henry transformed Melrose into a writer's and artist's colony that flourished between the 1920s and 1940s (Mills 1977; Gallien 1966). Her guests included Sherwood Anderson, Alexander Woolcott, Harnett T. Kane, and Rachel Field, and some of their works were conceived or written while at Melrose. Henry Chambers, Ada Jack Carver, Ross Phares, Ruth Cross, Ellsworth and William Woodward, Roark Bradford, William Spratling, and Rudolph Matas also visited. William Faulkner is reputed to have visited. Cammie developed friendships with Irma Sompayrac, who founded the Natchitoches Art Colony in 1926; with Caroline Dorman, "a local botanist," who wrote and painted; and artists such as Alberta Kinsey, who also stayed at the plantation. Dorothy Scarborough, who documented and wrote on Black folklore, visited Melrose and recorded songs by Black people (so-called negro songs) (Babb 1996, viii; Scarborough 1925). There was a list of the most prominent visitors in one of the rooms in the main house, which could be seen on the tour.

The most prominent visitor was Lyle Saxon, whom Cammie had met in New Orleans in 1923 and with whom she begun an extensive correspondence. He first visited the plantation in 1927 (Moore 1984, 21). Saxon was one of the most notable men of letters in Louisiana from the 1920s to his death in 1946 (Harvey 2003; Thomas 1991). Born in Baton Rouge, he worked as a journalist, and later as a features writer. His fiction and nonfiction drew heavily on Melrose materials. He traveled between New York and Louisiana frequently, and regularly wrote a book a year for many years. His books include *Cane River, Children of Strangers* (1937), *The Friends of Joe Gilmore* (1948), and *Old Louisiana* (1950). He was a state director of the Federal Writers Project of the 1930s and left many diaries and letters. His novel *Children of Strangers* played a significant role in popularizing the Cane River area beyond Natchitoches Parish (Chance 2003; Thomas 1991).

Grace King, a well-known writer of short stories and novels, born in New Orleans and whose family had a plantation in St. Martin Parish, also visited. Henry E. Chambers—author of several histories of Louisiana—sent Cammie many scrapbook fillers. Harnett T. Kane used her collections for some of his writings, and along with Saxon, he popularized Cammie's efforts (Kane 1945).

And then there was François Mignon, the self-proclaimed "Frenchman" who arrived in 1939 and stayed for decades, through 1970. Mignon designed and cared for the gardens, especially the large gardens between the African House and Ghana House (Gilley 2000, 43). He served as assistant librarian, supervised plantation affairs, and helped Cammie gather information for her scrapbooks. He also worked on the maintenance and improvement of buildings, aided with requests, and entertained Cammie's guests. He strongly encouraged Cammie to write a diary for the entire year of 1934, even typing it up (Cammie Henry Diary 1934).[9] He is regarded as instrumental in encouraging Clementine Hunter to pursue her painting, and once she got underway in the late 1940s, he became her unofficial agent for decades (Wilson 1990). Throughout much of the time he was at Melrose Plantation, Mignon wrote his own essays and reflections, including a column in the local newspaper, "Plantation Memo."

Following Cammie's death, Mignon assisted the APHN with the promotion of Natchitoches tourism and helped raise funds. He was also a central figure in "propagating" much of the history—and many of the myths—about Melrose, including historical accounts for the African House and the Ghana House. He lived in the Ghana House for a while (Macdonald and Morgan 2006).

Mignon stayed at Melrose through 1969, when Cammie's son John Hampton Henry Jr., then owner of the plantation, died. Mignon was asked to leave by the family members who inherited it and the plantation was sold at auction to Southdown Land Company, which donated it to APHN (Mills and Mills 1973, 53). He remained in Natchitoches in a house provided by one of the local women (Cammie Henry Center records). He continued to write and publish, especially in newspapers. He helped the APHN in their work, attended meetings, helped raise monies, and provided information, much of which was later found to be exaggerations or myth.

A plantation as big as Melrose could not function without a large, stable, and varied workforce, and Cammie employed many African American tenants and servants to fulfill these roles.[10] Clementine Hunter was one of these workers. She began, like all the other Black people at Melrose, as the descendant of enslaved persons, and her early role, like many of them, was to serve white people. In fact, it was much more than an early role—she continued to serve white people until she was more than fifty years old. She cooked and served for Cammie Henry, and almost certainly for Cammie's children, for whom she also made toys. During Cammie Henry's lifetime, Clementine Hunter had been known to her primarily as a menial worker—first in the fields, then in the main house—and as a beneficiary of Henry's generosity and kindness.

The majority of Black people working at Melrose—cooks, cleaners and maids, field-hands and laborers, drivers, and skilled men—did not become famous. They did the clearing, planting, picking, piling, chopping, and storing; the cutting, cleaning, cooking, and serving; the washing, ironing, and folding; they made the beds, swept the floors, dusted the furniture, and cleaned the windows. Someone had to maintain the gardens and the stables. They carried out all the domestic labor that was necessary to make the household conducive to reading and writing, collecting and storing, and binding and weaving.

The Black residents lived in cabins on the plantation or in the nearby vicinity. They had been born enslaved or were the children and grandchildren of the enslaved. After Cammie Henry's death in the 1940s, many remained on the plantation continuing the menial work to which they had been confined, and the subordinate roles in which they were imprisoned, as did so many other Black men and women across the parish, the state, and the South (Clayton 1990; Jones 1986; Carson 1974; Keyes 1950).

The archives in the Cammie Henry Center and elsewhere contain numerous photos, names, and descriptions of the Black workers, the roles they played, and their contributions to life at Melrose, but not much more. For example, the Anne Malone collection has photos of many Black people in what looks like the 1920s. The majority are from the Lyle Saxon album. Some are from Melrose scrapbooks, and some are by individuals, some unattributed. Many photos appear in Rolonda Teal's book, which does an excellent job of conveying the breadth (but not depth) of Black contributions to the upkeep of the plantation (Teal 2007). Short stories also exist about some of the workers, for example, Israel and Jane Suddath (Dollar 1998; Cammie Henry Diary 1934). A book by Clayton (1990) contains four photos of "[f]ormer slaves living around Natchitoches," including "Uncle Israel Suddath" age 106, of Melrose (Clayton, 227).[11] Many of them appear in paintings by Clementine Hunter.

Clementine Hunter was born in 1886 or 1887 at Hidden Hill Plantation (later renamed Little Eva Plantation), near Cloutierville, Louisiana.[12] Her name was originally Clementine Reuben and she was the daughter of Janvier Reuben and Mary Antoinette Adams (Gilley 2000). Her parents called her Clemence. She was the oldest of seven children. She lived in various places around the immediate region as a child. As an adult she spent most of her life at Melrose. Like her mother, Clementine Hunter also had seven children, (two of whom died at birth) and several grandchildren. She was married twice. She began working in the fields and picking cotton around Natchitoches at an early age, and was taught by her father, working with her family "from one field to another" (Gilley 2000, 55). She was proud that she could pick cotton well and said that it gave her time to think about other things—the Lord, praying, singing, anything. Her parents pushed her to attend school, but she kept running away and returning to the cotton fields.

Clementine went to work at Melrose around the year 1900, when she was fourteen years old. She worked for almost three decades in the fields picking cotton; then later, in 1928, she became a domestic, working as a washerwoman and a cook, and looking after the gardens. She also helped out with other tasks. Although she arrived at Melrose in a similar way to the majority of Blacks there—as low-level workers in a racially paternalistic system—and although she lived in much the same circumstances as the majority of her fellow workers, Clementine Hunter became the most well-known Black person at Melrose, perhaps the only Black person there post-slavery about whom anything is said in detail at the site.

During her lifetime and career, Hunter painted miscellaneous and sundry items, including window shades, or canvases, along with "the insides of cardboard boxes found at the Melrose store, ironing boards, wooden roofing shingles, lamps, buckets, spittoons, etc." (Gilley 2000, 60). Her work portrayed four main categories: work, play, religion, and other (Wilson 1990). In her career as a painter, she completed more than 5,000 original paintings on a range of subjects: "workers in the fields, women doing laundry, children at play, plantation animals, funerals, weddings, baptisms, and honky tonk dances" (Gilley 2000, 60). She did not stop painting until she was very old, even when her old age meant the act of painting became physically painful for her. In addition to painting, she made dolls, sewed clothes, weaved baskets, and made quilts.

After Cammie Henry died in 1948, Hunter remained at Melrose for several more decades. Mignon suggested that she paint the murals in the African House, which she completed in 1957. He also suggested "she paint the ceiling and large crucifixion scene in the Ghana House, and a frieze on the outside of it, on wood fiber panels a foot wide by eighteen feet long" (Gilley 2000, 46). She had tremendous creative success with her work, which was popular throughout the South, the United States, and beyond. Although she first sold her paintings for twenty-five cents, they later sold for thousands of dollars (Wilson 1990). But she never did much long-distance traveling, even when famous. She was invited to many art shows (most of which she declined). In 1986, she was awarded the degree of honorary Doctor of Fine Arts by Northwestern State University, which she personally accepted. But she respectfully declined an invitation to the White House from President Jimmy Carter.

During her time at Melrose, Hunter had lived in various cabins on and off site. She left Melrose in 1977 and moved to a cabin in the vicinity, where she continued to paint. This cabin was relocated to the Melrose site in 1978, while she moved to another cabin nearby (*Natchitoches Times*, 1978). This cabin is still located at Melrose, and is furnished with much of her furniture, along with newspaper photos and clippings of her achievements.

Clementine Hunter lived to become 101 or 102 and died January 1, 1988. She was buried in a mausoleum she had picked in St. Augustine cemetery, in a spot next to the grave of François Mignon. Her story is central to the story told at Melrose and she is a central person in the video *Women of Cane River*. One side of her life that receives little or no attention at Melrose is her social analysis of plantation life. As one author has suggested, "Clementine was a social historian in many ways, even though she could not read or write" (Gilley 2000, 9). Key aspects of this social history analysis are addressed in discussion on the Ghana House later in this chapter.

HERITAGE TOURISM AFTER THE WRITER'S COLONY

During the time that Clementine Hunter's creativity was soaring, the fortunes of Melrose were in decline. Annual festivals and holiday events began in Natchitoches as early as the 1920s. Groups such as the "Belles in Calico" and the "Ladies in Calico" led the march. The "Ladies in Calico" were elite white women from Natchitoches who established and ran annual Christmas tours of homes and promoted the restoration and public display of important buildings. They became the "Ladies of Natchitoches" and finally the Association for the Preservation of Historic Natchitoches, which became the owner and operator of Melrose. Melrose was deemed to be of historic importance and romantic appeal, and they worked rapidly to restore the main house and to celebrate Cammie Henry's work and the writer's colony. They saw the value of highlighting the history of legally free people of color, and they promoted information about exceptional (mainly white) women, such as Cammie Henry and Kate Chopin. Promoting significant information on Black people (or working-class whites) was not their concern, although Black people continued to perform roles in the work to which they had always been confined.[13]

Many of the women that worked to save, restore, and promote Melrose had known Cammie Henry personally. Some had been close friends or associates, and some knew François Mignon (Cammie Henry Center records). They included other famous local (white) women, such as Caroline Dorman, Ora Watson, and Ada Jack Carver (Becker 2018).

By the 1960s, with several decades of experience behind them, the APHN acquired Melrose. Natchitoches women worked with local and state notables. Some of the women had husbands, brothers, or sons in prominent jobs—lawyers, architects, businessmen, and politicians—who assisted them with their work by facilitating contacts, helping with legal and technical matters, designing and drafting, and providing advice (Cammie Henry Center records). Through these networks, they developed influence with people inside and outside the state, which led to them securing state and federal funds. The APHN assessed the extent of monies needed to refurbish Melrose and they worked tirelessly to secure funds. This involved tremendous amounts of work, and many women made personal sacrifices and suffered the consequences. But it was done in the way that these things are normally done—via access to wealth, as well as social and cultural capital.

One of the most active among this group was Ora Watson, who had been a professor at Northwestern State University in Natchitoches. A sampling of her letters gives a taste of the amount of work being carried out to preserve Melrose. In a letter to Mr. Richer Brown, Vice President, Tracy-Locke, Inc., June 16, 1972, Watson indicates that "we have just completed roofing the big House, at a cost of almost $8,000! We had to use cedar shakes, but it was really the labor that cost; the shingles were only about $1,500" (Cammie Henry Center records). Also, "We have been trying to raise money in various ways such as benefit teas, card parties and soliciting donations." They also planned "a Plantation Party at Melrose" (Cammie Henry Center records).

In a letter dated February 22, 1972, to Mr. George Leake, Chairman, Louisiana Historical Preservation and Cultural Commission, Watson described the situation at Melrose and said of Melrose "It consists of the main house and six other houses on six acres of land" and adds that "[a]ccording to the professional estimates we have, about $100,000 will be required to restore Melrose properly. That will include restoration of the gardens, building several fences and some walkways and putting a hard surface on the parking area" (APHN Folder 21, "Melrose Correspondence 1960–72"). In a letter dated June 17, 1972, Watson comments that "since leaving Northwestern in 1970, I have devoted my entire time to historic preservation in the Natchitoches area" (APHN Folder 21, "Melrose Correspondence 1960–72").

And the women wrote to people at the highest levels of political office. For example, a letter dated June 16, 1972, from Mrs. Lyndon B. Johnson to Mrs. Watson says that since her husband's heart attack, she has wiped out all things on her calendar, not already committed, so she could spend more time with him. But she sends $10.00: "I would like to think I could at least add one shingle and a nail on the roof of the big House and am enclosing my check for $10.00!" (APHN Folder 21, "Melrose Correspondence 1960–72"). In this way, the APHN rallied around to raise funds and develop Melrose, had several buildings restored, and a history of the plantation written (Mills 1977). In 1974, the site became the property of APHN. Their efforts led to the site being designated a National Historic Landmark in 1974 (HSR, August 2005). As mentioned earlier, the plantation opened for tours in 1986.

HERITAGE TOURISM AT MELROSE PLANTATION

At the start of the twenty-first century, Melrose Plantation organized its heritage tourism around two guided tours, one of the Main House and one of the grounds; and it had a well-stocked gift shop. When my research began in 2007, visitors could also walk without guides around the site and enter several buildings, but by 2011, this practice had been ended due to fear of damage to the buildings.[14] However, where time allowed and upon request, site tour guides happily provided a tour of the other buildings of the site.

Discussion of buildings was a major theme at the site, with a focus on their history and distinctive Creole architecture, including French Creole design and style, and the distinctive material of bousillage. However, these details were restricted to a limited number of buildings, specifically, the Yucca House, the African House, the main house, and the kitchen ruins. We typically heard little to nothing about other buildings at the site. In what follows I describe the information provided about each of these buildings on a typical guided tour.

The Buildings and Twenty-First-Century Slave Cabins

As can be seen in the site map, after arriving in the parking lot, visitors walked down a path passing the weaving house to the left, and then turning

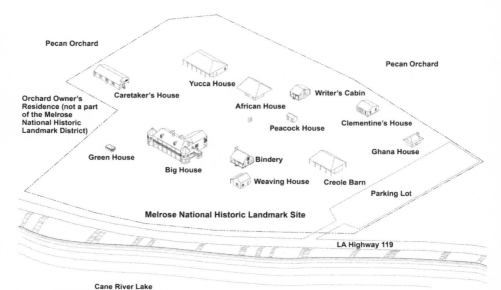

Map of Melrose Plantation. © Library of Congress, Prints & Photographs Division, Historic American Buildings Survey, HABS LA-2-69-F.

to the right to enter the bindery/gift shop. Visitors began their visit to the site at the shop, which is where they purchased tickets and where the guided tour began.

The Main House

The most important building at the site—the one that got most attention in terms of time and detail devoted to it—was the main house. Of course, there was the extremely unusual variation at Melrose of the master-enslavers having been legally free people of color. The main house on the site was not the original house from the colonial period at Yucca Plantation but rather was built in the 1830s by Louis Metoyer, the "mixed-race" son of Marie Thérèse Coin Coin (Mills 1977). He lived in it until the 1840s, when the plantation was sold to the Hertzog family. Since that time, the main house has been occupied mainly by elite white residents, although it almost certainly had Black residents, some of whom were enslaved, in the antebellum period. The house benefited from major additions and modifications since slavery ended, including substantial renovations carried out by Cammie Henry in the early twentieth century.

The guided tour of the Main House consisted of a fifteen-minute video entitled *Cane River Women* presented on a television in the basement of the house, and a tour of the house lasting thirty to forty-five minutes.[15] The video described the wonder and beauty of Cane River, the history of settlement and plantation growth and the prevalence of an agricultural way of life in the parish. Then it moved on to discuss each of the three exceptional women as well as mention of Kate Chopin. It provided details of their individual biographies and their unique contributions to the region and to the world. There were some photos shown of the women, except Marie Thérèse Coin Coin, and there was a video clip of a very elderly Clementine Hunter. The overall tenor of the video conveyed how exceptional these women were and their humanistic contributions to making the world a better place.

After the video was shown, the tour continued throughout the main house, covering several floors and most of the rooms. The tour focused mainly on Cammie Henry's life and work, including some information on the writer's colony. It covered the architecture and history of the house in some detail. And it covered Clementine Hunter—including details about the series of paintings that she did which were now in the *garçonnière*, located upstairs in the Main House. In many respects the tour was typical of the majority of plantation heritage sites across the South, with its focus on the lives of the elite owners, their families, important (white) visitors, and details of the

The Main House at Melrose Plantation.

architecture of the house and of its furniture and contents. We heard anec-
dotes about individual experiences, idiosyncrasies, relationships, and aspirations. As was usual on other tours, at the end, visitors are invited to visit the
plantation grounds and to enjoy the gardens. The main difference between
this tour and most of the others is that the elite owners were legally free
people of color; and that a Black woman, Clementine Hunter, got so much
attention. No other plantation heritage site discussed a Black person, especially a Black woman, in such detail in the main house,[16] although the story
of Clementine Hunter is framed as that of an exceptional or atypical Black
person (see Alderman and Modlin 2008).

Much of the initial information about Cammie Henry comes from the
video. Cammie Henry was born January 14, 1871, in southern Louisiana,
where her parents owned a plantation. She attended Natchitoches Normal
School and met her future husband, John Henry, there. John Henry belonged
to a wealthy agricultural family and he and Cammie inherited four plantations. They had seven children: six boys and one girl. The docent told us that
"Cammie Henry had a deep abiding interest in people of all races." She also
had a deep passion for historic preservation, including buildings. She scoured
the country looking for "old log cabins" and brought several of these cabins
to Melrose. After her husband died, she turned Melrose into a writer's colony.

A list of the prominent writers (all of whom were white) that stayed at
Melrose was on the table in the basement room, and the docent mentioned
several of them. Chief among them were Lyle Saxon, a notable Louisiana
writer, and François Mignon. Saxon became a close friend of Cammie Henry,
visited many times in the 1930s, and wrote some of his important works at
Melrose Plantation (Harvey 2003). He mainly stayed in Yucca House, which
was remodeled by Cammie Henry for him. He stayed in Yucca House over
a period of ten years. Mignon also lived and wrote in Yucca. In the 1930s,
François Mignon came to Melrose, telling locals that he was French and
could not return to France because of the Germans. He continued to live at
Melrose for another forty years, through the 1970s. In the 1980s, some fifteen
years after he died, some research was being done and it was found out
that he wasn't French at all. His name was Frank Minet, and he was born in
New York. (On a later tour, a different docent simply described Mignon as a
Frenchman and did not acknowledge that this was a deception).

Much of Cammie Henry's original furniture was still in the house, as
were several of Clementine Hunter's paintings, and these were described in
detail. Before we left the basement, we were told that although it was now a
room in the house, it used to be a basement proper and held carriages. It was
used in this way because of the threat of flooding in the nineteenth century.

It was changed later when flooding was no longer an issue. Cammie Henry wanted it to be more prominent. We were told that the bindery is where she taught people to do binding.

Upstairs we visited several rooms. In one of them, we were told that Dr. Judith Miller visited a lot and stayed in this room. She was a missionary in Africa and Japan for a while. She had a special chair made for her because she had polio. The chair was very crooked. It was made by a "craftsman" on the plantation to fit her specifically and was made at Cammie Henry's request.

One of the rooms had a fireplace, and another was a bedroom in which we were provided with the details about the bed and a rolling pin. The docent in passing mentioned that the "Calico Ladies" donated furniture to Melrose. There was a high bed, built that way to enable it to catch the wind and breezes from the window. We passed another bedroom, part of the wrap around porch, but did not go in. The docent informed us that we could go in if we wanted to do so.

We then went out to the porch, where we were told that Cammie Henry lived in the house for thirty years with no indoor bathroom. The bathroom was added in the 1930s. All of this part of the house was added by Cammie Henry in the 1930s. We were also told that Cammie Henry's bedroom, and maybe even the whole section of the building, was brought to Melrose from another plantation—the Marco Plantation—to become part of the house.

Initial details on the tour about Clementine Hunter were provided in the video, and most of the information about her paintings is provided when visitors arrive in the garçonnière, located upstairs in the main house. There were more than a few of these original paintings in the garçonnière, including one of a Black Jesus. The video tells us that "she was a tiny Black woman over ninety years old," and that she was a painter of "plantation primitives." We were told about many of the subjects that Clementine Hunter painted, and how her art captured the way of life of many rural Blacks. There was a section in the video, of thirty seconds or so, with Clementine Hunter talking. The video also mentions the African House murals.

When we entered the garçonnière, we were told that it was a common room on plantations—originally designed for boys as they became older and stayed out late. It provided them with a separate entrance so as not to disturb other family members. On other sites, the garçonnière was typically located across the river. Overall, the idea was to keep the noise down.

When the docent talked about the paintings in the garçonnière, and in the African House, we were told that Clementine Hunter painted geese, cattle, a Black Jesus Christ, and the Calico Ladies of 1970 who got the plantation. She also painted good angels and bad angels. Some of these are in the African House. In 1939, she could not read or write, because she had refused to stay at school. Over time she learned to do some writing, and then she was able to sign her name to the paintings. Some of her paintings were selling for thousands of dollars at the start of the twenty-first century. At the end of the tour, we were led downstairs to the back of the house and invited to tour the gardens. When we left the main house we could see a barn and "slave bell." On some tours the docent pointed to the bell and mentioned it; on others, it was ignored.

Yucca House

The Yucca House was another distinctive building on the site and one that was central to its history. Although it was not presented during the tour as a slave cabin, it functioned as a slave cabin for a long time, there is evidence that enslaved people lived in it, and a high likelihood that other enslaved persons visited and even slept there. A dispute was ongoing as to whether it was first occupied by Marie Thérèse Coin Coin or her son, Louis Metoyer. Most accounts at the site say that it was Marie Thérèse Coin Coin who built and first lived in the house. They relate that she was legally free at the time she lived there. However, we know that Marie Thérèse Coin Coin had spent most of her life enslaved. Research that had recently been made available suggested that it was highly unlikely that Marie Thérèse Coin Coin lived in the house and that it was probably first occupied by Louis Metoyer (MacDonald et al. 2006a). These scholars argue that there is no concrete evidence that Coin Coin lived there and a lot of evidence to the contrary. In either case, I believe that it is also likely that whoever lived there first knew enslaved persons who were family members or friends who also lived or stayed in this house.

More importantly, after the Metoyers built a big new house, Yucca House clearly functioned as a slave cabin. For example, during one of the tours I took part in, visitors were told that after the main house was built (in the 1830s) Yucca "became a house for slaves." And we know from records at the Cammie Henry Center that at least two enslaved persons—Israel Suddath and Jane Suddath—lived in Yucca House for long periods of time, both during slavery and after it ended.

The visit to Yucca House was a significant part of the tour, and it was the first building visited as part of the grounds tour. At the site, it was described in detail as the home that was built and/or lived in by Marie Thérèse Coin Coin. She was already legally free before she built and/or occupied the house. The details provided about the house were a combination of architecture and resident history—covering slavery, when Marie Thérèse Coin Coin lived in it; the Jim Crow period, when Lyle Saxon and then François Mignon lived in it; and through to the 1960s, when Mignon continued to live in it. The

Yucca House at Melrose Plantation.

lead-up to these details was mainly about gardening—as we were told that there are lots of flowers in this vicinity of the cabin, and the docent told us the names of many of them, including ginger lilies. The house's name and the original name of the plantation—Yucca—come from the local yucca plant, which grows in abundance in this vicinity.

We were told that Yucca was the original home on the plantation and was made of red clay bricks that were "hand made by slaves" and baked in the sun. The wood used in its construction is cypress; bousillage was also used. According to the docent, the wood was put together without the use of nails and the beams took six years to construct. The house was used as a hospital in the Civil War. The docent also said that Yucca House was the only plantation house in the area with a porch wrapped all the way around it. Yucca has a detached kitchen and two fireplaces. During my tour of the site in October 2007, the house was under restoration and the interior was empty. The entire floor was gone, and renovations were being made to the ground underneath to give the building stability.

On one of my early tours (October 2007), the docent was Betty, a Metoyer family member. After the contextual details about the garden and Cammie being the third owner of the site, Betty then told us she was going to do an impersonation of Marie Thérèse Coin Coin and narrate a story. She did not tell us the source of the story. She then said the following:

I was born a slave. I met a Frenchman, a white man, aged twenty-five, and became mother of five kids. In 1778 he purchased me. Then my freedom. Then freedom for my kids. Most of my life I spent as a house servant. I had lots of protection. He gave me a tract of land. I settled in a small cabin on sixty-eight acres. I secured the freedom of my children and grandchildren. Our family was not accepted as white or black, therefore we intermarried, Indian and some Chinese in our family. Our family built a church in 1803, it was the only church built by people of color in the USA. Our family owned over five hundred slaves.

She then told us that the cabins were brought to Melrose by Cammie Henry. This house, Yucca House, was used as a guesthouse by Lyle Saxon over a period of ten years. François Mignon from France lived here for thirty-two years. She gave us details of the Henry family and its descendants. She did not mention that Uncle Israel and his wife—two former enslaved persons—lived in the house. Another docent informed us that "this building has had more prominent writers in it than any other building in the USA," and gave a list of some of the names, including Lyle Saxon and François Mignon.

The house in 2010, of course, looked very different from the past, and especially the antebellum period. There is a drawing of the house in Lyle Saxon's semi-autobiographical book, published posthumously in 1948, in which Yucca was presented as "Saxon's Cabin on Melrose Plantation" (Saxon 1948, 22). Although the book provided no details about the cabin, it does contain a drawing of the interior under the caption "Interior of Saxon's Cabin" (ibid., 39). This drawing of the interior indicates the transformational nature of the renovation that Cammie Henry undertook. In this drawing, the room looks like an extremely comfortable living room in a well-to-do house. There is a huge mirror, hundreds of books, some on shelves that run floor to ceiling, a fire burning in the hearth, two comfortable armchairs and a sofa, a small table, and two small lamps on small tables. The overall image conveyed is of extreme comfort bordering on what must have been, in the 1940s, luxury. In the drawing, there is also a huge portrait of Grand-pere Augustin on the wall, and it is almost certainly the one that once hung in the St. Augustine Church. Later on, in the book, there is a very high-quality drawing (so that it almost looks like a photo) of the "Gallery of Saxon's Cabin" (ibid., 118).

The African House

The most fascinating structure at Melrose was the African House, which is a key location in the tour of the site and was highlighted in the website

The African House at Melrose Plantation.

and site literature as the most authentic African-style house in the United States in the twenty-first century. It was visually striking both because of its unique structure and style of construction. It was bound to capture attention, because it was so distinctive vis-à-vis other buildings around Natchitoches, Louisiana, and the South. Because of this, it was perhaps the most well-known of all the structures at the site. All the major promotion material on Melrose, including items produced by the site itself, have photos of the African House. It was also important because it housed a fascinating collection of Clementine Hunter paintings—the so-called African House Murals. There was almost nothing like it at any other plantation heritage site across the South (Shiver and Whitehead 2005). Nothing, that is, that strikes us so visually as being African, or that claims such an authentic African provenance. I was tremendously impressed when I first saw it during my site visit in the late 1990s.

In 1969, when the APHN submitted the nomination form for Melrose Plantation to be listed on the National Register, they noted that "[t]he grounds of Yucca Plantation, now known as Melrose Plantation, contain what may well be the oldest buildings of African design built by blacks, for the use of blacks in the United States" (HSR, August 2005, appendix, 5). They also stated that "it is a unique, nearly square structure, directly in the rear of the Big House and may have been intended as a stable on the ground floor and quarters or storage above" (ibid.).

But this celebrated building was juxtaposed against the slender information we heard about it at the site. In the site's promotional literature, and
during the tour, we were provided with only the most rudimentary and
incomplete information about the building and its history. This was in stark
contrast to the details we received about the main house. This may be noticeable to the attentive visitor to the site. There was also the irony that although
it is presented as the most African building in the nation, it was used as a
jail for enslaved persons. And an even greater irony awaits the more probing
visitor who looks into the historical background of the house, with several
local experts asserting that it is not African at all but French (MacDonald
et al. 2006a; Morgan et al. 2006).[17]

As part of the tour, visitors typically went to the African House immediately after Yucca House, which had already alerted visitors to the "African
origins" narrative prevalent at the plantation. Visitors entered the African
House downstairs, where some interior items are briefly described—then
proceeded upstairs and saw the spectacular murals, which were described in
extensive detail. Details about the African House could also be obtained from
the various leaflets and from the tour itself. On our tour, as we approached
the building the docent told us that the bottom half of the building was brick
"handmade by slaves" and the top half was stone. It was used as a jail for
slaves "when they were bad" she said. We were told that the African House
originally had no stairs; it had a ladder instead. Afterwards, it was used as a
guesthouse. This building was opened to the public in 1974. (When I visited
it in the late 1990s, the upstairs was not available for viewing, perhaps due
to renovations.)

We spent just a couple of minutes inside the ground-level room, which
had beams over the walls and ceiling. There were markings on the wooden
windowsill, like scratches. The docent said, "We think these were made by
slaves to mark how many days they had left in jail." There was an armoire,
with lots of markings on it, including the names, ages, births, and deaths of
children. There was a desk and wardrobe in this room along with a number
of records. The desk of François Mignon was also in the room.

Most time in the African House was spent upstairs—at least fifteen to
twenty minutes—with the docent providing details about Clementine Hunter,
and much more detail about the murals. We stood upstairs, surrounded by
the murals, which cover all the walls on all four sides. They are the originals
and were done by Clementine Hunter in the 1950s, and later restored in the
1970s. The circular room is distinctive and impressive.

We were told that Clementine Hunter was a "primitive artist," and her
paintings reflected that style of art. In the tradition of primitive artists, the

African House Murals.

artist paints the most important things or people bigger than other things or people, and this was evident throughout her work. Clementine Hunter was born on Hidden Hill Plantation (a local plantation) and came to Melrose to work. The work conditions here were generally believed better than at other plantations, said the docent. Clementine Hunter's name is now known worldwide for her art. She died on New Year's Day, 1988, at the age of 101. She was buried locally. We were also told that Clementine Hunter served coffee to Lyle Saxon and François Mignon.

The African House murals are important in the world of primitive art and there are numerous publications about them (Shiver and Whitehead 2005; Giley 2000; Lyons 1998; Wilson 1990). The docent told us brief details of many of the paintings, what and who was painted and why by Clementine Hunter, and why some people were painted big and others small. For example, there was a painting of a tiny overseer in a house and the docent said, "She did not think very highly of him." Other paintings portrayed a fight scene, washing day, the main house, and several images of the African House. The docent said that "she [Hunter] was a Catholic and always painted Baptist scenes."

One of the paintings had a scene in which a man is drowning. His head was bigger than his body because his head is more important, said the docent. Another painting had a wedding scene—the bride was larger than the groom because she was more important to Clementine Hunter. The docent highlighted one mural in which "all the women are working, and the men are not." The docent added that by the end of her life experiences Hunter had come to conclude that men were worthless! One of the murals had the Ghana House in it, and the docent mentioned this and gave us a brief description of it. One of the figures is Cammie Henry's son. He was the overseer, and that day, Clementine Hunter was not happy with him. Also, there was a photo of a painting in which Cammie Henry was painted small. We were not told why.

Another mural had a woman's underwear on the line to dry—yellow with green trim. This, said the docent, was an inside joke about a local woman who wore these kinds of colors. Most women's "draws" were supposed to be white and Clementine Hunter was having a joke. Another painting had a juke joint—it still exists in the area but was no longer open. Still another painting had a man with a gun! We were told that every single person in this picture was someone that Clementine Hunter knew. Clementine Hunter herself was in the picture, bringing coffee to Lyle Saxon. François Mignon was in the picture too.

We were told that one of the characters in the painting was "Uncle Israel," who was at the top of the picture. He was "the last slave" to live at Yucca, said the docent, and he lived on the plantation until he died.[18] Also Marie Thérèse Coin Coin was in the picture, and she was painted very big. Some of the murals have cabins in them, but no mention was made of them. The docent said that these are all paintings of Clementine Hunter's world. What was her world, asked the docent, rhetorically? And responded that it was a world of fields, picking cotton, and it was also a religious world.

The Kitchen Ruins

The kitchen ruins were located close to the main house, although all that was left was half a fireplace and some tiles on the floor. This was unfortunate, because kitchens at these sites were typically where more information was provided about Black people than any other location (Eichstedt and Small 2002, 95–97 and passim). They were places where Black people, especially women, often slept. The tour of the kitchen at Melrose Plantation did not function in this way and no information was provided about it or about a young Baptist preacher who in the 1960s "robbed the store" and set fire to the kitchen. He was arrested and went to jail for fourteen years. It is reported that the kitchen was still a free-standing structure in 1965, when it was burned down, and it seems that many of Cammie's scrapbooks perished

The Kitchen Ruins at Melrose Plantation.

with it (HSR, August 2005, 18). As we left the "kitchen," the docent rang a bell, but said nothing.

The Bindery/Gift Shop

This cabin was organized as a reception area for visitors to the site and as a bookstore and gift shop. It was the second building seen when visitors entered the site. They had to go there first to purchase tickets for the tours, and so it was usually the first building that visitors entered.[19] The bindery/ gift shop was extensively stocked with a range of tourist merchandise, like postcards, mugs, souvenirs, and coffee-table photo books, for example, on Clementine Hunter. There were also prints of Clementine Hunter portraits, many of which feature the African House, as well as soaps, dolls, and other sundries. There were lots of general books on the history of Louisiana, including its architecture, and some academic books, including several on the Civil War period.

This cabin was not part of any tour and usually no details about it were volunteered by site staff. Cammie wrote that it used to be a slave cabin on a different plantation and was brought to Melrose Plantation in the 1920s or 1930s to serve as her bindery (Cammie Henry Diary 1934).

The Bindery/Gift Shop at Melrose Plantation.

The Weaving House

The weaving house was the first building that visitors saw when they entered the site from the parking lot. It was not part of the tour and there was a small sign on it directing visitors to the gift shop/bindery to purchase tickets before proceeding on the tour. When I visited in 2007, visitors could go inside the cabin and it had many items inside it; by 2010 it was usually closed, and visitors needed to consult a docent in order to enter it. It was labeled the "weaving house" and was presented as the place where Cammie Henry did her weaving in the 1930s and 1940s. One or two small plaques provided brief information about Cammie Henry and her life as a weaver, and photos with captions.

The roof was impressive—it looked like slate or wood. The house was slightly elevated at the base and had mold up the side for several inches. The front had an overarching roof and four poles holding it up. Inside the weaving house was a series of items—a large wardrobe, a massive weaving loom, a spinning wheel, a small chair, and other small pieces of furniture. There were several photos of Cammie Henry; for example, Cammie at her loom. There was a photo of Cammie Henry and another of Ora Watson inside the weaving house. There was a black and white photo of the Ghana House in

The Weaving House at Melrose Plantation.

a beautifully laid out garden on the wall of the weaving house. There was a plaque on the wall that read "Restored in 1973—In loving memory of Nettie Hubier Russell by her daughter Ora Vesta Watson."

The Ghana House

During the period of research, the Ghana House remained unlabeled, was not described in any of the promotional literature, and was not part of any tour, guided or unguided. Interpreters took visitors to see it if they requested a visit and the interpreter had time. It was located off to the side of the site, a hundred yards or more away from the main path, and a typical visitor was not likely to notice it unless looking for it. It was occasionally mentioned in passing during the visit to the African House, because it is in one of the murals there. On one of my tours, the docent said that the Henrys had used it as a wash house. We were also told that it has not been restored yet, which implied that it was under consideration for restoration. In the application for inclusion in the National Register, APHN described the Ghana House as follows:

The Ghana House is a one story, one room structure of heavy squared logs laid horizontally and dove-tailed at the corners like the upper story of the African House. The double pitched, hipped roof with

Ghana House at Melrose Plantation.

wide overhanging foundation consists only of four stones supporting the sills, one at each corner of the building. This small building is of interest because of its wall construction. (6)

Like the African House, it was a visually striking building, although it was much smaller than the African House. I was able to explore the outside and inside of Ghana House in 2008. The docent informed me that there used to be paintings inside the building, but many of them were taken to the main house at some point. The docent also said that there might have been paintings on the outside of the house. He mentioned that there was no art inside it at this point. He opened the house and we entered it. There were simply bare walls and a few stored items. There was a sign above the door that reads "GHANA," on the side facing away from the garden. The docent explained that the house has a "double pitch hit room" and that its style was straight out of West Africa and that construction took a long time.

There is significant information about this house in books and documents. Like the African House, it was not a straightforward story, as some of the details of the cabin were contested—intensively contested—and had been for a long while. There was contradictory information about the origins and nature and history of Ghana House available from other primary sources.

Information about the house is available in newspapers from the 1950s and 1960s, and some information is summarized in Mills 1977. Mills has a photo of "Ghana House" and says it is "[t]ypical of the slave housing provided by Isle Brevelles' planters *de couleur*" (italics in original); also, that "its date of construction is unknown, but it is generally believed to be among the oldest area structures" (ibid., unpaginated illustration following page 54). He continues that it was originally erected on the Spanish grant given to Pierre Metoyer, third son of "Marie Thérèze Coincoin," and "the cabin was removed to Melrose in the 1930s. There it was dubbed 'Ghana House' by writer-in-residence François Mignon, in honor of the African slaves who inhabited it" (ibid.).

Several sources indicate that the Ghana House was not original to the site and was moved there in the 1930s (MacDonald et al. 2006a; Morgan et al. 2006). Some specialists say it is not African at all, but a simple log cabin (Morgan et al. 2003, 52). Others say that it is French in origin. It became clear that it was brought to the site by Cammie Henry and had no specific name at that time (Cammie Henry Diary 1934).

The "Female Writers Cabin"

Almost nothing was said about the female writer's cabin during the tours, and it was typically not mentioned or opened except upon request. Before one tour in 2007, the docent pointed to the cabin and told the visitors that it was "a typical slave cabin" saying it was made of a round cypress log with river

The "Female Writers Cabin" at Melrose Plantation.

mud. He added that it had been brought into the site from elsewhere and was used by some of the women writers. I was able to inspect the building in 2009. The door into it was locked, but I could see through the glass windows. I saw several pieces of contemporary furniture inside, a sofa covered with red cloth of some sort, a chair, an armoire, and a few other items.

The Barn

There were several other structures on the site, the biggest of which was the barn, and a small cabin that served as a restroom, which the docent said used to be a cabin, but they have no information about its origins or function. There is archaeological evidence extant about some of these cabins and other dwellings, but typically no information was provided about them during the tour or in the promotional literature for the site (MacDonald and Morgan 2006, 139).

Clementine Hunter's Cabin

Clementine Hunter's cabin was not a part of any guided tours during the period of research and was typically not mentioned by docents, except occasionally to say that it was there. I visited it several times, upon request, and entered it. On one occasion, I was joined by a docent who provided some information about it. The cabin at the site is one that Hunter lived in when she moved off the site, about three-quarters of a mile from Melrose. The cabin was brought to Melrose in the 1970s, and at that time, the plan was to make it a museum, but that had not yet happened.

When I visited it, the cabin was bright white as if it had been recently painted and seemed to be constructed of horizontal white wooden boards. The front window was framed by bright green shutters, with an entry way to a front porch. Inside the front porch was at least one green door and another green-framed window. The porch itself was enclosed except for the entryway and a window to the outside. Three or four white wooden steps led to the porch entrance. The cabin was shaped like a simple rectangle. From the outside it didn't appear to be very big. The roof was a brownish red color. It was difficult to tell if it was made of sheet metal or wood. Two small trees stood in front outside of the window and the house was surrounded by grass.

The cabin had four rooms that felt extremely small when you entered them, especially after touring the main house. Inside the cabin the main information provided was about Clementine Hunter's art and life. There

Clementine Hunter's Cabin at Melrose Plantation.

were beds, pieces of furniture, framed photos, and other items. In one of the rooms, there was a series of newspaper clippings on the wall, covered in see-through plastic, and some black and white photos of Clementine Hunter. Most of the information described Clementine Hunter, especially after she became a primitive artist. The house, while not in disrepair, had a feeling of age—it had not been kept up.

There were two items of furniture in one room: a small wooden chair near the window on the right and an unidentified piece of furniture, also wood, near the window on the left. Above this piece was another framed portrait—perhaps of Clementine Hunter holding a rooster. There were two poems on the wall in one of the rooms in the cabin.

One of the rooms was a bedroom. The floor was covered with brown wooden planks and the walls were brown horizontal wooden boards. There was a full-size bed, the frame of which was very basic. There was one thin mattress and a colorful quilt covering it—the quilt was checkered with colors like orange, pink, red, grey, and yellow. The window was framed with white wood and there was a simple wooden bedside table with a framed portrait on it. There also appears to be a colorful painting on the wall focused on a Black person. Beneath the bed was a white pot—perhaps a chamber pot. The room was very small, and from the vantage point of this picture, could barely fit more than the bed. The overall impression conveyed was very much in accord with previous images of Clementine Hunter, that of a highly talented artist who lived a modest and humble life.

. . .

In this chapter, I have argued that heritage tourism at Melrose Plantation operated under a narrative strategy of symbolic annihilation. In that regard it was very different from the two other study sites in Natchitoches. It did not fit neatly into any simple category of sites in Louisiana (or the South), and representations of slavery and slave cabins were more complicated there for a variety of reasons. The site's depictions of slavery and slave cabins, legally free people of color, and the three exceptional women are complex, multifaceted, and contradictory. At Melrose, one could argue that slavery was relatively incorporated into representations and discussions, because visitors hear significant details about slavery at the site; but that is not my conclusion. I argue instead that both slavery and slave cabins at Melrose were symbolically annihilated. This is because slavery was mentioned in such a circumscribed and problematic way through the experiences primarily of one person—Marie Thérèse Coin Coin—and her descendants, the Metoyer family. And it is because the slave cabins were literally annihilated as slave cabins per se, being overwhelmingly presented as writer's cabins occupied by white people after slavery ended.

A clear and consistent message was conveyed that the institution of slavery in Melrose and in Natchitoches was different (and by implication better) than elsewhere in the South because it allowed greater flexibility in its racial classification and in the opportunities it afforded people of color, including women—to become legally free, and once legally free, to rise in the social hierarchy. Slavery there also offered better opportunities for white women. Heritage tourism at Melrose devoted far more attention to elite owners of color, to differences between French Creoles of color and other Creoles (implied to be white), to Anglos (as opposed to all white ethnics), and to women rather than men.

Representation of slave cabins at this site were the most obscure and abstruse of the three sites in Natchitoches. At Melrose Plantation the former slave cabins were both everywhere and nowhere: everywhere because they were physically present at the site, images of them appeared in promotional literature, and they appeared in many of Clementine Hunter's paintings. Nowhere, because they were not referred to as slave cabins per se and virtually nothing was said about them as spaces lived in by the enslaved. Yucca House was the exception, because although it functioned as a slave cabin for a significant period, especially in the antebellum period, it began as the home of Marie Thérèse Coin Coin once she was legally free, and it is this story that dominates the representation. None of the other former slave cabins on the site (weaving house, bindery/gift shop, Ghana House, or female writer's cabin) were included or referred to in the formal tour.

Other structures with spaces where the enslaved may have lived in the past, such as the main house or the African House, were not discussed as spaces in which enslaved people lived. The cabins in Clementine Hunter's portraits (or other painted objects) were not addressed in any significant way either. Instead, the emphasis was on their design, the artwork contained within them, and the (mainly white) tenants who stayed there after slavery. With the cabins symbolically annihilated and with such convoluted representations of slavery, Blacks, and people of color, the opportunity was lost to provide a more detailed focus on slavery; to reveal some of the many complexities of legally free people of color owning enslaved people; to create the conditions for a more critical debate on slavery and its legacies; and to explore the role of slave cabins and what they mean, including the continuum of accommodations lived in by the enslaved.

Beyond the treatment of Marie Thérèse Coin Coin and Clementine Hunter as individuals, Melrose Plantation focused only marginally on Black people, provided very few humanizing details, and almost no critical comments on the institution of slavery. As at most other plantation heritage sites, visitors heard very little (or nothing) about the lives of the majority of the enslaved on the site and little about the majority of the buildings. No significant details about them were given on tours, and no significant images or mention of them occurs in the main house. It is fair to say that except for discussion of the Metoyer family, slavery is also symbolically annihilated. Black people at the site are consistently marginalized. No significant information is provided about the fact that the most residents at the site were Black, and we also hear almost nothing about Black people (or working-class whites). As a result, the opportunity is lost to articulate Black voices and Black visions in ways that individualize and humanize Black people.

Several staff at Melrose said that they would like to do more research and tell many additional elements of the Melrose story. Of course, unlike at the two previous sites, they did not say that more attention should be given to post-slavery than slavery, because almost all attention was already given to post-slavery.

Gender clearly shaped the organization and presentations at Melrose Plantation, but again in more complex and convoluted ways than at the other two sites. I argue that the site was explicit on exceptional women and yet evasive on gender. We heard some passing mention of the constraints faced by elite white women—they were excluded from the political realm, confined largely to the household, and expected to be dedicated wives or mothers. Most attention, however, was spent on praising the women's drive and dedication in saving and restoring houses, organizing activities such as the Festival of Lights, and promoting heritage tourism in the parish. These activities actually resonated with the gender roles typically assigned to (white) women.

We heard even less about Black women—about their lives and experiences of under slavery, confined to agricultural and domestic menial labor and living under the constant threat of sexual violence and the possibility of their children or family members being sold. We heard almost nothing about their experiences under Jim Crow segregation, where they had de jure freedom but were still subject to the most entrenched social constraints and threats of violence. The fact that Clementine Hunter spent her life through her fifties doing servile work is almost an aside in how she is represented.

Nor did we hear about the ways in which the relative success of elite white women (during and after antebellum slavery) was based to a large degree on the labor of Black women, especially their domestic labor. We heard almost nothing about the many circuits of intersectionality or race and gender that prevailed at all times in Natchitoches history. Individual stories were told about motivated, dedicated, and highly energetic women who made things happen, but these stories were wrenched from the gender division of labor and presented as individual accomplishments.[20]

Understanding the distinctive patterns of heritage tourism at Melrose involves recognizing the unique history of the site, the fact that it was owned by legally free people of color for a substantial period of time, and the histories of Cammie, Clementine, and Coin Coin. These facts provide the substance to most of the representations.

Several of the factors that explained Oakland and Magnolia were also clearly relevant to Melrose. As at the other two sites, the APHN and its predecessor organizations grounded their activities squarely in the elite paternalist southern heritage promotion of Natchitoches generally, but of course, with the distinctive story of the Metoyers and the three exceptional women.

Staff were strongly influenced by their beliefs and experiences of visitor priorities. The site was more popular and had more visitors than the other two sites, so why change? Resources were also relevant—and Melrose struggled more than the other two sites because it did not receive the same resources as the NPS sites. This meant fewer opportunities to hold tours, provide additional activities, or undertake research. A lack of significant Black involvement in the site, was also a factor, especially involvement by professionals with relevant experience in public history. There had been one or two Black workers over time and there continued to be Cane River Creole descendants working at the site (though they did not define themselves as Black). Additionally, the harsh reality of racism and racial inequality under Jim Crow had created very different priorities and opportunities for Black people in the region leading to very different forms of heritage organization in Black communities. And finally, there was the state. As a private, not-for-profit site, operations at Melrose did not fall under the jurisdiction of the NPS, and staff had far greater flexibility over how it was run. But NPS did provide some support—in the form of funding, technical advice, and informal collaborations.

CONCLUSION

Historical tourism was a project conceived of by whites for white con-
sumers. . . . (so that) . . . Tourists could enjoy the picturesque spectacle
created by servile African Americans without needing to understand
them. Indeed, an exaggerated concern for African Americans might
have interfered with the tourist experience. To acknowledge the black
past, at least as understood by blacks, would have raised knotty questions about the legacies of slavery as well as current race relations,
thereby subverting the carefully nurtured images of gentility, romance
and nostalgia that sustained southern tourism. (Brundage 2018, 264)

In this book, I have provided a description and analysis of how slavery and
twenty-first-century antebellum slave cabins were presented in heritage tourism at three major heritage sites in Natchitoches, Louisiana, at the start of
the twenty-first century. Oakland Plantation, Magnolia Plantation Complex,
and Melrose Plantation were highly visible, highly visited, and very popular
heritage sites in the parish. All three sites were open to the public; all three
possessed a wide range of original eighteenth- and nineteenth-century buildings and structures from plantations built on slavery; all three provided
guided or unguided tours and a range of activities that presented detailed
information on southern history, southern plantations, and slavery; all three
highlighted the distinctive Creole culture of the region and did so in ways
that foregrounded the roles of elite white men and women historically; and
all three possessed and displayed several twenty-first-century antebellum
slave cabins, as well as other spaces in which the enslaved slept or lived.

These heritage sites—and the twenty-first-century antebellum slave cabins
and spaces located on them—are the physical and institutional embodiment of social forgetting and social remembering. They remind us of the
subordinated and exploited status of enslaved Black people throughout the
late nineteenth century, as well as struggles over the legacy of that status.
My analysis highlighted some of the contested dynamics of public history

as well as the contemporary struggles and historical precedents to those struggles reflected in those dynamics. The ways in which they constituted an important component of twenty-first-century southern heritage tourism offers striking insights into the nature of representations and discourses of slavery at these sites. Bringing slave cabins to the analytical foreground and highlighting their ambiguous roles under slavery and their marginalized roles in heritage tourism today provides a more compelling illustration of the continued significance of resource imbalances and contested struggles in heritage tourism than does consideration of heritage sites' mansions alone, or of slavery alone.

Throughout the book I have foregrounded information on the range of twenty-first-century antebellum slave cabins and other spaces at the sites in which the enslaved slept or lived. I defined this range as a *continuum of coerced accommodations*, a concept that provides greater insights into the web of unequal relations between owners and the enslaved on the plantations. I identified and evaluated the reasons why the twenty-first-century antebellum cabins were central to the sites at this present time; and I offered an explanation of why each site treated them as it did. I did this because the framing of the cabins as distinct structures rather than as a continuum of living spaces also disposes of uncomfortable issues that threaten the (white) tourist experience. And of course, there is the issue of what thoughtful consideration of the slave cabins can add to our analysis that might be missed by a focus on slavery in general. I also compared representations of slavery at the sites with representations of the slave cabins. The primary goal of the book was not about the history of the cabins and other spaces in which the enslaved lived or slept, though a brief history was provided. Rather it was about the social organization of the plantation heritage sites during the field research period (2007–2011), the nature and distribution of the range of spaces on these sites, and how and why variations in the representations of slavery and slave cabins at that time occurred in the way that they did at the sites.

Southern heritage tourism at plantation heritage sites in Natchitoches raises compelling questions about public history, collective memory, and the legacy of slavery. First, why was so much attention devoted to elite whites and to the buildings in which they lived as compared with the amount of attention devoted to Black residents and the buildings and spaces in which they lived? Black residents were the majority population at all times and the buildings they lived in were the majority of buildings (and spaces) in which they slept or worked at all times. This differential attention raises questions about the past in the present; how have the long-entrenched patterns of racial inequality and segregation in the South shaped priorities at these sites? This includes understanding the historical trajectory of the sites since the legal abolition of slavery. A second question concerns how gender shaped the representations at the sites, including representations of white and Black women. A third question concerns the extent to which Black voices and Black visions could be heard and seen at the sites. Fourth is the issue of legally free people of color who owned enslaved people themselves. And finally, there is the question of the role of the state in shaping representations of heritage tourism.

Underlying all these issues are questions about how power and access to resources lead to certain types of social remembering and social forgetting. In the instance of slavery and its legacies, it involves what I describe as the *cumulative institutionalization of neglect*. For example, the sites reveal how social contexts shaped by the material and institutional dynamics of race and gender inequalities remain central in the particular outcomes that emerge in public history, and in the continued bias towards highlighting elite whites. The sites thus provide us with an opportunity to think more about the role and possible consequences of heritage tourism in Natchitoches, in Louisiana, and across the South more generally.

In this final chapter, I summarize my main findings and highlight some issues that they raise about the social contestation of the public representation of slavery and slave cabins at these sites, as well as issues of public history elsewhere in the US South. My research provides insights into patterns prevalent at that time and allows for a comparison with developments since then, at those sites and others across the South, especially in light of the dramatically increased attention memorials to southern history have attracted in recent years. I close with several key developments in the United States around slavery, public history, and collective memory in recent decades.

HERITAGE TOURISM IN NATCHITOCHES

When I carried out research at the start of the twenty-first century, Natchitoches was promoted widely as the oldest permanent European settlement in the Louisiana Purchase territory. It was an important regional tourist center, incorporating urban and rural attractions and an extensive cultural heritage area. There were historic buildings, natural resources, social and cultural events, museums and interpretive centers, and related activities. Tens of thousands of visitors arrived in Natchitoches each year to enjoy these cultural activities. Public and private institutions across the town, the state, and the nation were active in the promotion and delivery of tourism activities. The

National Park Service (NPS) brought significant resources to Natchitoches in the form of finances, personnel and management, technical advice, and research. NPS continued to play a central role in many of these activities and was the owner of two of the most visited sites in the parish—Oakland Plantation and Magnolia Plantation Complex. By the start of the twenty-first century, the town and parish had lost the economic benefits of agriculture that they used to enjoy. The local elite and professional residents recognized the tremendous economic benefits of presenting the region's historical past in a form that tourists could visit and admire.

Several themes were prominent in heritage tourism in Natchitoches during my field research. One theme highlighted architecture, language, religion, music, and food, and other aspects of the cultural lifestyle and legacy of the French, and of (elite) French Creole families. Several aspects of slavery and its legacies were also mentioned, including descriptions of the multitier racial hierarchy that was prevalent during slavery (whites, mixed-race, and Black populations). The so-called Cane River Creoles—a group with mixed origins—became rich and powerful master-enslavers and even attained the dubious distinction of owning more enslaved people than any other legally free people of color in the South. Notable locals were also highlighted, especially those who achieved national or international acclaim. These included people like Louis Juchereau de St. Denis, the founder of Natchitoches, and John Sibley, the "Indian Agent" of the New Orleans Territory. Less typically than elsewhere in the South there were also stories of exceptional women, such as Marie Thérèse Coin Coin, Cammie Henry, Clementine Hunter, and Kate Chopin.

I chose to study Natchitoches for several reasons, which I will recap here. First, slavery and its legacies played an indispensable role in the establishment and growth of the parish and heritage tourism about these legacies was a vital component of the parish's economic activities at the start of the twenty-first century. Second, plantations and associated activities were central to the promotion of heritage tourism during my research, and the three plantations in this study had sixteen twenty-first century slave cabins on site, along with at least thirteen other spaces in which the enslaved lived or slept. Third, the treatment of slavery and slave cabins varied considerably across the three sites, as did site management. At Oakland and Magnolia plantations, the slave cabins qua slave cabins figured far more prominently in heritage tourism than at Melrose Plantation. At Melrose Plantation, the slave cabins were difficult to recognize as slave cabins per se, because they are primarily represented as log cabins once occupied by the white writers who were guests of Cammie Henry, owner of Melrose at that time. These differences in ownership and/or management enabled me to explore how contrasting representations came about and why they continued to exist.

Fourth, extensive official and other documentation, rich primary data, and significant secondary publications on the history of the parish and the organization of heritage tourism were readily accessible. It's also important that site officials and the local archivists were welcoming and supportive as I did the research. Finally, despite all its compelling intrinsic features, slavery and its legacy in Louisiana in general, and Natchitoches in particular, have attracted far less scholarly attention than other areas in the South, especially the upper South. We know far more about the history of Virginia, North Carolina, and South Carolina than we do about Louisiana. We know far more about the history of New Orleans than we do about any other area of Louisiana, and we know more about the history and legacy of sugar plantations in the southern section of Louisiana than about other crops or regions elsewhere in the state. There are few studies of contemporary plantation sites and heritage tourism in the state, outside of New Orleans and the River Road. I have sought to rectify this relative neglect.

I wrote this book with four specific goals, and I took account of four different themes. My first goal was to describe the nature, role, and signifi- cance of the twenty-first-century slave cabins at these three major plantation heritage sites at that time. I accomplished this by providing an overview of the nature of heritage tourism and public history in the parish at the present time, by describing how the attention devoted to slavery and slave cabins at the sites compares with the attention devoted to elite white life- styles and culture, and by looking at how the representations of slavery at the sites compared with their representations of the twenty-first-century slave cabins.

My second goal was to explore and assess how representations of slavery and slave cabins at the sites could help us examine the reconfiguration of the past and rearticulation of history in the present. How were historically entrenched institutions and structures of racialized and gendered inequality and power reproduced in the conditions of the present? And how were the stories, and discourses at the sites during the research—including the most common themes, stories and details—shaped by these patterns of inequal- ity? In other words, I described and analyzed some of the ways in which the physical structures of the past were deployed in the tourist industry of the twenty-first century. I examined how questions of public history (including silences and omissions) were incorporated into tourism, and I raised ques- tions about collective memory (how certain aspects of southern history are willfully remembered and others willfully forgotten).

My third goal was to describe the historical trajectory of plantations and cabins since their construction under slavery, through the Civil War and postbellum periods, and how they became incorporated into heritage tourism. The fourth goal of the book was to examine the legacy and representations of the people of mixed European and African origins—the so-called free people of color, specifically the Metoyer family, who owned enslaved people in the parish. Some of the descendants of this family still lived in Natchitoches at the time of research, and some family members played roles in the tours and the organization of the site.

As I grappled with these questions, I engaged with four important themes. The first theme concerned how gender ideologies and roles structured the social organization and representations of the sites, including in presentations, the gendered division of labor in management and administration, and how both have been shaped by history. This included consideration of intersectionality, that is, the ways in which race and gender interacted to shape life roles and outcomes. I described how gender ideologies shaped the treatment and presentation of slavery and the slave cabins, with regard to elite whites and enslaved Black people. I described gendered images and discourses and how gender shaped the establishment and preliminary priorities of the sites as they become incorporated into heritage tourism. These issues were particularly relevant, given the power inequalities prevalent in the Jim Crow period and their immediate legacy in the post–civil rights period.

The second theme concerned representations of ethnic identity in the history and culture of Europeans that colonized the region—including those with Spanish, French, and Anglo ancestry and identity. These differences were presented as points of distinction and interest. This included the manifestation of these differences in the lives of the elites, in their architecture, cultural practices, family structure, language, and religion, as well as food, music, and clothing.

The third theme addressed what I have termed Black voices and Black visions. I asked questions about the sources of evidence and information upon which the current representations in heritage tourism of slavery and slave cabins at the sites were based, and I assessed to what extent evidence and data from Black people were the basis of or included in the presentations. We know that historically the majority of residents at the sites were Black people and that most of the residences were also lived in or worked in by Black people (including people of mixed origins). How much of the information from websites, promotional literature, on signs and placards at the sites, and expressed by tour guides during tours, was based on evidence or insights from the Black residents, and especially from Black women, at the

plantation? How much information came from narratives, biographies, folktales, songs, or religious texts created by Black people? Did we see images
from art, sculpture, drawings, or songs of Black people that lived at the site
(or elsewhere)? Overall, I set out to discover to what extent the Black people
resident at these sites were individualized or humanized. Questions of this
kind provide keen insights into the nature of discourses and representations,
as well as into underlying issues of power and access to resources.

The fourth theme concerned the role and influence of the state. Two of
the three sites studied (Oakland and Magnolia Plantation Complex) were
owned and managed by the National Park Service. The third site (Melrose
Plantation) was owned and managed by the not-for-profit Association for the
Preservation of Historic Natchitoches. I have described the role and influence
of the state in shaping treatment and representations of slavery and the slave
cabins; how state ownership shaped the information presented at the sites,
the knowledge collected about the sites, and the resources available to them;
and how the state became involved in the establishment of the three sites.

I collected a wide range of data for this book about the history of the
sites and their operations during my research and I carried out a number of
interviews. I also used a range of research methods. More details about both
are provided in the Appendix.

OAKLAND, MAGNOLIA, AND MELROSE: AN OVERVIEW

During field research, all three heritage sites were open to the public and
were visited by people from across the region, the nation, and the world.
All three had a wide range of original eighteenth- and nineteenth-century
buildings and structures built while they were slave plantations, including
a main house, outbuildings, and gardens; all three had twenty-first-century
antebellum slave cabins with three at Oakland (one of which is in ruins),
eight at Magnolia, and five at Melrose. They also had a range of other spaces
in which the enslaved slept or lived (for example, workspaces such as the
kitchen or blacksmith shop and spaces in the main house such as the basement). There were guided house tours at Oakland and Melrose, and a self-
guided tour of the grounds at Magnolia.

The number of buildings that existed when I started the research was a
fraction of what once existed at the sites, because most of the original buildings had deteriorated over time, were destroyed during or after the Civil
War, or lost to accidents such as fires. A higher proportion of buildings in
which the elite whites lived survived, and/or were preserved, and elite white

residents of the parish mobilized to ensure that. But some of the former slave cabins were also identified and preserved. The former mayor of Natchitoches, Bobby DeBlieux, played an important role in saving them. The cabins at Oakland and Magnolia were original to the site, but Cammie Henry brought in the cabins at Melrose from other sites in the 1920s and 1930s.

All three sites offered fascinating case studies of how twenty-first-century antebellum slave cabins survived and became part of heritage tourism by virtue of having had new life breathed into them by white people a long time after slavery ended. It is an interesting twist of fate that many of these cabins that existed at the start of the twenty-first century existed because white people socially valued them, and found a way to identify, preserve, and incorporate them into heritage tourism. This happened earlier at Melrose (around the 1920s) through Cammie Henry's activities and her writer's colony. It happened far later at the other two sites (in the 1990s). At Oakland and Magnolia, Bobby DeBlieux played a crucial role in retaining the cabins on the sites. The "log cabins" at Melrose were valued by Cammie Henry as part of her quest to preserve an architectural and cultural history of the antebellum period. They were not used nor preserved as slave cabins.

Slavery and the twenty-first-century antebellum slave cabins featured centrally in the activities or exhibits at all three sites. All three sites possessed and displayed several twenty-first-century antebellum slave cabins—and other spaces in which the enslaved lived or slept. Site visitors heard about the existence of the cabins, they got to see them if they wished to do so, and even go inside some of them, and they learned basic details about the former residents of the cabins at different points in history, including during slavery and Jim Crow.

The distinctive Creole culture of the region was highlighted at all three sites, in ways that promoted the historical roles of elite white men and women. This was achieved by foregrounding and naming prominent families, important events in which they were involved, and details of their contributions in politics, industry, economics, and culture. At all three sites, elites were the main focus of attention. At Oakland and Magnolia, this meant primarily elite whites, and especially men. At Melrose, it meant legally free people of color. At all three sites, ethnic differences among elites were central—at the first two sites, ethnic differences within the white population (between French Creoles and Anglo-Americans) were called out, while at Melrose it was ethnic differences between Creoles that were people of color, and Creoles that were white. In addressing elites, the sites focused on elite housing and architecture, elite family members and their individual roles and biographies, and cultural patterns associated with elites, for example, management of the plantations and entertainment and consumption.

At all three sites, gender was a major structuring variable of visits and representations. Visitors heard about the appropriate and socially allocated roles and spaces for elite white men and women, and boys and girls; what jobs they did (men in plantation management and economics, women in domestic management and entertainment); what rooms they occupied; and what other roles they played. We also saw images of men and women in these roles in the form of portraits or paintings.

The gendered roles of Black men and women got far less mention, but we did hear about and see some images of Black people at the sites, and we did hear some Black voices and see some Black visions. For example, we heard about some of the work done by Black women in the kitchen of the main house; we saw images of Black men and women (and even children) working in the fields; and we occasionally heard individual names of Black workers. Visitors were sometimes told that men were more likely to occupy crafts positions (for example, carpenter or blacksmith) and women more likely to be cooks and nannies. We also saw some images of Black men and women in these roles, for example, in drawings hanging on the walls of the cabins or in the plantation store. At Melrose Plantation, visitors also saw a wide range of paintings by Clementine Hunter, many of which portrayed Black men, women, and children. The representations of Black people are more limited and impersonal, and they pale in substance, range, and significance when compared with representations and voices of elite whites (or in the case of Melrose, elite legally free people of color). With the exception of Melrose Plantation, we hear very little personalizing or humanizing information about Black people, in contrast to the details and insights that are shared about the elite white residents.

A perceptive visitor could see that gender operated differently in the Black community than it did for elite whites. There was far less of a distinction between the socially allocated roles of Black men and women as compared with roles for elite white men and women. For example, visitors saw images of Black women, like men, doing similar kinds of work in the fields.

While the sites shared many of these practices in common, there were important differences between them. The major difference was between Oakland and Magnolia on the one hand, and Melrose on the other hand. Oakland and Magnolia adopted similar strategies for representing slavery and slave cabins—relative incorporation. Relative incorporation meant that information was provided to visitors about slavery and the slave cabins, and how they functioned as key elements of plantation life under slavery.

Information was provided about some of the interactions of plantation residents of all racial and ethnic backgrounds, for example, while working or during recreation. Visitors also heard information about women and the way gender shaped their lives. This information was available on the online web site, in site promotional literature, in various locations at the sites (including temporary exhibits), and during the tours. In addition, the docents at these sites were able to respond to general questions from visitors to the site about slavery, slave cabins, and enslaved people.

However, slavery and the slave cabins were not yet "fully incorporated" into either of the two plantations. They remained in clear second place compared with the amount and quality of information provided about elite white lives, including living spaces. This was reflected, for example, in the overall framing of southern history at each plantation, as well as in the details provided about specific buildings and residents. At Oakland Plantation, there was only one guided tour, which centered primarily on the Main House, and it focused on the lifestyles, culture, thoughts, and feelings of its elite white residents. Many of these elite whites were personalized and individualized in the guided tours. At Magnolia Plantation, information about the cabins was perfunctory, and far more attention was devoted to the plantation store. Information and access to the cabins at both sites was uneven and inconsistent. They were typically closed or locked and had no exhibits or exhibits that were rudimentary. For the most part, visitors did not hear any significant personalizing or individualizing information about the enslaved or other Black residents of the site. Nor were women—especially Black women—and gender given any serious consideration.

Melrose was more complicated than the other two sites. I have argued throughout this book that slavery and the slave cabins at Melrose were symbolically annihilated, rather than relatively incorporated. And although women—Black and white, mainly elite—were mentioned everywhere, the significance of gender and race ideologies and social organization was absent.

In contrast, the information on southern heritage presented at Melrose focused far more on key episodes in the twentieth century than it did on slavery. Slavery was mentioned several times, but in highly individualized and particularistic ways. Melrose visitors almost certainly left with little general information about slavery at the site, in the parish, or in Louisiana and the South. The information at the site was also distorted and partial—a common practice across the South. There was a major difference from the other two sites, where visitors mainly heard about elite white residents. At Melrose, they heard a good deal about elite legally free people of color, but in the end the majority of information was still about elite whites, because they were the dominant group in the periods after slavery ended.

With regard to slavery, Marie Thérèse Coin Coin and the history of the Metoyers was the fulcrum of discussion. We heard about the unique community of legally free people of color that became rich and powerful, in large part because they owned enslaved people. We learned they were part of a wider network of similar families; we learned they became richer than many local elite whites; and we learned that this wealth and status was quickly eroded once the number of Anglo-Americans increased in the region in the antebellum period. We also heard a great deal about the unique social initiative institutionalized in Cammie Henry's writer's colony. Here, the focus was on Cammie Henry as an eccentric, determined, and successful individual committed to the preservation of (certain aspects of) southern heritage.

As a result, slavery and the former slave cabins at Melrose Plantation were both everywhere and nowhere: everywhere because we saw images of them in the site literature, in Clementine Hunter's portraits, and because they are physically present. And yet, they were nowhere, because at no time were they highlighted as slave cabins per se, or as part of the continuum of accommodations in which the enslaved lived or slept.

The way gender shaped the organization and presentations at Melrose Plantation was also more complex and convoluted than at the other two sites. I just argued that the site was explicit on exceptional women and evasive on gender. This meant we heard a great deal about exceptional women, but almost nothing about gender. There was some passing mention of the constraints faced by elite white women—they were excluded from the political realm, confined largely to the household, and expected to be dedicated wives or mothers. But most attention was spent on praising the women's initiative, drive, and dedication in saving and restoring houses, organizing activities such as the Festival of Lights, and generally promoting heritage tourism in the parish. These activities resonated with the gender roles typically assigned to (white) women. We also heard about proud mothers who dedicated their lives to ensuring success for their offspring, as raising children is a responsibility typically assigned to women.

THE SOUTHERN GENTILITY NARRATIVE

I have made it clear throughout this book that the dominant narrative for framing the history at these sites (and in Natchitoches more generally) was that of southern gentility, elite white lifestyles, paternalism, and romance.

My colleague Jennifer L. Eichstedt and I collected evidence of this kind of framing in our previous research on plantation museum sites. In that work we argued that sites in general and house tours in particular

> overwhelmingly focus on aspects of antebellum white southern life that maintain a vision of the genteel, honorable South. This framing relies on the language of romance, wealth, honor, and the chastity of white southern women and is created through a focus on architecture, furniture, and accoutrements such as paintings, chandeliers, candelabras, dishes and so on, which all demonstrate the tastes and refinement of the white elite; an additional and equally important focus is on the codes of conduct that guided family life and social interaction. (Eichstedt and Small 2002, 59)

We highlighted some of the variations in different regions across three states—Virginia, Georgia, and Louisiana (Eichstedt and Small 2002). Natchitoches has its own unique features, but the underlying foundation of this framing remained essentially the same. First was an emphasis on the unique and distinctive history of Natchitoches as a town and parish, highlighting its humble origins, its founding (and "founding fathers") and expansion, its trials and tribulations, and its eventual success (for whites). It highlighted the distinctive, impressive, and indeed beguiling aspects of the French (and the Spanish) presence and legacy in the parish, especially as reflected in architecture, religion, family, and food. Heritage tourism in Natchitoches also highlighted favorable and romantic aspects of the plantations' histories.

Second was an emphasis on the history of elite and wealthy families, especially the families that established, built, and expanded Natchitoches in ways that led to its success. This included identifying family changes over generations: challenges, failures, and successes. It meant emphasizing how individuals and families struggled (as pioneers, clearing land and developing trade routes) for what was right and best for them and the parish. Insights into family fortunes over generations were key. They were often thwarted, with great consequence (the Civil War), but nevertheless persevered. The humanity, dignity, and kindness of elite, wealthy families and individuals and their legacies were emphasized.

All of this was, of course, gendered. We heard about the men who headed the families, the marriages and wives, and the children that took over the family fortunes or losses, and persevered. The fact that by the end of the twentieth century, some of these families had unbroken ownership of the plantations for several hundred years was all the more impressive and romantic.

Third were the life histories of outstanding individuals and succession over multiple generations, including the Prud'hommes at Oakland, up to and including the Prud'homme family members who sold the plantation to NPS in the 1990s. Sometimes we heard about the elite women on the plantation—for example, Jean Pierre's wife, Catherine Lambre—but not as often or in as much detail as the men. At Magnolia, we heard about several generations of Lecomtes and Hertzogs: about Jean Baptiste Lecomte, who established the plantation; Ambroise Lecomte I and Ambroise Lecomte II, who continued it; up to and including Betty Hertzog, who in fall 2011 was still living in the private main plantation house adjacent to the site. We heard about the family relationships between the Lecomtes and Hertzogs—for example, the marriage of Atala Lecomte to Matthew Hertzog after slavery was legally ended—and how the merging of the families sustained their wealth, although the plantations were divided into different units. We heard about the Hertzog who built the plantation store after the Civil War. At Melrose, we heard about many (white) individuals involved, among them the writers at Cammie Henry's writer's colony—Lyle Saxon, François Mignon, and others. Visitors heard their names, saw their faces, and enjoyed the rich details of their lives. For example, we saw images of Cammie Henry, François Mignon and others in photographs in the Weaving House. And, of course, we heard the story of Bobby DeBlieux, who was so central to the success of heritage tourism in the parish.

Again, we sometimes heard about the elite women on the plantation, for example, Ambroise II's wife, Julia Buard, his second wife, Lise Victorie Desiree Sompayrac, and Sally Hertzog, who died in 1960. The most compelling individual stories probably come from the women at Melrose, each one of whom, we were told, through sheer hard work, dedication, determination, and perseverance, rose above their circumstance (or in the case of Cammie Henry, survived after the loss of her husband) to do great things—for family, for community, for the parish, and for posterity. Without Marie Thérèse Coin Coin, we would have no fascinating story to tell of the rise and fall of the Metoyers; without Cammie Henry, we would not have the documents that relate the history of the parish (or the state); and without Clementine Hunter, we would not have the folk art that provides such rich resources for documenting rural Black life.

Clearly then, this narrative was heavily shaped by established gender conventions where men and women, especially wealthy white men and women, do what they are supposed to do, that is, what society expects them to do. There was a consistent focus on elite white women whose proper role was in the household as wives and mothers, taking care of household niceties, dressing appropriately, and remaining within these proscriptions. In all of this, Black women were generally ignored, both in the ways they were denied similar privileges (never able to stay in the domestic realm) and in the way their labor provided an indispensable basis for elite white women's domestic achievements (by providing the cooking, cleaning, and childcare).

And fourth, the arrival of NPS in the 1990s to save the plantations from what looked at the time like certain doom and destruction is both evocative and romantic, because it rescued and has made public a legacy of great importance to the elite white population in Natchitoches—a legacy that might otherwise have been lost forever. The family stories were thus kept alive and accessible, and the physical legacy—buildings and family heirlooms—were saved and protected for posterity. What could be more romantic than that?

EVASION, ERASURE, AND EUPHEMISM

One of the problems that confronted heritage sites in Natchitoches was how to deal with the difficult, unpleasant, embarrassing, and outright shameful history of slavery and segregation and with the embarrassment or guilt that may have arisen from confronting these facts. How to treat the seizure of land that rightfully belonged to Native Americans? How to deal with the then legal practice of capturing, transporting, and enslaving Africans and with the legal practice of slavery? How to address the inescapable exploitation of men, women, and children and the range of abuses constituent to that exploitation? And to deal with the inveterate suffering and pain—all of which were sanctioned by Christian churches and authorities? These issues are especially troubling if one was implicated in them—by virtue of family, community, ethnic, racial, or national identity. They are not abstractions but concrete, practical problems that must be addressed when websites, tourist literature, panel descriptions, photographs, and posters are being created, and when tour scripts are being written. In Natchitoches, these questions had to be confronted by management and staff at the sites, by the tourist agencies, by the city and parish government, and by the National Park Service itself.

Since stories cannot tell everything, one of the main functions of a dominant narrative is to highlight the items that are necessary and integral to a story and make it clear what items should be conveyed by euphemism, avoided, or completely annihilated. There was no significant mention at any of the sites of slavery per se as an inherently and inescapably exploitative, violent, or unjust system; no mention of the endemic and entrenched violence and brutality of the system; and no mention of sexual assault and rape. The goal, it was clear, was not to linger too long on the harsh and unsavory elements of the past, but rather to highlight the grandeur, charm, and individual successes.

In Natchitoches, coercion, violence, and brutality (especially involving sexual abuse) were almost never mentioned; injustice was almost never mentioned. There was very little mention of racism, except to imply it was less severe in Natchitoches than elsewhere in Louisiana and the South. There seems to have been an absolute ban on mentioning any specific brutality, violence, or abuse—especially sexual abuse—that might have happened at the sites during slavery or legal segregation. It was as if violence or brutality never occurred and/or was never documented. As if no one was ever whipped or beaten, as if enslaved families were never separated, as if no one died prematurely. To the contrary, all we hear are neutral summaries or complementary evaluations of the roles and lives of the elite family members. Consultation of the records demonstrates otherwise.

Instead, visitors were told that exploitation and abuse occurred elsewhere in the South, but not in Natchitoches. We were told that high rates of mortality through overwork were characteristic of the sugar parishes of Louisiana or the rice counties of Georgia, but not the cotton fields of Natchitoches. We were told that violence was the purview of other master-enslavers, as was sexual abuse, but not the eminent families of Natchitoches. And we were told that a rigid racial system was typical in Anglo states, but not in the multitier racial system of Natchitoches.

Throughout this book, I have described several ways that these issues were handled in heritage tourism. A range of justifications were deployed, just as they were under the system of slavery itself.[1] At the three main sites in Natchitoches, several discourse strategies and rhetorical styles were deployed. Most of them can be treated under the rubrics of euphemism, evasion, and erasure. But how do we begin to analyze these evasions, erasures, and euphemisms?[2] Throughout the book, I have explored what was said and done at the sites. In this section, I pay more attention to what was absent at the sites. Given that choices had to be made about what to include and what to exclude, what is missing can reveal buried or ignored issues. In representations and discourses of race, silences and absences are an increasingly important set of issues. I describe some of these tactics here.

One issue is what is said—and the particular choice of words—and another issue is what is not said. What is not said raises questions of intentionality—because silence or absence might be intentional or unintentional. The evidence collected for this book did not allow me to document intentionality with any confidence, but I can offer some observations.

At the three sites, I have identified various strategies of trivialization and deflection (say very little), relative incorporation (say more than a little, but still not too much) and symbolic annihilation (say nothing). I also described how the cursory and stilted representations of slavery and of the cabins were typically merged into a vast ocean of detail about experiences of elite whites and their families. Overall, elite whites were humanized and individualized, while the majority residents of the plantation—Blacks and people of mixed origins—were marginalized. And again, all of this was gendered.

Several discursive tactics were employed at the sites described in this book. The general approach involved saying as little as possible about slavery and slave cabins or about the majority of Black residents. It involved not mentioning brutality, violence, or other disagreeable aspects of slavery; and absolutely not mentioning any culpability on the part of the family members themselves. And there was no attempt to articulate the range of accommodations for the enslaved, or to explore their implications.

How else were these tactics used? First were the evasions and erasures. Both involved silence, but they had different elements. Silence meant that nothing was said, but sometimes it may not be obvious that something needed to be said. And at other times things were begging to be said. For example, it may not be obvious to staff or docents that they should mention that slavery was an unjust system, or that all the Black people at the site were in subordinate positions, while all the white people were in positions of power. It may not be obvious to mention that Clementine Hunter was a fieldworker and cook for almost fifty years because those were the only jobs available for Black women on plantations in Jim Crow Natchitoches, and it may not be obvious to mention that François Mignon was able to achieve what he did because he was male, white, and privileged.

Erasures were also silences and evasions, but the difference was intentionality—erasure is deliberate. I argue that it occurred when there was a compelling or obvious reason to say something about a topic although that can't be proved on the basis of the evidence I have at hand. But I think it is highly plausible. For example, as I mentioned there was the almost complete erasure of any mention of brutality, especially sexual brutality. There was the almost complete erasure of mention of the institutional injustice. There was almost complete erasure of mention of the racism of slavery or the racism of Jim Crow legal segregation and enforced inequality. The few exceptions to these common practices were in one or two exhibit panels: at Oakland in the exhibits in the slave cabin and plantation store; at Magnolia in the exhibit in the slave hospital/overseers' house. There was also mention of such issues in one or two of the available leaflets. Even such limited mentions are missing at Melrose where there was no acknowledgement whatsoever of exploitation, brutality, violence, or oppression.

Second was the use of euphemisms like "servant" and "worker." Some of these euphemisms result in trivialization and deflection of fundamental aspects of slavery. For example, Marie Thérèse Coin Coin's relationship with Metoyer, and the fact that she was mother to his children, was treated euphemistically and the undeniable race and gendered power relations—a powerful white man and an enslaved woman of color—were ignored. This included some elements of trivialization and deflection. The story of Coin Coin was described in such a way as to suggest that sexual relationships between free white men and enslaved women were based primarily on romance or love, rather than power inequities or coercion. In other words, what was said at the site was sanitized and romanticized.

Overall, these strategies functioned to marginalize, neglect, or erase Black people, about whom we hear very little: few names, little or nothing about their thoughts or ambitions, their humanity, nothing about their acts of heroism or resistance, and almost nothing about cultural or other affirming activities (such as religious beliefs and practices, gardening, or income-earning practices) in which they were involved.

OAKLAND, MAGNOLIA, AND MELROSE: AN EXPLANATION

At the end of each chapter in this book on each of the sites I mentioned several factors that help us understand why the sites organized heritage tourism in the ways that they did. To summarize: Why did all three sites privilege the lives and culture of the minority of elite (primarily white) people who occupied the sites? Why did the majority of residents at the sites—overwhelmingly Black people at all times—get only secondary attention compared to elite whites? And why was the information about Black people—with one or two exceptions—general, abstract, and often stereotypical? Why did we hear so much about the main houses at each site, so little about the slave cabins, and even less about the other spaces in which Black people slept or lived on the sites? Why did relative incorporation prevail as the predominant narrative strategy at the Oakland and Magnolia sites, and why was symbolic annihilation the main narrative strategy at Melrose? In terms of representations of the lives of Black people—and of the slave cabins and later on the quarters—what were some of the strengths of the sites that could lead to more inclusive, accurate, and representative narratives? What improvements could be made without substantial resources? And what improvements could be made with resources?

The site management and staff offered several reasons for the prevailing patterns at that time. At Oakland and Magnolia, they pointed out that in the 1990s, at the time that sites were being made public heritage sites, the decision was made that their primary focus would be the mid to late twentieth century. They also highlighted their perception of visitor priorities, maintaining that visitors were primarily interested in the main house and came to hear about elite lifestyles, architecture, and gardens. The NPS superintendent did express her desire to go beyond a romanticization of southern history, but my interpretation is that she felt the sites had already done a great deal to avoid that. Beyond this point, and more generally, staff expressed regret about limited resources—including evidence on Black lives under slavery—especially in the context of a deteriorating economy at that time. Better conditions would have enabled them to do more and deeper research.

Staff at Melrose offered few explanations for the nature of the representations that prevailed there—it was as if the appeal of Coin Coin, Cammie, and Clementine was obvious. The site was more popular than the other two sites and operated under the clear belief that its narrative focus was exactly what visitors wanted. The docents told their stories with enthusiasm and creativity and the visitors seemed enthralled by it all. Who could oppose such a long-standing tradition? And so why should they change? The state did not require it, and APHN did not require it. Even the Texans who visited the site—of whom there were many—did not seem to mind being the butt of some jokes by tour guides, from their smaller, poorer neighbors in Louisiana. None of the staff at Melrose suggested significant changes around the underlying issues of southern gentility and elite lifestyles.

The explanations at Oakland and Magnolia have some merit, but I highlight several other factors that I believe are more compelling. These factors apply to Melrose as well. The most compelling is that all three were founded and continued to operate under the thrall of southern gentility, including a preoccupation with elite whites, paternalism, and romance. Narratives of southern gentility were irrepressibly gendered, and paternalism highlighted the honor and chivalry, economic achievements, graciousness and decency of men, and the motherhood, domesticity, and beauty of women. These narratives also insisted on avoiding any mention of the brutality, violence, and exploitation, under the system of slavery—and later of Jim Crow segregation—that enabled these elite lifestyles. This framing was like a cloak—one could even say a straitjacket—that prescribed or dictated the elements deemed important at each site. This dominant narrative severely constrained representations at the sites and greatly impeded a more open-minded and balanced approach. The sites thus lost the opportunity to promote a far more inclusive focus on Black people, as such a focus could not avoid critiquing the limited scope of such ideologies. By embracing this approach, the sites secured material benefits from their (mainly white) visitors.

A second factor was staff beliefs about visitors' interests, which they thought were the main houses, the elite lifestyles, and the architecture and glamor of plantations. This is clearly a major issue and highly suggestive. However, evidence from other sites indicates that many visitors are appreciative when more substantial information is provided on the lives of Black people. Such evidence has increased since the period in which this research was conducted (through 2011) and so beliefs about visitor priorities have almost certainly been modified.

A third factor arises from resource limitations, both evidentiary and financial. The fact that Oakland and Magnolia were owned by the state—in the form of NPS—meant that some resources were available. Without state resources, the sites would not have been purchased and set up for heritage tourism in the 1990s. Significant amounts of money were spent purchasing the sites, carrying out renovations, restoring and preserving buildings, carrying out research, and paying staff. Whatever deficiencies the sites revealed during my research, it is abundantly clear that they would have been far worse without the NPS or may never have come into existence at all.

Resource limitations were greater at Melrose than at the other two sites. Melrose staff expressed a desire to carry out more research, organize more activities, and hold more tours, but sufficient resources were not there. The facilities at the site were deteriorating, maintenance costs were increasing, and visitor numbers were barely holding steady (for example, Hurricane Katrina in 2005 reduced the number of visitors to the state, and the economic recession from 2008 exacerbated the situation). The potential for symbolic or significant change in representations of slavery and slave cabins seemed far less likely at Melrose Plantation than at the NPS sites.

A fourth factor was the lack of Black people involved in the sites; that is, Black people with knowledge, experience, and in many respects, greater sensitivity to the volatile issues that heritage sites cover. It is clear that some individual Black people were involved as staff or interpreters, but that is not the point. Looking at sites across the state and across the South, when Black people are systematically involved, and in ways that are collective and institutional, sites tend to be far more inclusive and representative of a wide range of Black experiences (Benjamin and Alderman 2017; Eichstedt and Small 2002). I suspect that the greater involvement of Black people in Oakland and Magnolia accounts for their more balanced coverage than at Melrose.

The fifth factor was entrenched racial inequality. All three sites were based in plantations that had subordinated and exploited Black people for centuries, first under slavery, then under Jim Crow, both with state-sanctioned racial discrimination. All three emerged as tourist sites during entrenched racial inequality in which Black people were expected to accept these conditions (i.e., "know their place") politically, economically, and socially, under threat of sanction, violence, or brutality. Despite its *Natchitoches twist*, Black people have always been subordinated to whites in the parish and they remained so at the time of my research. Contributing to or taking part in heritage sites that ignored the violence and exploitation of slavery—and of Jim Crow— and proudly boasted of racial tolerance in Natchitoches for people of mixed African and European descent in particular, and Black people in general, was hardly a priority for local Black people, either in the past or by the start of the twenty-first century.

Black people were far more concerned with their safety and survival, material needs, employment, education, housing, and health, than with heritage representations of the kind embraced in Natchitoches in the public realm and at these sites. Black people in the parish and across the state had their own cultural celebrations, mainly in their own communities, and that's where they put their efforts. I suspect that if Black people had not been restricted, besieged, or tormented by racism and had been involved in the transformation of the sites into heritage sites, we would have heard less about elite whites, architecture, and gardens, and far less about Cammie Henry and elite legally free people of color. I suspect we would have heard a very different story about Marie Thérèse Coin Coin, one that highlighted the power and domination of the white men that shaped her life, and her resistance to it; about the continued resistance and resilience of Black people and of maroons under slavery; far more about Clementine Hunter and her perspective on Blacks and whites and more about Uncle Israel and Aunt Jane; and far more about the meaning to Black people of the kitchens, cabins, and spaces in which they organized their lives.

I suspect all this because this is what the limited evidence tells us in Natchitoches. For example, when some of the quarters were taken down in the 1940s because they were dilapidated, interviews with Black people living there revealed that they were against that destruction. Although (white) people with power saw only the physical state of the cabins, Black people valued them and did not want them destroyed (Malone 1996). The importance of the cabins and their emotional value to Black people was also foregrounded in Clementine Hunter's work. Similar insights are evident in memorials and museums organized by and for Black people across the South (Glymph 2020; Clark 2005; Franklin 2001). The cabins—and later the quarters—are remembered as places of community, shared experiences, and family; they are also remembered as places of relative independence, autonomy, and decision-making free from the wretched surveillance and unrestricted violence of white racism. These heartfelt recollections, memories, and stories about living in plantation quarters are central features in many of the works of one of Louisiana's most famous novelists—the multiple award-winner Ernest Gaines. And they are the thing that comes back, and about which he revels, over and over again in his interviews.

I'm reminded of my visit to other sites in Louisiana where I was some-times greeted by docents who told me that the "big house" wasn't open at that time. When I said that I had not come to see the big house but the cabins, they responded incredulously, saying something like—"Why would you want to see them, there's nothing there!" (Small 2012, 16). I still stand behind my statement that "Whether or not there is something there, is not a matter of fact, but a matter of social valuation" (ibid., 16). And I believe that throughout this book I have demonstrated that the social valuations that prevail at the three sites studied here are not shared by very many Black people—or as increasing evidence is revealing—by many white people either.

The final factor concerns the role and influence of the state. I have described several aspects of this role for the NPS sites and argued that these have been beneficial overall in getting the sites up and running, financing research and maintenance, and establishing goals and criteria to achieve some kind of inclusiveness in representations of southern history. Melrose, as a private, not-for-profit site, was a different matter. Management was not required to consult with others to the same extent as at the NPS sites about what was appropriate or advisable; it did not operate under the same man-dates as the NPS sites, nor was it evaluated in the same way or with the same consequences. The state was not completely absent, however. Its main influ-ence came in the form of limited funding, some technical knowledge, and a supportive, informal relationship of cooperation with Cane River Creole National Historical Park. This resulted in collaborations, professional rela-tionships, formal and informal projects, and other types of mutual support and advising. The remoteness of Natchitoches, its small community identity, shared goals of heritage promotion, and the proximity of the sites to one another helped sustain this relationship. It is difficult to believe that Melrose would have remained as it is if it had been subject to state involvement of the kind that occurs at the NPS sites.

CHANGING THE GRAND NARRATIVE

In principle, making changes to representations of slavery and slave cab-ins at all three sites—to make them more accurate, comprehensive, and

inclusive—would not require significant effort or resources. More fundamental changes could be made in the medium and longer term, especially
those that require financial resources. Management and the staff at the sites
said such changes were their primary goals. In the more than ten years since I
completed my research in Natchitoches, significant changes have been made
at many similar plantation heritage sites across the South. Obstacles remain,
as I have mentioned, but they are not insurmountable. I mention some of
these changes in the epilogue to this book.

The thorniest obstacle remains how to remove the preoccupation and
obeisance to a narrative of southern gentility, elite white lifestyles, paternalism, and romance. This would require far greater attention to socio-economic
and gender stratification within the white population—including across
ethnic groups. And it would require far more attention to Black people at
the sites, which would be difficult without more attention to the slave cabins
and to what I have called the continuum of coerced accommodations for
the enslaved. Making these changes would open up many other questions, as
I've mentioned, that site management and staff may be reluctant to address,
and visitors may dislike.

In addition, raising these issues would lead to a more immediate recognition of questions of power and access to resources as we examine: 1) who
lived in the main house and why, as compared with who lived at the back of
the main house, and why; and 2) who decided whether the main house (and
elite whites) or the slave cabins (and enslaved Blacks) should get the most
attention at the heritage tourism sites. These considerations were already
being discussed at other sites in Louisiana—such as Frogmore and Laura—
during the period of research, and attention to these issues has increased
since then (Moody and Small 2019; Carter et al. 2014; Dwyer et al. 2013).
Bold innovations have taken place at Whitney Plantation, which provides
what must be one of the most comprehensive and inclusive representations
of the lives of enslaved people at any plantation heritage site in Louisiana.

Visitors to the sites in Natchitoches could not have failed to recognize
just how little information there was about enslaved people, how stifled and
muffled Black peoples' voices were; or how few Black visions were presented
and how blurred and hazy such visions were. More Black voices and visions
would have conveyed far more accurate representations of Black people's lives
and given them far more nuance and texture. I argue that as we seek more
comprehensive understandings of the lives of the majority of site residents,
and more details about the majority of buildings and spaces that functioned
as accommodations, the slave cabins can offer some of the most promising
sources of information. We are far more likely to find alternate sources and

accounts of the lives of the enslaved in the slave cabins. Consideration of slave cabins directs us to a wide range of Black voices and Black visions, including documentary and non-documentary sources. It also directs us to issues of material culture as the basis for apprehending the experiences, ambitions, and perspectives of Black people. Evidence from other sites in Louisiana and across the South reveals that when slave cabins are given more attention in contemporary heritage tourism, we are more likely to hear from Black voices (from documentary sources such as slave narratives, folktales, and spirituals) and from Black visions (in art, craft work, and sculpture).[3]

If these initiatives were accompanied by a move away from the almost exclusive focus on slave cabins as separate, distinct units of accommodation, in a way that incorporated and addressed some of the other locations in which the enslaved regularly slept and lived, tremendous opportunities for far more nuanced descriptions of life for everyone on the plantation would be opened up.

The life and accomplishments of Clementine Hunter offer an example and a path forward, but as I have mentioned already, the narrative structure at Melrose would need to change for that to happen. Clearly each site does not have a Clementine Hunter, but they do have other people whose lives are worthy of discussion. In her art, Hunter demonstrates that there are other ways to represent the lives of the majority of the residents on the plantation than the representations that were most common at Melrose (and at the other two sites), and that there are other ways to represent slave cabins and the tenant houses in which Black people lived. Her work reminds us emphatically that the majority of people at the plantation were Black, not white, and that the majority of accommodations at the plantation were lived in by Black people. She is a cultural critic who offers alternate sources, a different voice, and a hidden transcript to those that prevail for the site as a whole. In multiple ways, she offers an antidote to the partial and distorted representations of slavery and slave cabins that prevail at Melrose. Her work also reminds us of the benefits of moving away from the limitations of archival documentary sources, and into other areas of data, evidence, and interpretation—including art, where one can use creativity and innovation to convey important issues and lessons.

In Hunter's body of work, we find a much wider panorama of Black life, Black agency, Black aspirations, and Black joy than anywhere else. Most of the buildings we see in her art were built and lived in by Blacks, including churches, kitchens, juke joints, and both slave cabins and tenant cabins. Black people are invariably prominent—in the fields picking cotton, in churches, in homes, and in music. Unlike on the plantation generally (and most other plantations), one struggles to locate an image of a benevolent or munificent white person in her paintings.

Another clear opportunity for improvement could be found in the role of tour guides (Cook 2015). The tour guides at the sites had significant potential for more accurate and inclusive attention to slavery and slave cabins. Most tour guides followed pre-written scripts that privileged the issues I've mentioned and sustained the dominant narrative style. They highlighted key issues, told stories, and pointed to important artifacts inside houses and grounds. They modified the tone—from serious and melancholy, to humorous and frivolous—as they saw appropriate. They could and did foreground issues important to them, for example, around gender, or race, or race and gender. They often showed empathy. They were constrained by a variety of factors—but they did not operate in a narrative straitjacket. They were in a powerful position to influence or adapt the general scripts and to shape, direct, and even control conversations and discussions, especially where visitors—Black and non-Black—asked questions (Alderman and Modlin 2015).

Several scholars have highlighted the flexibility and performative nature of tour guide roles, including the ways in which they can display empathy (Benjamin and Alderman 2017). At some sites, tour guides insist that the cabins are an indispensable component of the tour. During my research, the tour guide demographic was dominated by southern women over the age of fifty. This is slowly changing. There is clear evidence that tour guides are more attentive to the details of slavery than ever before. In other words, they have the potential to break free from the chains of southern mythology.

Finally, there are vast amounts of information—documentary and non-documentary—which could be consulted for more comprehensive representations at the site. These include significant collections of documentary material from all periods of Natchitoches history at various parish repositories, including the Cammie Henry Library and the NPS collection. There is also significant evidence at other archives in the state, for example, at Louisiana State University and the state archives. This includes first-hand evidence of a wide range of social practices in the cabins and quarters, such as religious beliefs, material possessions, musical instruments, and diet.

There are significant non-documentary sources of evidence in Natchitoches and elsewhere—such as archaeology, architecture, and art—that reveal the texture of Black lives under slavery and beyond. Substantial amounts of information about the slave cabins at the three sites have already been obtained via archaeology. Research on the cabins has more accurately dated them and has revealed evidence about cultural, religious, and labor practices (Brown 2006; MacDonald et al. 2006a, b; St. Clair 2006). One of the most

significant disputes in Natchitoches during my research arose from the findings of archaeologists, a challenge to the idea that Yucca House was built
by Marie Thérèse Coin Coin (MacDonald et al. 2006a, b; MacDonald and
Morgan 2001).[4] Staff at all three sites have already drawn considerably on
this evidence, and again many say they would like to draw on it far more,
but don't have the resources to allow for that. Opportunities could be found
for accessing these resources without requiring significant financial input.
A study of slave cabins can turn our attention away from the limitations of
documentary records and toward consideration of material culture (Franklin
2019; Singleton 1985).

Finally, it should be remembered that all three sites in Natchitoches are
public sites, two owned by the NPS and the third by a private not-for-profit
organization—APHN. Evidence from a range of researchers has demonstrated that publicly owned sites are more likely to provide better representations of both slavery and slave cabins than are privately owned sites, with one
or two exceptions (Bright et al. 2016; Cook 2016; Small 2012). This reflects the
legal and consultative requirements under which many publicly owned sites
operate. One finds the best examples of relative incorporation, and options
that can be built upon and extended, at such sites. I have demonstrated that
some of the important achievements at the NPS sites in Natchitoches arise
because they are public, while Melrose Plantation falls way behind because
it is not an NPS site. The lesson here is that we should encourage public sites
to take a decisive lead on these issues, while recognizing that some private
sites are also receptive to these changes.

EPILOGUE

DEVELOPMENTS AT PLANTATION
HERITAGE SITES SINCE 2011

Research has continued on plantation heritage sites in Louisiana of the kind described in this book since my fieldwork was completed in 2011, but I have not been able to identify any published research on Natchitoches since then.[1] I don't seek to summarize all research here, but let me make several points. Most research has been on the River Road plantation sites, and it offers important insights, though is not attentive to the specifics of Natchitoches or representative of Louisiana as a whole. Some recent research involves site observations, and interviews with site owners, managers, docents, and a wide range of visitors (Alderman and Bright 2016; Potter 2015). This research provides insights into how the changing economic and political context in the United States has influenced the sites, including increased professionalism and national networking across sites and museums. And it reveals the continuing tensions at the sites over the range of issues covered. There is some focus on the cabins, but none of these studies have cabins as the primary focus.

My examination of published research and current websites of many Louisiana heritage sites reveals many continuities in the practices I have described in this book and in my previous research. Some of these findings are described in my recent publications.[2] It's true that there is far more attention to issues of race, racism, and the experiences of the enslaved and more information on the slave cabins at the sites than in past. There has been a series of marked symbolic and some substantive improvements in attention to slavery and to the enslaved. For example, a number of sites that had original cabins and typically kept them in the back of the site have brought them physically to the front, while some sites have constructed new cabins—Oak Alley Plantation is one example. Yet, these developments are subordinate to the continued prevalence of southern gentility, elite white lifestyles, paternalism, and romance as the dominant frames for representations at the sites, and a stubborn resistance to fundamental change in this framing continues. At present, few sites can claim to give equal attention to the lives of the enslaved or other Black people as compared with elite whites; and few sites give priority to slave cabins. A similar conclusion is revealed in some recent research (Benjamin and Alderman 2017; Bright and Carter 2015).

The most striking exception to this trend is the Whitney Plantation on the River Road, which was opened in 2014. This site swims almost totally against the tide of the typical plantation heritage site, not only in Louisiana, but also across the US South. The site incorporates discussion of slavery and the lives of the enslaved in a substantial way and prioritizes them over all other residents of the plantation, including the owners (Moody and Small 2019; Commander 2018). At Whitney Plantation, the ways in which the plantation's existence and success were primarily based on exploiting enslaved Black labor is a central feature of the narrative. The range of experiences and treatment of most of the enslaved is described and issues of brutality, violence and economic exploitation are frequently mentioned. So too are the ways in which the lives—and often family members—of the master-enslavers and the enslaved were intertwined in social, familial, and sexual relationships. Issues of agency, autonomy, and dignity are also central.

This site comes closest to what may be called *full incorporation* of slavery (Small 2012, 12). Its existence has raised the question of whether this represents a fundamental turning point for other plantation heritage sites in Louisiana and elsewhere. I have found no persuasive evidence to suggest that that is happening. Several sites have made it clear that they do not intend to make a significant change to the current and long-established portrayals of grandeur, architecture, and elite white lives (Alderman and Bright 2016).

There is evidence of greater attention being paid to the lives of the enslaved at the sites outside Louisiana, at least at a number of sites. For example, Walcott-Wilson argues that more inclusive representations are emerging across the South, including attention to cabins, for example, at Boone Hall and Magnolia Plantation sites in South Carolina (Walcott-Wilson 2020). This includes attention to the role of tour guides. Walcott-Wilson examined the emotional labor of tour guides at plantation heritage sites, especially their interactions with visitors. She describes the adverse effects and psychological stress on tour guides and others working at the sites, both when interacting with visitors, and also while working on their own. She mentions experiences of affection, revulsion, and exhaustion (Walcott-Wilson 2020, 74–75).

Emotions of this kind are common because "The plantation heritage site industry was not created to interpret 'difficult histories,' but to obscure them" (Walcott-Wilson 2020, 75).

DEVELOPMENTS IN US POLITICS AND SOCIETY SINCE 2011

Several dramatic national developments over the last decade have substantially increased discussion of race and racism, and of public history, monuments, and the legacy of US slavery today. This includes the horrific 2015 killings of nine African American women and men in a church in Charleston, South Carolina, by a twenty-one-year-old white supremacist who was an avid supporter of the Confederacy. It includes the Confederate flag flying on a Confederate monument near the state building in Charleston, South Carolina, that was eventually removed, after its position there was initially defended by Governor Nikki Haley. It includes the murder of George Floyd in Minneapolis in May 2020, and before him the killings of Breonna Taylor in Louisville, Kentucky, in March 2020 and twelve-year-old Tamir Rice in Cleveland, Ohio, in 2014—and several other African American men and women (Clinton 2019; Cook 2017).

It includes debate over the thousands of monuments to the Confederacy across the US South in public squares, government and private buildings, ports and harbors, rural communities, and cemeteries (Clinton 2019; Cook 2017). There are schools, street names, and a vast number of private houses that honor (mainly male) Confederate heroes and events. And it includes debate over the Confederate flag, which continues to be flown prominently by a wide spectrum of organizations, groups, and individuals. The flag was both visible and prominent in the activities of some of the most extreme rightwing groups, including the domestic terrorists who ransacked the Capitol in Washington, DC, on January 6, 2021. These highly politicized incidents and horrific crimes have highlighted continuing racial tensions, antagonism, and conflict. Following several other incidents, further demands were made to remove monuments. During this time, President Trump consistently opposed such calls, and mockingly added "Who's next? Washington, Jefferson?" Plantation heritage sites of the kind described in this book have not garnered similar public attention at the national level, although they have been important at local levels.

Recent surveys indicate that a majority of American people want these monuments kept in place. Several prominent politicians acted to defend them, many others simply kept silent, and several politicians acted to remove them. For example, in May 2017, the mayor of New Orleans, Mitch Landrieu, removed four Confederate monuments, including one of Robert E. Lee, and made a powerful statement justifying his action. Early the following year, he published a book decrying the monuments as deceptions (Landrieu 2018). Monuments were also removed from, across North Carolina.

Demands that military installations currently named after Confederate military personnel be renamed were met with immediate rebuke from then-President Trump. At least ten military bases named after Confederate generals have been identified, including Fort Bragg in North Carolina, (named after Braxton Bragg, a slave owner); Camp Beauregard and Fort Polk in Louisiana; and Fort Lee in Virginia (named after Robert E. Lee, commander of the Confederate Army). Many say that these Confederate generals were traitors, and the bases should be named after military personnel that actually promoted national unity. Others have suggested they should be named after Native Americans.

President Trump continued his strong opposition to the renaming of military bases, but several senior military officers—including some currently serving and retired officers—went against Trump. In January 2021, the president vetoed the Defense Spending Bill that included a provision for the bases to be renamed, but Congress overrode the presidential veto—largely along party lines. The bases will be renamed, and it will be forbidden for any base to fly the Confederate flag. At the same time, George Floyd's murder and the expansion of the Black Lives Matter (BLM) movement have kept issues in the public eye and have also brought them to far greater international attention as BLM movements and demands sprouted in nations across Western Europe.

Several other incidents have kept discussion active; for example, the opening of the National Museum of African American History and Culture in Washington, DC, in 2016. Located in an impressive building on the National Mall, the museum addresses a wide range of African American life and culture, covers extensive historical periods, and houses an original slave cabin from South Carolina. It had already been revealed in 2008 that Fairfield Plantation in low country South Carolina, which had been home to more than 200 enslaved persons, was the ancestral home of First Lady Michelle Obama. Evidence obtained by a genealogist employed by President Obama's campaign staff revealed that her great-great-grandfather, Jim Robinson, was born on the plantation and remained enslaved until the Civil War. He later worked as a sharecropper. Like so many other African Americans, the First Lady knew very little about her family's history. The evidence reveals that there were multiple slave cabins, and many of them had been assembled on a so-called slave street.

The activities of Joseph McGill, an African American who had worked as a park ranger, are also relevant. McGill participated in reenactments of Civil War battles—as a Union soldier—after being inspired by watching the movie *Glory*. Since 2010, McGill has devoted a great part of his life to helping preserve, conserve, and publicize slave cabins. He has done this by sleeping in extant slave cabins, across the US South and elsewhere (for example, in Minnesota), that were built during slavery. He requests permission of the owners, and then spends the night or several nights sleeping in them, no matter how rough or uncomfortable. Some of the current cabins are in terrible condition, but he values their authenticity and believes that if his ancestors could tolerate them for their entire lives, he could tolerate them for several nights. He sometimes wears shackles. He has persuaded friends and others to join him and invites groups of school children and others to visit the cabins. He tries to imagine the harsh realities of the enslaved, their hopes and dreams, and their plans for survival and escape.

McGill's goal is to save the cabins and ensure that people are aware of their history and significance before they disappear. He wants more public discussion of the cabins and of slavery and to encourage southern whites and Blacks to talk to one another. Already in his sixties, he expects to continue doing this as long as he can. As a result of the public visibility of his work, many cabins have been saved and restored. He originally called his work the "slave cabin project." Seeking to avoid the perpetuation of stereotypes, he changed the name to the Slave Dwelling Project, its current name in 2023.

Dramatically increased attention to the role of universities in US slavery—founded or funded by owners of plantations (including Thomas Jefferson) and having owned or used enslaved labor for their development—has also increased in the last ten years. Several professors and alumni of universities began commenting on these issues, and momentum gained as top administrators, including several university presidents, developed the issues further (Harris et al. 2019). One of the first was Brown University, where its then-president—African American scholar Ruth Simmons—established a commission to look into the university's history of involvement in slavery. That history was found to be substantial, and the university published a report in 2006. Several other universities followed—with conferences, reports, exhibitions, funding, or monuments—including Emory, Yale, Princeton, Harvard, Duke, and the University of North Carolina. They had varying results, but significantly increased public discussion and attention.

The establishment of the Universities Studying Slavery Consortium developed during this period and added further momentum. The consortium began with a University of Virginia (UVA) presidential commission, followed by a working group and then the consortium. It became national and not long after became international, as universities across Great Britain such as Liverpool University and Bristol University joined. Several universities across the United States—including some of the most prestigious—began to actively consider ways to not only research their histories, but also ways to rename buildings, remove monuments, and commit financial and other resources to address issues of inequality, access, and equity for Black students at the present time. The then-president of Harvard University, Drew Gilpin Faust, organized a conference and invited internationally renowned author and journalist Ta-Nehisi Coates. Coates has written on these issues, most notably on reparations. Student protest on campuses and beyond pushed many of these issues, highlighting the need for truth, and making it clear that even though some of these histories generally were known, they were not typically part of official histories of these universities.

One of the most prominent initiatives is that of Georgetown University; its president, Jack DeGioia, formed the "Working Group on Slavery, Memory, and Reconciliation" in 2015. It was revealed that Maryland Jesuits had owned plantations and used funds to establish and sustain Georgetown University. Later on, facing financial ruin in the 1830s, they sold almost all of the 272 enslaved persons they owned to two planters in Louisiana. A Georgetown graduate—Richard Cellini, who had never thought much about race and less about slavery—carried out research and located descendants for those sold to Louisiana. Cellini started the "Georgetown Memory Project," hired a team of genealogists and tracked down 212 of the original group that was sold. The majority lived in southern Louisiana, in the vicinity of the plantation where their ancestors had been sold. The group GU272 was formed by students at Georgetown, and more than 500 direct descendants, living or deceased, were located. Georgetown University granted legacy status to all the descendants, with preference for admissions in the same way as for children of alumni. Sandra Green Thomas—president of GU272—said this was not enough. Karran Harper-Royal became executive director of the GU272 Descendants Association, which was established in 2017. She works with Georgetown University to find a way forward.

There were also developments at the University of Virginia, in Charlottesville. UVA was founded in 1819. Thomas Jefferson, James Monroe, and James Madison were central to it. Monticello is nearby and many school buildings were built by enslaved persons. In 2013, UVA established a commission to examine its history with slavery. Its role is officially acknowledged, and a stone memorial planned to honor the approximately 5,000 enslaved that labored at the university during a period of almost fifty years. It should be noted that in each of these debates, there was significant opposition to renaming, including from extremely wealthy alumni of the schools, some of whom threatened to withdraw funding if buildings were renamed.[3]

Many of these discussions inevitably—and in many instances immediately—led to outrage over increasingly visible evidence of racial inequality, injustice, and discrimination, in particular in the area of police treatment of, and violence against, African Americans, as well as the astronomical rates of incarceration of Black men. The public health crisis arising from the COVID-19 pandemic significantly increased attention to similar issues. Many commentators have highlighted the direct links across these institutional terrains, and the direct links between past and present. This has led to increased calls for reparations.

Finally, although it commands far less public attention than Confederate monuments, the issue of reparations has also figured more prominently in public debates in recent years. Several books and articles, both scholarly and in the popular press, have appeared, and there have been a series of television and media discussions and debates. Award-winning writer and journalist Ta-Nehesi Coates was at the forefront of these debates. The issue of reparations was a key issue in discussions about Democratic contenders for the presidential nomination in 2016—especially Bernie Sanders and Hillary Clinton, both of whom refused to support demands for reparations. In contrast, in May 2021, California Governor Gavin Newsom established a task force to study and develop reparation proposals for African Americans.

AFTERWORD

> The representation of plantations as dynamic and diasporic spaces is an underrepresented perspective in the interpretive context of national heritage in the United States. Specifically, there are gaps in the interpretive sphere that limit how plantations are seen, understood, and experienced today by visitors to former antebellum plantation sites. These gaps exist because the production of knowledge about plantations has primarily been articulated from a plantation owner perspective—typically that of the white male elite. This perspective is branded, marketed, and projected to the general public as a product and an asset of historical significance without critique. (Jackson 2012, 135)

The white South erected the ideological and institutional edifice of white supremacy as a basis for most of the prevailing and hegemonic narratives relayed about southern history at heritage sites and museums today. This edifice is far more encompassing and extensive than memorials and museums—it was and is reflected in political debates, historical accounts, literature, and research productivity. It has always included extremist and fanatical elements—as with the fanatical supporters of Confederate monuments and flags—as well as more mainstream and nuanced ones. Many elements of these narratives are direct, blunt, and offensive, while others more tempered and characterized by omissions, evasion, and euphemism. But all were and are predicated on similar principles—an honorable southern society built on chivalry, decency, and honor, a benign slave system of paternalist planters and faithful, complacent, and happy slaves, alleged northern aggression, and the Lost Cause. Central to this narrative are racist and gendered narratives—white men as the founders of the civilized United States, the defenders of white womanhood against a perceived Black threat, and perpetrators of violence against Black women.

Current developments in the United States remind us that the legacy of slavery and the Civil War remains ever-present; and that public history and collective memory have important consequences in contemporary life, including questions about who controls public history. They remind us that history is not dead and buried. We are still living history, still living the past in the present, and struggles over historical facts, meaning, and legacies are immediate, palpable, and consequential.

Plantation heritage sites of the kind I've described in this book continue to play a significant role in the dominant narratives of southern history. Compared to Confederate monuments and memorials, plantation heritage sites have far more impact and consequence, given their vast infrastructure, the far more subtle narratives deployed, and the massive numbers of visitors. They have so far failed to attract the kind of public or national attention, evaluation, or criticism that Confederate monuments have received. I believe these sites—and the twenty-first-century antebellum slave cabins on them—need more attention too.

As I mentioned in the preface, I began empirical field research on representations of slavery in Georgia in the summer of 1996 when the Olympic Games were taking place. The state government and business leaders were looking for ways to keep the millions of visitors in the state, spending money after the games ended. Promotion of southern heritage was a key mechanism, and after all, wasn't Georgia home to the most famous plantation main house that never existed—the magnificent house named Tara in *Gone with the Wind*? Georgia was not the first state to use its version of southern history to attract or retain national and international visitors. And like many other states before it—most notably South Carolina and Louisiana—it was largely successful.

Times have changed since then. The sites have been critiqued, significant changes have occurred, and we can document vastly improved professionalism at many sites. But I contend that the underlying foundation of southern gentility remains. Despite noticeable improvements since 1994, plantation sites still fail to tell a full or balanced story. Their silences remain too loud, their evasions too obvious, their euphemisms too pervasive, and their marginalization of slavery too entrenched for me to be convinced of any fundamental transformation. Several sites clearly remain committed to symbolic annihilation, and they remain too wholeheartedly under the thrall of southern gentility. For reasons of economics, of politics, and of personnel, it is unlikely they will realize fundamental change any time soon.

At present, Black people in the United States do not have the resources to fundamentally challenge or shape museums and memorials, inside or outside the South, nor to undermine the ideological grip of southern gentility prevalent at plantation heritage sites. For most African Americans, there are bigger problems than heritage and museum exhibits, and far more immediate priorities than slave cabins. Police and gun violence, mass incarceration, community decay, challenges in education, and the appalling levels of poverty, all exacerbated by the public health crisis, are clearly far greater priorities. But we are fortunate that there are still dedicated individuals, institutions, and communities who recognize that even in the face of such threats, we must still dedicate some of our time and energies to providing accurate, extensive, and inclusive knowledge and information about slavery and its legacies. We should be thankful that they continue to mount a strong fight.

APPENDIX: RESEARCH METHODS
AND DATA COLLECTION

The four main approaches used to collect evidence and information for this book were participant observations at sites, analysis of site documents and photographs, formal and informal interviews, and analysis of documentary records in historical archives.[1] I have relied heavily on work by the scholars of African American Studies and African Diaspora Studies who have refined these methods and data collection techniques for studies of Black populations and for research on the changing nature of racialized discourses and images. I drew on social historians of African Americans (Berry 2017; Harris and Berry 2014; Glymph 2008; Dusinberre 1996; Hine 1994) and historians of collective memory (Blight 2001, 2002; Brundage 2000, 2005). I drew on museum studies (Coombes 1994) and discourse analysis (Stanfield 2011). I benefited substantially from innovations in the use of nondocumentary sources such as material culture (Franklin and Lee 2019; Franklin 2017, 2001; Battle-Baptiste 2011; Singleton 1985). I was particularly attentive to work that focuses on gender and the experiences of Black women, including visual analysis (Mitchell 2020; Glymph 2019; Finley et al. 2018; Farrington 2005; Hall 1997).

The majority of the data for this book were collected on the contemporary distribution of twenty-first-century antebellum slave cabins in heritage tourism in Natchitoches, including the recent history of the three plantation heritage sites that are the primary focus of the book. Significant data were collected on the history of the cabins and the sites from their establishment several centuries ago through to the present day. This allowed me to provide detailed descriptions of the cabins at the start of the twenty-first century, in the context of the sites as a whole, including information on their social and geographical location, the construction materials utilized, their relative states of repair or disrepair, and the nature and extent of renovation, restoration, and preservation. Most importantly, it allowed me to provide information about how the cabins were represented at the sites compared with other buildings.

I collected information from websites, promotional literature (both on site and from other sources); signs and placards on site; exhibits and displays in various buildings; observations on guided and self-guided tours; interviews, both formal and informal; and historical archives. I made detailed notes of the visual images at the sites, including portraits, paintings, photographs, and drawings. I also took hundreds of photographs at each site, including of the interiors and exteriors of all cabins. Some of these photographs are presented in the book, but much larger numbers—more than five hundred—were used for review and assessment, including confirmation of detailed texts.

I have been collecting data on plantation heritage sites across the South since the early 1990s and had already visited more than forty sites in Louisiana, including the three sites in this book, before I began fieldwork for this particular project in 2007. Prior to research in the United States, I worked on representations of slavery and its legacy in museums in England; later on, I worked on similar issues in the Netherlands (Nimako and Small 2009b; Small 1997, 1994a, b). I began identifying potential research sites and collecting documents for this project in 2004, building on experience from research for a previous study in the United States (Eichstedt and Small 2002). I began fieldwork and archival research in the spring of 2007, visiting more than thirty-five sites in nine states across the South. I also visited archives, libraries, and state and private museums in several of these states. These visits provided me with an overview of the range of slave cabins then incorporated into heritage tourism across the South, and the various tactics of incorporation and/or marginalization deployed at different sites. Some initial findings from these visits have already been published (Small 2015; Small 2012; Small 2011).

In the fall of 2007, I began more intensive research in Natchitoches, visiting the parish multiple times—and for periods of several months at a time—between August 2007 and August 2010. I continued to collect information online, and via correspondence and phone calls through the fall of 2011. Archival research on Natchitoches was also conducted in a range of archives across the state, including Hill Memorial Library at Louisiana State University in Baton Rouge and the Louisiana State Archive, also in Baton Rouge. Dr. Angela Lintz Small assisted me in my field research for several months in the spring of 2008, and several graduate and undergraduate students also assisted with site visits and online searches (see acknowledgments).

While I sought out the best data available for answering my questions, I also made particular efforts to identify evidence and information that documented Black voices and Black visions, including those reflected in material culture. By Black voices I mean sources of documentary data left by African

Americans, such as narratives, folktales, biographies, memoirs, and oral testimony, including the so-called slave narratives (Craft and Craft 1999; Clayton 1990; Starling 1988; Levine 1977). By Black visions I mean information, ideas, and evidence contained in creative culture such as art and sculpture, and material culture, including archaeology and architecture (Franklin 2019; Battle-Baptiste 2011; Farrington 2005; Franklin 2001; Singleton 1985), and photographs (Teal 2007; Hall 1997). These data form a significant component of the evidence collected for this study.

I went to each site at least ten times. I took part in guided tours by a range of tour guides, as well as my own self-guided tours. I observed docent and tour guide presentations at the sites during normal visitor sessions with a random range of visitors. During the visits, I paid attention to the social geography of the plantation and the physical location of the cabins vis-à-vis other structures at the site. As has been mentioned, none of the cabins were in their original antebellum locations, having been relocated on multiple occasions over the last 150-plus years. Was signage for the cabins clear and obvious? What kinds of information—texts and images—were provided about the slave cabins and their residents?

I paid particular attention to the information provided by the docents and noted what items on the tours—both inside and outside the buildings—they highlighted. I noted the common elements of tours, as well as variations across tours. I paid attention to issues that were always or frequently discussed and to questions that arose from visitors; and I identified messages, direct and indirect, communicated in the tours. I was also keen to find out what issues were marginalized, anaesthetized, or annihilated.

I did not make audio or video recordings of tour guide presentations or interviews, as I felt this would have been too intrusive and would have disrupted the natural flow of the tours. However, I took extensive written notes during the tours, and expanded upon those notes as soon after the tour finished as possible. I often dictated summaries and impressions from the tours into my digital audio-recorder for accuracy and better recollection. Quotations from interviews in this book are not verbatim but the nearest approximations based on my notes and verbal summaries. Taking notes and photographs did not usually attract attention or disrupt tours because often there were teachers and/or school children also taking notes. Everyone was taking photos all the time. I was asked what I was doing on less than a handful of occasions (by a visitor rather than a tour guide, because guides knew ahead of time that I was a researcher) and I indicated that I was a researcher. Sometimes people asked a few more general questions, but typically nothing more. It was mainly unproblematic.

I collected a wide range of private and public documents, most of which focused on the organization and management of the sites at the time of research. I also collected materials about when the plantations began to transition into tourist sites. Many documents were collected from records at the sites themselves. Others came from local organizations and associations and from city and state tourism agencies. These include information from websites, promotional and tour literature, brochures and leaflets, and documents prepared for regular and special events, celebrations, and anniversaries. They also include scripts for tours at the sites. The majority of these documents were public. Private documents included in-house reports by management and staff, memos and minutes of meetings, and notes on activities prepared for and used by management and staff. These documents were private but not confidential in the sense that they were not typically available to general visitors but could be examined upon request. They were provided to me at the discretion of the management. I was not denied access to any documents that I requested. The documents provided information going back to the antebellum period and earlier. Among them were detailed archaeological and architectural history reports.

Information on the nineteenth- and twentieth-century histories of the sites was obtained from the Cammie Henry Center, the Natchitoches Genealogical and Historical Society, Natchitoches Public Library, the Hill Memorial Library at Louisiana State University in Baton Rouge, the Louisiana State Library in Baton Rouge, and several public libraries in Alexandria and Baton Rouge, including East Baton Rouge Public Library and West Baton Rouge Public Library. This included data from manuscript collections; national, state, and parish records; census records; newspapers; and magazines. I also consulted biographies and autobiographies, memoirs, and leaflets. An extensive range of secondary publications on these periods were consulted, including journal articles, books, dissertations, and theses.

I reviewed photographs produced by owners, residents, and visitors to the sites over the last century or so. Some of these provided information on the Black residents of the sites—residents who did not normally appear in the narratives at the sites or in the documentary records (Teal 2007). For example, in photographs of events for elite whites—parties, celebrations, anniversaries—there were often Black servers or waiters, and I was able to locate names and get further details about them. Some photos also included names, labor roles and other roles performed, and insights into family relationships.

The archives consulted include a vast amount of data in many different forms: official and unofficial records; manuscript collections; newspapers;

diaries and memoirs; minutes of meetings; correspondence; financial transactions; probate records; work schedules; and purchases and sales. The data
included personnel information, social organization, tour formats, and tour
texts and photographs. I accessed statistical information and official data
from the city, county, state, and federal levels.

It will come as no surprise to historians that the information in these
archives is frequently incomplete, but there can be unexpected and produc-
tive discoveries too. For example, I discovered multiple boxes of documents
in the NPS regional headquarters in Natchitoches, including extensive store
records, receipts for purchases of food and other goods, and payments to
laborers and residents of the plantations in the early and mid-twentieth
century. These laborers were most often Black or of mixed Black and white
origins. I was informed by the site docent that many of these records had
initially been sent to the University of North Carolina at Chapel Hill, but
that the archive there wanted only the nineteenth-century materials, and so
the twentieth-century material was returned to the NPS.[2]

I also obtained information and insights from material culture, in particular from archaeology, architecture, and art. For example, I found more than
ten archaeological studies that had been carried out at the sites, including
several dedicated exclusively to the "slave and tenant quarters." I located
at least twenty Historical Structure Reports or archaeological and architectural histories of buildings at the three plantations. These studies revealed
information on the changing construction, design, and structure of the cabins, including consideration of African influences and insights into human
agency, cultural practice, and resistance by the inhabitants. The studies
supplemented documentary sources, but also fundamentally challenged or
directly contradicted evidence from other sources. For example, tour guides
and interpreters typically represented master-enslavers and their families as
good, decent, and honorable people, and the enslaved population as largely
happy, well-fed, and even faithful. But archaeological studies, and representations in art, provided evidence of dissatisfaction, hunger, resistance, sabotage,
and sometimes violence and brutality.

Similar evidence and insights were revealed in art. At Melrose Plantation, Clementine Hunter's art and life provided a necessary corrective to
the limited representations of Black life provided by those who owned or
managed the plantation. These insights arise only if one reads between the
lines, because Hunter's art on display at the plantation was narrowly interpreted. At the site she received detailed treatment as an "exceptional Black,"
in stark contrast to the lack of attention given to the majority of Blacks at the
plantation. This attention was highly individualized, and none of it located

her in the context of subordinated Black female labor in Jim Crow America. A different set of messages was conveyed in her art, where we saw family, culture, work, leisure, and pleasure, as well as strong and independent Black women in the foreground. We also saw critical portrayals of the white power hierarchy on the plantation, with white people, if they appeared in her art at all, in the background. In interviews and in her biography, we find evidence of her subordinate status on the plantation and hear her voice as a Black woman who grew up deep in the belly of rural Jim Crow.

Formal and informal interviews were conducted with management and staff, including volunteers. When I got to sites, I informed site personnel of my research goals and issues. I did not give out detailed information about the goals of my project, partly because it was not requested, partly because I felt it was not wanted, and partly so as not to increase the risk of researcher effect (for example, by discussing controversial issues). After I had made initial requests for interviews, respondents were asked to fill out human subjects' permissions. Only one person refused to sign the forms.[3]

Formal interviews were recorded where possible and followed a list of specific questions. Formal interviews took place with the site superintendent of the Cane River Creole National Historical Park, two site interpreters, and two other site docents. I conducted one interview with the docent at Melrose Plantation. I conducted three interviews with Bobby DeBlieux, the former mayor of Natchitoches. He also generously took me on a driving tour of the Cane River area and provided me with several important documents and other information. Informal interviews involved more general questions and discussion. I also took part in a number of conversations with experts, scholars, and others associated with the sites and the cabins, including academic experts, professional archaeologists and architects, and managers and organizers of tourism. These included Dr. David Morgan, Dr. Nancy Morgan, Rolonda Teal, and Mary Lin Wernet. Some of these individuals had conducted or were conducting research on plantation or other heritage sites in Natchitoches, elsewhere in the state, or elsewhere in the South. Some were working for local or state agencies involved in heritage tourism. I also looked at transcripts of and/or recordings of interviews carried out by others.

I did not carry out any interviews with site visitors, nor did I plan to do so in my research design. This would have required far more resources than I had and would have entailed a more complicated methodology. Such interviews would most certainly have produced useful information, for example, about what the sites and images meant to visitors, why they visited, and what they got from the visit. Other scholars have conducted interviews of this kind—during the period of my research and since then—and have raised important issues and provided key insights (Bright and Carter 2016; Bright et al. 2016). Exploring how visitors responded to the sites was not one of my goals; however, as I took part in tours, I heard many comments from visitors and also took part in informal discussions with visitors during tours.

Although I did not carry out a typical ethnography for my research in Natchitoches—with long-term immersion in a community—I was present at all the sites on multiple occasions over several years; I took part in many guided tours with groups of visitors, often with the same tour guide; and I was also frequently present at sites for long periods in unstructured ways. During many of my visits, I spent time wandering around the site, observing the outsides and insides of buildings, making notes, and taking photographs. Staff saw me on multiple occasions and knew that I was doing research, and I was more than happy to inform them ahead of time of my research plans. In this respect, my research has some resemblance to ethnography, and so the question of researcher effect arises.

Researcher effect has been the subject of much discussion in the literature, including in several of my own writings (Small 2011; Stanfield 2011; Eichstedt and Small 2002). The main question is how to minimize the impact of the researcher on the people being researched so as to get the most accurate and reliable data. This is especially significant in a context in which a researcher of color is working with white respondents on a possibly controversial topic. While not always controversial, discussing the legacy of slavery is almost always highly charged. There is a potential for greater problems when the research involves a woman (especially a woman of color) conducting research on men (especially white men). Some of these issues applied to my research. For the project to be successful I needed the cooperation of site workers and management. This required maintaining cordial relations and avoiding issues that might lead to feelings of unease or discomfort, in order to facilitate cooperation.

In practice this was not always so simple. What do you do if staff members say something with which you fundamentally disagree (that "slaves" were happy, or that "slave masters" were good people)? What if they used language that you find offensive (like "mammy") and what if they confidently state information that you know to be entirely incorrect? What if the staff member asks you for advice? Many did ask for advice and wanted to know if their site was doing a good job and how it could be improved; and they asked for comparisons with other sites that were doing better. Every occasion risked the possibility that your response could cause discomfort or unease. There were no easy answers to these questions. From the point of view of completing research, the best that I can say is that I tried to avoid causing offense or controversy.

I strongly suspect that there was researcher effect in this project, although I can't be sure how extensive it was. I come to this conclusion from my analysis of the literature, from my own extensive ethnographic work and interviews, and from concrete experiences during the research process. To begin with, evaluations of researcher effect commonly convey that greater insights are achieved when the race and gender of the researcher and the subjects are the same, especially where the topic concerns race, gender inequality, or discrimination. At the three sites I researched, the majority of staff and volunteers were white, a majority of them were southern, and significant numbers of them were clearly aged sixty years or older at that time. Thus, I was a Black man conducting research on overwhelmingly white subjects. And I am a foreigner too, manifestly clear from my accent. All the docents knew I was doing research while on their tours, and I suspect that it affected their presentations. My co-researcher on a previous study found that she was addressed in different ways than I was, because she was white, northern, and female (Eichstedt and Small 2002).

However, unlike my experiences at other sites in Louisiana and across the South, none of the staff expressed surprise that my main interest was an examination of the cabins, not the main houses. That's because in Natchitoches it was clear that the cabins were important parts of the sites.

It is difficult to know the full extent or impact of the researcher effect on my project. In my professional interactions in Natchitoches, I found the vast majority of my respondents to be overwhelmingly polite and responsive to my questions. No one openly refused to answer my questions, and no one refused to provide documents that I requested. All staff generously offered information and insights and guided me to other avenues of information. Many people volunteered additional information. At the Cammie Henry Archive, Mary Lin Wernet was extremely generous and attentive to my archival needs. In addition, as a Black British man with an English accent, I was often welcomed in ways that may not have been extended to an African American. Many people raised questions about architecture and archaeology in Great Britain or asked about mansions there. Overall, I am satisfied that the use of multiple methods helped offset some of the likely researcher effects. Information from site staff, while important, was just one source of data, and tour presentations were just one part of my work.

In framing the contours of this project, in identifying the best sources of data that would reveal the information I wanted, and in deciding on the best methods to collect these data, the problem that faced me was *how to confront the past in the present*? How to confront the past, in terms of how many cabins existed and the experiences of their inhabitants? How to confront the present in terms of the organization, exhibits, and displays about such cabins at plantation sites today? And how to apprehend the ways in which the past was represented at the sites today? As I began preparations for this research, it was clear to me from the start that multiple methods would be necessary. I found that the use of multiple research methods for collecting evidence offered unique advantages that offset the disadvantages of any one method.

TERMINOLOGY

In this book, I avoid using some of the language typically used in analyses of slavery and its legacies. For reasons I have explained in more detail in early publications, I find that language which is often represented as neutral or descriptive, or which is used unreflexively, in fact conceals relations of power authority, even domination (Nimako and Small 2012; Small 2011, 1994a; Eichstedt and Small 2002). This is common for gendered language (Collins and Bilge 2016; Collins 1991). Rather than lend support to such practices, I chose a different terminology, even if readers are not accustomed to it. In fact, use of this language is designed to unsteady the comfort level with long-established and problematic concepts, and to change the frame of reference so as to raise questions. Rather than using *slave master* or *planter*, I use *master-enslaver* and *mistress-enslaver*; rather than *slave*, I use *enslaved*; rather than *free people of color* I use *legally free people of color*; in place of *abolition*, I use *legal abolition*. I do continue to use *slave cabin* because I think it conveys the subjectification of the enslaved that was intended and typically achieved by master-enslavers. However, if any of these words are used in primary documents, I cite them as originally stated, as is conventional.

Throughout the book I have used the words *Black* and *white* several times; I also used the word *mixed-race*. Of course, we have to be very precise in our understanding of their meanings, as they varied over a wide range of time periods and contexts (King O'Riain et al. 2014; Forbes 1993; Davis 1991). This is more important in Louisiana, including Natchitoches, than many other places in the US South, because racialized categories and definitions there were far more varied than elsewhere in the US South (Schweninger 1996; Dominguez 1986; Berlin 1984). More legally free people of color achieved greater economic standing in Louisiana than elsewhere in the US South. There were substantial power, resource, and status imbalances between Blacks and people of color under slavery; and those imbalances continued long after slavery was legally abolished. I use the word *Black* to mean a person believed to be "pure Black" by contemporaries during and beyond slavery—even though we now recognize that the idea of a pure race is largely a social fiction. I use the word *mixed-race* to mean a person of mixed European and African origins, and occasionally some Native American ancestry. I use the word *white* to mean a person believed in that period to be "pure white," regardless of the European nation to which they traced their roots. Throughout the book I distinguish between white people with French, Spanish, and English ancestry, where ethnicity was significant. The literature on these topics is extensive (Hodes 1999, 1997; Dorman 1996; Forbes 1993; Davis 1991; Dominguez 1986).

NOTES

PREFACE

1. As the gallery developed, I occupied roles as guest curator and as a member of the Advisory Board, and I wrote several chapters in the gallery's catalogue. I was also a member of several local Black organizations, including the Consortium of Black Organisations and the Federation of Liverpool Black Organisations. I was invited to occupy these roles because I was at the time the only Liverpool-born Black person with a PhD and because my PhD dissertation (University of California, Berkeley, 1989) had been written on slavery in the Caribbean and the United States. I was also a full-time academic at the University of Massachusetts Amherst. These roles and my specialist knowledge gave me multiple perspectives on the issues.

2. The word *creole* refers to a variety of mixtures—people, language, music, and other aspects of culture—of Africans, Europeans, and sometimes Native Americans. It first meant people believed to be of exclusive European origins born in the Americas, to distinguish them, and treat them as subordinate to Europeans born in Europe.

3. During field research in fall 2007, I visited several cabins in the vicinity of Baton Rouge, Louisiana, which still had African American occupants. During fieldwork in 2010 and 2012, local residents again insisted that many cabins remained occupied.

INTRODUCTION

1. I use the terms *master-enslaver* and *mistress-enslaver* instead of *slave master* and *slave mistress* because it shifts the frame of understanding and helps us to "unmask the ways that dominant language obscures the reality of enslaving human beings" (Eichstedt and Small 2002, 4–5). See Appendix for more details on choice of terminology.

2. One recent author tells us, "In the aftermath of slavery, black bodies remained extremely vulnerable; when living black bodies ceased to be valuable property, dead black bodies became valuable property" (Adams 2007, 87).

3. Antebellum Natchitoches had both slave cabins (mainly rural) and slave quarters (mainly urban) during the course of its history. The physical remains of both types were still extant in Natchitoches during the research period. This book focuses primarily on

the plantation slave cabins, which were greater in number than the urban quarters, and which were more centrally incorporated into heritage tourism in the parish at the time of research.

4. I prefer the term *legal abolition* to *abolition*, and I draw a distinction between legal abolition and emancipation. Legal abolition meant the end of legal slavery and did not lead to the circumstances conducive to emancipation—which would have included opportunities for political, economic, and social equality (see Nimako and Willemsen 2011; Foner 2002, 1988).

5. Bousillage is a local material made from a mixture of red clay and Spanish moss. The French borrowed the idea from Native Americans of using clay kneaded with moss as a substitute for stone (Miller and Keel 1999). Bousillage was common in Natchitoches, as well as along the River Road (Badin Rocque 2006. See also Sexton et al. 1999). Outside Natchitoches and Louisiana, enslaved persons also lived in stone cabins, for example, in Maryland, Texas, and Tennessee (Strutt 2010; McDaniel 1982).

6. Maroons were escaped enslaved persons—and their descendants born free— that set up short- or long-term communities outside the immediate control of the plantations.

7. We cannot know the precise number. This is an estimate based on an assumption of 9,434 enslaved persons living in cabins occupied by an average of five persons. To this number we need to add enslaved persons living in kitchens, artisan shops, barns, and in quarters in the main house. See Fogel and Engerman 1984. There are some variations specific to Natchitoches, which I describe in chapter 1.

8. As one scholar of slave cabins elsewhere has observed, "During the antebellum era the number of slave houses in the Southern landscape far exceeded the number of owners' mansions, a situation that is significantly reversed today" (Strutt 2010, 231).

9. This number refers only to purpose-built structures designed primarily or exclusively as accommodation for enslaved persons. It does not refer to the wide range of other structures or spaces in which the enslaved lived and/or worked. In field research in Virginia, Georgia, and Louisiana from 1994 to 2001, my colleague Jennifer L. Eichstedt and I identified twenty-first century antebellum slave cabins at about one-third of the 120 public heritage sites we visited (Eichstedt and Small 2002, 98).

10. See Hahn and Wells 1991, 35.

11. The main house at Oakland was built in the 1890s, after the original main house was burned down by Union troops during the Civil War; the kitchen at Oakland Plantation is known as "the cook's cabin." The kitchen at Magnolia Plantation is on private property and is not accessible to the public.

12. The main house at Magnolia Plantation was also on private property and not usually accessible to the public.

13. This concept refers to the range of accommodations and spaces inhabited by the enslaved—including on the one hand, separate, distinct, and purpose-built accommodations (typically called slave cabins) and, on the other hand, spaces in other structures in which the enslaved lived or slept, including the main house, kitchens, carpenter and blacksmith shops, barns, and other structures.

14. Alderman and Modlin (2008) highlight the long-entrenched patterns of inequality that directly influence what is remembered and what is forgotten.

15. Nottoway Plantation in Louisiana and The Antebellum Plantation in Georgia both address slavery while symbolically annihilating the slave cabins at the sites. In contrast, Boone Hall in Charleston exemplifies a deep engagement with the substance of slavery via its substantial incorporation of slave cabins into representations of slavery at the site. Innovative work at the Whitney Plantation in Louisiana, which opened in 2014, exemplifies how this can be done in a far more inclusive way.

16. In the epilogue to this book, I describe some of the most important events and public discussions in the last decade.

17. There are several variations of the name Prud'homme used in the range of documents over the entire period of their presence in Natchitoches, including "Prud'homme" and "Prudhomme." For the sake of consistency, I use "Prud'homme" throughout the book, unless citing a primary document, in which case I use the original spelling.

18. These states are Louisiana, Florida, Georgia, South Carolina, North Carolina, Virginia, Maryland, Alabama, and Mississippi.

19. A video produced in 1980, entitled *Cane River Women*, documents the lives of Marie Thérèse Coin Coin, Cammie Henry, Clementine Hunter, and Kate Chopin. It is shown to visitors to Melrose Plantation at some point during the guided tours.

20. Significant but limited scholarly work has been published on the history of the Cane River Creoles. Almost none of this research addresses slave cabins. See Mills 1973; Mills and Mills 1973. Research on the various buildings on the plantations, much of which focuses on the cabins, has been carried out, including the various Historic Structure Reports produced by the National Park Service, as well as Macdonald et al. 2007.

21. An initial summary of some of the methods used for this research appeared in Small 2011.

22. Work has significantly increased in the last decade (Alderman 2018; Benjamin and Alderman 2017; Bright, Alderman, and Butler 2016; Alderman and Modlin 2013). These studies are primarily about the River Road. There are several PhD dissertations on contemporary heritage sites in Louisiana, including Handley 2004 and Miller 2004.

23. There were some exhibits about legally free people of color, but they were not typically about those who owned enslaved persons. For example, some exhibits at museums in New Orleans address the lives of legally free people of color. In Virginia, the Booker T. Washington National Monument documents the life of the most powerful Black man in the United States at the end of the nineteenth century. Born enslaved, with a white father, he became legally free, and his fame largely applies to the period after slavery was legally abolished; see Small 2012. There is also a house museum in Natchez, Mississippi, dedicated to William Johnson, a legally free person of color who owned sixteen enslaved persons.

24. Definitions of *relative incorporation* and *symbolic annihilation* are provided in future chapters. The criteria that would enable us to describe a site as *full incorporation* are described in Small (2012, 12). As I mention in a following chapter, the Whitney Plantation, which opened in 2014, comes closest to full incorporation.

CHAPTER ONE:
SLAVERY AND HERITAGE IN NATCHITOCHES

1. As with the name "Proudhomme" there are also variations of the name "Lecompte" in primary documents including "Lecomte." Again, for the sake of consistency, I use "Lecompte" throughout the book, unless citing a primary document, in which case I use the original spelling.

2. Examples can be found in Vlach 1997, 1993; Dell and Vlach 1986.

3. This number is based on the census figures of 9,434 enslaved persons, living in cabins occupied by an average of five persons. This number does not include persons living in kitchens, carpenter and blacksmith shops, and barns.

4. Northrup's account is the basis for the 2013 movie, *12 Years a Slave*, directed by Steve McQueen.

5. At least the right to vote for men. The right to vote for women had to wait another forty-five-plus years.

6. The main book on the history of Melrose written by Gary Mills says its original name was Yucca Plantation (Mills 1977). Other writers drawing mainly on this source repeat this assertion, but evidence has emerged to indicate there is no definitive proof that this was the plantation's original name.

7. In explanations offered to visitors to the heritage tourism sites at the three plantations in this study, guides invariably mentioned economics, mechanization, devastation of crops, and even the competitive international prices of crops as the reasons for outmigration by Black workers. They almost never mention racism, racial discrimination, or Jim Crow legal segregation.

8. A punkah is a fan that was used to keep flies and insects away from meals.

9. As mentioned in the introduction, the video *Cane River Women* documents the lives of Marie Thérèse Coin Coin, Cammie Henry, Clementine Hunter, and Kate Chopin. (See *Shreveport Times* 1980).

CHAPTER TWO: OAKLAND PLANTATION

1. I was given tours of the facility on several occasions, including during my site visits in 2007 and 2010.

2. During my research visits to the site I saw at least two different exhibits on slavery in the cabins. In October 2007, the cabins were locked, but opened upon request, and had no exhibits in them. By March 2008, there was an exhibit in one slave cabin. This included several small table exhibits with photos and text describing slavery in Louisiana in general. When I returned for a visit in August 2010, there was a larger exhibit in the same cabin. It is clear that Peggy Scherbaum, the site's chief interpreter, already had significant plans underway to increase the representations of slavery at the site before I visited there in 2007. For example, she already had in place plans for a major conference that took place at the Rural Life Museum in Baton Rouge in April 2008, which brought together experts on these issues from around the state and the nation.

3. Family tradition is the basis for asserting this original name, although there are no documents to confirm this. See Big House, HSR 2004, 16. There are several general histories of Oakland Plantation and its buildings. For further information, see Haynie 2002; Miller and Wood 2000; Miller and Keel 1999; Miri 1998a, b; Keel et al. 1997.

4. The symposium "What Are We Saying? Discovering How People of African Descent are Interpreted at Louisiana Plantation Sites," was held at the Louisiana State University Rural Life Museum in Baton Rouge. It was attended by scholars, NPS staff, and others, and explored representations of slavery across Louisiana sites, and elsewhere in the South, with a view toward sharing information and cultivating cooperation across sites. A severe medical problem prevented me from attending.

5. The Oakland Plantation site map says "Gabe Nargot was the last person living at Oakland who had been enslaved here," and one of the reports notes that the cabin was "the residence of Mr. Gabe Nargot, the last surviving slave of the plantation" (Miller and Keel 1999, n.p.; see also Gijtano 2007).

6. Details of the cell phone tour were obtained from the two Cane River Creole National Historical Park interpreters who created it—Nathan and Tarona. They also provided me with the verbatim script for the tour, and a list of the goals and objectives. I interviewed them and took the cell phone tour myself in August 2010.

7. In this chapter, I treat the main house first, because it is given the most attention at the site. There is a so-called mammy room in the main house where an enslaved person slept on a regular basis. This is described in a later section.

8. There are rooms like this at sites elsewhere in Louisiana and across the South, for example, Nottoway Plantation in Louisiana and the Antebellum Plantation in Stone Mountain, Georgia. See Eichstedt and Small 2002.

9. Edwards and Kariouk 2004; Vlach 1997, 1993; Dell and Vlach 1986.

10. In Toni Morrison's book *Playing in the Dark*, she comments on the practice in American literature by which all people of color have their ethnic identity mentioned, while white peoples' identity is left unstated, because it is assumed to be obvious and universal.

11. Eichstedt and Small (2002, chapter 7) describe various types of relative incorporation. See also Small 2012. Two examples of sites in which slave cabins are "fully incorporated" are Frogmore in Louisiana and the Booker T. Washington National Monument in Virginia.

12. For example, compare the fifteen or so historic structure reports and other reports conducted at Oakland Plantation, or the ten at Magnolia, with the much smaller number done at Melrose. This reveals the investment required and also the obligations under which the NPS must conduct its business. In this case, the state was a relatively progressive agent.

CHAPTER THREE: MAGNOLIA PLANTATION

1. Some of the details of these relationships were described in chapter 1.

2. Examples of twenty-first-century brick slave cabins can be found at Boone Hall Plantation in South Carolina.

3. In interviews and discussions with Bobby DeBlieux, he told me that it was clear from the start of his involvement that the cabins would be part of the site. There was little discussion and no opposition to their inclusion. He added that growing up in Natchitoches he had seen tenants' cabins everywhere along the Cane River, but that by the 1960s most of them had disappeared.

4. Details provided here come from the same sources as the cell phone tour details in chapter 3. I completed the cell phone tour at Magnolia Plantation in August 2010 while touring the site.

5. It was common to arrange slave cabins in grid formation across the South (see Rehder 1999; Vlach 1993), but even where slave cabins survived into the twentieth century, such formations did not typically survive. A few exist today. For example, Evergreen Plantation in Louisiana still has more than eight cabins in the form of a so-called slave village. Boone Hall, South Carolina, has several cabins currently described as a "slave street."

6. This is the case with all of the cabins at Melrose Plantation, as will be explained in chapter 4.

CHAPTER FOUR: MELROSE PLANTATION—COIN COIN, CAMMIE, AND CLEMENTINE

1. Although the Metoyer family and the Cane River Creole community that they led are well known in the community and by scholars of legally free people of color, the research that has been conducted on the families is limited and a great deal about them is yet to be uncovered. Some of these issues are discussed in this chapter.

2. There is clear evidence that Mignon was born in New York in 1899, and did not, as he claimed, spend his childhood in France. It's possible he may have never visited France at all. See Ford 1991.

3. Melrose Plantation is the only "publicly accessible cultural heritage site at which the history of Cane River Creoles is currently presented to the public" (MacDonald et al. 2006, 46).

4. It is claimed that by 1830, the Metoyers and affiliated families owned 287 enslaved persons who worked more than 500 acres of improved land (Mills 1977, 108). In the United States, there are a few contemporary tourist sites that mention legally free people of color, especially prominent individuals, although none that address legally free people of color that owned enslaved persons. The Booker T. Washington National Monument in Virginia and the home of William Johnson, in Natchez, Mississippi, are two such sites.

5. This number is based on my definition of a slave cabin, and it is not clear if the managers and interpreters at the site would accept this definition. See the introduction for a discussion of how I define slave cabins.

6. The site claimed that Yucca House was original, but this claim was in dispute. See MacDonald et al. 2006.

7. A team of archaeologists from London and Louisiana examined the site in the late 1990s. They reported that aerial photographs from 1957 and the property map from 1877

helped them to document past locations of the "slave dwellings," which have clearly been moved over time (MacDonald et al. 2006a, 137).

8. Several books provide praiseworthy and romantic stories of Cammie's life in tremendous detail. They pay only passing attention to the multiple Black workers that made so much of her success possible.

9. In her diary, Cammie joked about how difficult it was to sustain writing a diary on a day-to-day basis for a year (Cammie Henry Diary 1934).

10. Cammie mentions many of them by name throughout her 1934 diary, a copy of which is in the Cammie Henry Center. I identified at least fifteen photos in the Melrose Collection at the Cammie Henry Center. Photos of many Blacks living at or working at Melrose are in Clayton 1990. Information about some of the Black residents is also provided in Dollar 1998 and in Teal 2007. And there are many vivid images of Black residents at Melrose—past and present—in Clementine Hunter's paintings.

11. There are varying estimates of Israel's age and date of death. The Historic Structure Report lists him dying in 1923 and says, "he was the last ex-slave to live at Yucca" (August 2005, 17).

12. There appears to be no evidence on her actual date of birth, which is estimated by most writers to be either December 1886 or January 1887.

13. Blacks and working-class whites played a significant role as laborers or agricultural workers, generating the wealth that financed and fed these families. At this time in Natchitoches, racial inequality was entrenched, and socially appropriate roles for Blacks reflected the will, wishes, and whims of elite whites. There were no Black people in political office, no significant Black businesses, and almost no Blacks in positions of authority in the police, courts, and business community. There was no significant involvement of Blacks in schools or colleges. It was, after all, the social formation of Jim Crow.

14. I first carried out research in Natchitoches in the mid-1990s, the details of which are provided in Eichstedt and Small 2002.

15. I provide details of the tour based on the multiple tours that I took between 2007 and 2010. The quotations should be taken as close approximations of what was said.

16. This is true for the 120 sites that Jennifer L. Eichstedt and I visited in 1996–2001 and for the tours I made to more than sixty sites in 2007–2008. Evidence from other research confirms this analysis—see Alderman and Modlin 2008; Harrison 2008; Mooney 2004.

17. At the time I wrote this, the issue had not been resolved. The tour guides continue to describe it as African in origin and nature.

18. The docent's statement was somewhat misleading. In fact, Israel was born enslaved, became legally free in 1860s, and lived at Melrose Plantation until the 1920s. When he died, he had already been free for fifty years.

19. In 2007 and 2008, when visitors entered the site, the weaving house was the first building that could be entered because it was typically unlocked, as were several other buildings. This had changed by 2010, when the weaving house and most other buildings could only be accessed by docents on guided tours.

20. Two other fascinating questions about the site also need to be addressed—was the African House originally based on an African design? And who has the right to tell the Melrose story? I briefly address those questions in the book's conclusion.

CONCLUSION

1. Under slavery, a series of racist ideologies were developed, including people of African origins being rendered to the realm of the inhuman in order to avoid confronting the harsh facts of injustice.

2. See Eichstedt and Small 2002 for several earlier suggestions on these strategies and tactics.

3. Examples include the Laura, Evergreen, and Frogmore plantations and the Louisiana Rural Life Museum, all in Louisiana; Boone Hall in South Carolina; Kingsley Plantation in Florida; and the Booker T. Washington National Monument in Virginia.

4. During my research, it seemed likely that the discussions arising from the new evidence would lead to challenges to several important contentions presented at Melrose Plantation.

EPILOGUE

1. I note that in February 2016 a conference entitled "Resistance. Escape. Community. Opposition to Enslavement in North Louisiana" took place in Natchitoches. Organized by the Cane River National Heritage Area, the keynote speaker was Sylviane A. Diouf, an international expert on the African diaspora.

2. See Moody and Small 2019; Small 2015.

3. And it's not only legacies of slavery that have been the basis for demands for renaming. For example, the Law School at University of California, Berkeley removed the name of John Boalt because of his virulent anti-Chinese racism. At the time of writing, the campus also approved the renaming of Le Conte Hall and Barrows Hall.

APPENDIX: RESEARCH METHODS AND DATA COLLECTION

1. I followed all standard protocols for academic research with human subjects as per university requirements.

2. At the time of my research, these records remained largely untapped and could provide vast opportunities for research on the lives and labors of Black men and women in twentieth-century Natchitoches.

3. Refusal is not uncommon in this type of research. The forms can be intimidating, and some potential respondents interpret the forms to mean they are signing their rights away. The person who refused later changed his mind and agreed to an interview.

BIBLIOGRAPHY

MANUSCRIPT COLLECTIONS

Association for the Preservation of Historical Natchitoches Collection
Bobby DeBlieux Collection
Cammie G. Henry Collection
Cammie Henry Center, Northwestern State University, Eugene P. Watson Library, Natchitoches
Cammie Henry Diary, 1934
East Baton Rouge Public Library, Vertical Files
François Mignon Collection
Hill Memorial Library, Louisiana State University, Baton Rouge, Mississippi Valley Collection
Lafayette Library
Melrose Collection
Natchitoches Genealogical and Historical Association
Natchitoches Public Library, Vertical Files
Prud'homme Family Photographs, Southeast Archeological Center, National Park Service, Tallahassee
Southern Historical Collection, Wilson Library, University of North Carolina at Chapel Hill
West Baton Rouge Public Library, Vertical Files

OBSERVATIONS AT PLANTATION SITES AND SLAVE CABINS

Ducournau Slave Cabin
Site visit, October 2007

Kate Chopin House
External site visit, Fall 2007
External site visit, Spring, 2008
External site visit, Fall, 2010

Magnolia Plantation
Site visit, 1997

Site visits, October 2007
Site visits, February 2008
Site visits, August 2010

Melrose Plantation
Site visit, 1997
Site visits, October 2007
Site visits, February 2008
Site visits, August 2010

Oakland Plantation
Site visit, 1997
Site visits, October 2007–December 2007
Site visits, February 2008–March 2008
Site visits, August 2010

Tante Huppe House
Site visit, February 2008

Badin-Rocque House, Natchitoches, Louisiana
Booker T. Washington National Monument, Virginia
Boone Hall Plantation, South Carolina
Fort Jessup, Natchitoches, Louisiana
Hampton Plantation, Baltimore, Maryland
Kingsley Plantation, Florida
Laura Plantation, Louisiana
Louisiana Rural Life Museum, Baton Rouge, Louisiana
Museum of Historic Natchitoches, Louisiana
Nottoway Plantation, Louisiana
Oak Alley Plantation, Louisiana
Oakley Plantation, Louisiana

INTERVIEWS

Robert DeBlieux, former Mayor of Natchitoches
Eric Ford, Site Manager, Cane River Creole National Historical Park
Dustin Fuqua, Cane River Creole National Historical Park
Laura Gates, Superintendent, Cane River Creole National Historical Park
Peggy Scherbaum, Chief Interpreter, Cane River Creole National Historical Park
Rolonda Teal
Site docent at Oakland Plantation
Site docent at Magnolia Plantation

Tarona Armstrong, Oakland Plantation

Nathan at Oakland Plantation

Edited Handson History video interview with Laura Gates, Peggy Scherbaum, Eric Ford, Rolonda Teal, and Greg Duggan

PRINTED SOURCES

Adams, Jessica. 2007. *Wounds of Returning. Race, Memory, and Property on the Postslavery Plantation.* Chapel Hill: University of North Carolina Press.

Alderman, D. H., and E. Arnold Modlin, Jr. 2008. "Special Issue: Museums, Narratives, and the Contested Memory of Slavery." *South Eastern Geographer* 48 (3): 338–55.

Alderman, D. H., and E. Arnold Modlin, Jr. 2013. "Southern Hospitality and the Politics of African American Belonging." *Journal of Cultural Geography* 30 (1): 6–31.

Alexander, Adele Logan. 1991. *Ambiguous Lives. Free Women of Color in Rural Georgia, 1789–1879.* Fayetteville: University of Arkansas Press.

Association for the Preservation of Historic Natchitoches. "Appendix B National Register of Historic Places. Nomination Form and Document." July 1969.

Araujo, Ana Lucia. 2020. *Slavery in the Age of Memory. Engaging the Past.* London: Bloomsbury Academic.

Babb, Arthur. 1996. *My Sketchbook, 1926–27.* Edited by Neil Cameron. Natchitoches, LA: Northwestern State University Press.

Battle-Baptiste, Whitney. 2007. "'In This Here Place': Interpreting Enslaved Homeplaces." In *Archaeology of Atlantic Africa and the African Diaspora*, edited by A. Ogundiran and T. Falola, 233–48. Bloomington: Indiana University Press.

Battle-Baptiste, Whitney. 2011. *Black Feminist Archeology.* Walnut Creek, CA: Left Coast Press.

Becker, Patricia Austin. 2018. *Cane River Bohemia: Cammie Henry and Her Circle at Melrose Plantation.* Baton Rouge: Louisiana State University Press.

Benjamin, Stefanie, and Derek Alderman. 2017. "Performing a Different Narrative: Museum Theater and the Memory-Work of Producing and Managing Slavery Heritage at Southern Plantation Museums." *International Journal of Heritage Studies* 24 (3): 270–87. DOI: 10.1080/13527258.2017.1378906.

Berlin, Ira. 1984. *Slaves Without Masters: The Free Negro in the Antebellum South*, New York: Oxford University Press.

Berry, Daina R. 2017. *The Price for Their Pound of Flesh: The Value of the Enslaved, from Womb to Grave in the Building of a Nation.* New York: Beacon Press.

Berry, Daina Ramey, and Leslie M. Harris, eds. 2018. *Sexuality and Slavery: Reclaiming Intimate Histories in the Americas.* Athens: University of Georgia Press.

Biographical and Historical Memoirs of Northwest Louisiana. (1890) 1976. Reprint, Marcelline, MO: Walsworth Publishing Company, Inc.

Blake, T. 2002. "Largest Slaveholders from 1860 Slave Census Schedules." Retrieved from http://www. usgwarchives.net/copyright.htm.

Blight, David. 2001. *Race and Reunion: The Civil War in American History*. Cambridge, MA: The Belknap Press of Harvard University Press.

Blight, David. 2002. *Beyond the Battlefield: Race, Memory, and the American Civil War*. Amherst: University of Massachusetts Press.

Bonilla-Silva, Eduardo. 2006. *Racism without Racists: Color-Blind Racism and the Persistence of Racial Inequality in America*. Oxford: Rowan and Littlefield Publishers.

Booker T. Washington—site promotional literature. Hardy, VA.

Breedlove, Carolyn. 1999. "Bermuda/Oakland Plantation, 1830–1880," MA thesis, Northwestern State University, Louisiana.

Bright, C. F., and P. L. Carter. 2016. "Who Are They? Visitors to Louisiana's River Road Plantations." *Journal of Heritage Tourism* 11 (3): 262–74.

Bright, Candace Forbes, Derek H. Alderman, and David L. Butler. 2016. "Tourist Plantation Owners and Slavery: A Complex Relationship." *Current Issues in Tourism* 21 (15): 1–18.

Brown, Kenneth L. 2006. "A Preliminary Report on the 2006 Excavations in the Quarters Community of the Magnolia Plantations, Cane River Creole National Historical Park, Natchitoches parish, Louisiana." Houston: University of Houston.

Brown, Kenneth L. 2008a. "A Preliminary Report on the 2007 Excavations into the Quarters Community of the Magnolia Plantation, Cane River Creole National Historical Park, Natchitoches Parish, Louisiana." Tallahassee, FL: The National Park Service; Cane River Creole National Historical Park, and the Southeast Archaeological Center, National Park Service.

Brown, Kenneth L. 2008b. "A Preliminary Report on the 2006 Excavations in the Quarters Community of the Magnolia Plantations, Cane River Creole National Historical Park, Natchitoches Parish, Louisiana." Houston: University of Houston.

Brundage, W. Fitzhugh, ed. 2000. *Where These Memories Grow: History, Memory, and Southern Identity*. Chapel Hill: University of North Carolina Press.

Brundage, W. Fitzhugh. 2005. *The Southern Past: A Clash of Race and Memory*. Cambridge, MA: The Belknap Press of Harvard University Press.

Brundage, W. Fitzhugh. 2018. "History and Memory in the American South." In *History, Memory and Public Life: The Past in the Present*, edited by Anna Maerker, Simon Sleight, and Adam Sutcliff, 251–73. London: Routledge, Taylor & Francis.

Burton, H. Sophie, and F. Todd Smith. 2008. *Colonial Natchitoches: A Creole Community on the Louisiana-Texas Frontier*. College Station: Texas A&M University Press.

Buzinde, C. N., and C. A. Santos. 2009. "Interpreting Slavery Tourism." *Annals of Tourism Research* 36 (3): 439–58.

Campbell, Edward D. C., Jr., and Kym S. Rice, eds. 1991. *Before Freedom Came: African American Life in the Antebellum South*. Charlottesville: Museum of the Confederacy and the University Press of Virginia.

Campbell, Randolph B. 1989. *An Empire for Slavery. The Peculiar Institution in Texas, 1821–1865*. Baton Rouge: Louisiana State University Press.

Cane River Creole National Historical Park. 2001a. Management Plan.

Cane River Creole National Historical Park. 2001b. Draft General Management Plan. Environmental Impact Statement, Louisiana. US Department of the Interior, NPS, Cane River National Heritage Area Commission.

Cane River Creole National Historical Park. 2007. National Park Service. US Department of the Interior. Natchitoches, LA: National Historical Park. GPO 2007-330-58/00607.

Cane River Creole National Historical Park. n.d. From Southern Plantation to National Park. National Park Service. US Department of the Interior. Natchitoches, LA: National Historical Park, n.p.

Cane River National Heritage Area. n.d. Côte Joyeuse: Tourist Leaflet.

Carson, John H. 1974. "The Economics of Racial Discrimination in Louisiana: 1950–1971." Baton Rouge: Division of Research Louisiana State University.

Carter, Perry L. 2015. "Where Are the Enslaved? Tripadvisor and the Narrative Landscapes of Southern Plantation Museums." *Journal of Heritage Tourism* 11 (3): 235–49. DOI: 10.1080/1743873X.2015.1100625.

Carter, P., D. L. Butler, and D. H. Alderman. 2014. "The House That Story Built: The Place of Slavery in Plantation Museum Narratives." *The Professional Geographer* 66 (4): 547–57.

Cizek, Eugene D. n.d. *The Architectural History and Origin of the Badin-Roque House, Isle Brevelle, Natchitoches Parish, Louisiana.* Natchitoches, LA: Robert Smith & Associates.

Clark, Kathleen Ann. 2005. *Defining Moments: African American Commemoration & Political Culture in the South, 1863–1913.* Chapel Hill: University of North Carolina Press.

Clayton, Ronnie W. 1990. *Mother Wit: The Ex-Slave Narratives of the Louisiana Writers' Project.* New York: Peter Lang Publishers, Inc.

Clinton, Catherine. 1982. *The Plantation Mistress: Woman's World in the Old South.* New York: Pantheon Books.

Clinton, Catherine. 1995. *Tara Revisited: Women, War & the Plantation Legend.* New York: Abbeville Press Publishers.

Clinton, Catherine, ed. 2019. *Confederate Statues and Memorialization.* Athens: University of Georgia Press.

Collins, Patricia Hill, and Sirma Bilge. 2016. *Intersectionality.* Boston: Polity.

Collins, Patricia Hill. 1991 *Black Feminist Thought: Knowledge, Consciousness, and the Politics of Empowerment.* New York: Routledge.

Commander, Michell D. 2018. "Plantation Counternarratives: Disrupting Master Accounts in Contemporary Cultural Production." *Journal of American Culture* 41 (1): 28–44.

Conrad, Glenn R., and Ray F. Lucas. 1995. *White Gold: A Brief History of the Louisiana Sugar Industry, 1795–1995.* Lafayette, LA: The Center for Louisiana Studies at University of Southwestern Louisiana.

Cook, Matthew. 2015. "Counter-Narratives of Slavery in the Deep South: The Politics of Empathy Along and Beyond River Road." *Journal of Heritage Tourism* 11 (3): 290–308. DOI: 10.1080/1743873X.2015.1100624.

Cook, Robert J. 2017. *Civil War Memories: Contesting the Past in the United States Since 1886.* Baltimore: Johns Hopkins University Press.

Craft, Ellen, and William Craft. 1999. *Running A Thousand Miles to Freedom: The Escape of William and Ellen Craft from Slavery.* Baton Rouge: Louisiana State University Press.

Crespi, Muriel. 2004. *A Brief Ethnography of Magnolia Plantation: Planning for Cane River Creole National Historical Park.* Washington, DC: National Center for Cultural Resources, National Park Service.

Davis, F. James. 1991. *Who Is Black? One Nation's Definition*. University Park: Pennsylvania State University Press.

De la Fuente, Alejandro, and Ariela J. Gross. 2020. *Becoming Free, Becoming Black: Race, Freedom and Law in Virginia, Cuba, and Louisiana*. Cambridge: Cambridge University Press.

DeBlieux, Robert B. 1986. "The Antebellum Complex in Rural Preservation: A Look at Magnolia Plantation." *New Orleans Preservation in Print*, November, 6–7.

DeBlieux, Robert B. 1993. "A Driving Tour. Down Cane River and through Kisatchie National Forest." Natchitoches Tourist Commission and US Forest Service.

Degler, Carl N. 1971. *Neither Black Nor White: Slavery and Race Relations in Brazil and the U.S.* New York: Macmillan.

Dessens, Nathalie. 2020. "Remembering in Black and White: Memorializing Slavery in 21st Century Louisiana." In *Traces and Memories of Slavery in the Atlantic World*, edited by Lawrence Aje and Nicolas Gachon, 128–43. New York: Routledge.

DeVore, Donald E. 2015. *Defying Jim Crow: African American Community Development and the Struggle for Racial Equality in New Orleans, 1900–1960*. Baton Rouge: Louisiana State University Press.

Din, Gilbert C. 1999. *Spaniards, Planters, and Slaves. The Spanish Regulation of Slavery in Louisiana, 1763–1803*. College Station: Texas A&M University Press.

Dollar, Susan E. 1998. *The Freedmen's Bureau Schools of Natchitoches Parish, Louisiana, 1865–1868*. Natchitoches, LA: Northwestern State University Press.

Dominguez, Virginia R. 1986. *White by Definition: Social Classification in Creole Louisiana*. New Brunswick, NJ: Rutgers University Press.

Dorman, James H., ed. 1996. *Creoles of Color in the Gulf South*. Knoxville: University of Tennessee.

Douglass, Frederick. (1845) 1988. *Narrative on the Life of Frederick Douglass, An American Slave. Written By Himself*. Cambridge, MA: The Belknap Press of Harvard University Press.

Du Bois, W. E. B. (1935) 1979. *Black Reconstruction in America, 1860–1880*. New York: Atheneum.

Eakin, Sue, and Joseph Logsdon. (1853) 1968. *Solomon Northup. Twelve Years a Slave*. Baton Rouge: Louisiana State University Press.

Edwards, Jay D., and Nicholas Kariouk. 2004. *A Creole Lexicon: Architecture, Landscape, People*. Baton Rouge: Louisiana State University Press.

Edwards, Jay D., ed. 2002. *Plantations by the River: Watercolor Paintings from St. Charles Parish, Louisiana by Father Joseph M. Paret, 1859 (In French and English)*. Baton Rouge: Geoscience Publications and Louisiana State University Press.

Eichstedt, Jennifer L., and Stephen Small. 2002. *Representations of Slavery. Race, Ideology and Southern Plantation Museums*. Washington, DC: Smithsonian Institution Press.

Ellis, Clifton, and Rebecca Ginsburg, eds. 2010. *Cabin, Quarter, Plantation. Architecture and Landscapes of North American Slavery*. New Haven: Yale University Press.

Estes, Craig. 1969. *Natchitoches*. Baton Rouge: Louisiana State University.

Farrington, Lisa E. 2005. *Creating Their Own Image. The History of African American Women Artists*. Oxford: Oxford University Press.

Ferguson, Leland. 1992. *Uncommon Ground: Archaeology and Early African America, 1650–1800.* Washington, DC: Smithsonian Institution Press.

Finley, Alexandra J. 2020. *An Intimate Economy: Enslaved Women, Work, and America's Domestic Slave Trade.* Baltimore, MD: University of North Carolina Press.

Finley, Cheryl, Randall R. Griffey, Amelia Peck, and Darryl Pinckney, eds. 2018. *My Soul Has Grown Deep. Black Art from the American South.* New Haven: Yale University Press.

Fleischner, Jennifer. 1996. *Mastering Slavery: Memory, Family, and Identity in Women's Slave Narratives.* New York: New York University Press.

Fogel, Robert William, and Stanley L. Engerman. 1984. *Time on the Cross: The Economics of American Negro Slavery.* Boston: Little, Brown.

Follett, Richard. 2005. *The Sugar Masters.* Baton Rouge: Louisiana State University Press.

Foner, Eric. 1988. *Reconstruction: America's Unfinished Revolution, 1863–1877.* New York: Harper & Row.

Foner, Eric. 2002. *Who Owns History? Rethinking the Past in a Changing World.* New York: Hill and Wang.

Foner, Laura. 1970. "The Free People of Color in Louisiana and St. Domingue: A Comparative Portrait of Two Three-Caste Slave Societies." *Journal of Social History* 3 (4): 406–30.

Forbes, Jack. 1993. *Africans and Native Americans: The Language of Race and the Evolution of Red-Black Peoples.* Chicago: University of Illinois Press.

Ford, Oliver. 1991. "Francois Mignon: The Man Who Would Be French." *Southern Studies* 2 (1): 51–59.

Fox-Genovese, Elizabeth. 1988. *Within the Plantation Household. Black and White Women of the Old South.* Chapel Hill: University of North Carolina Press,

Franklin, John Hope. 1943. *The Free Negro in North Carolina, 1790–1860.* Chapel Hill: University of North Carolina Press.

Franklin, Maria, and Nedra Lee. 2019. "Revitalizing Tradition and Instigating Change: Foodways at the Ransom and Sarah Williams Farmstead, c. 1871–1905." *Journal of African Diaspora Archaeology and Heritage* 8 (3): 202–25. DOI: 10.1080/21619441.2019.1726613.

Franklin, Maria. 2001. "The Archaeological Dimensions of Soul Food: Interpreting Race, Culture and Afro-Virginian Identity." In *Race and the Archaeology of Identity*, edited by Charles E. Orser Jr. Salt Lake City: University of Utah Press.

Franklin, Maria. 2017. "Archeology and Enslaved Life on Coke's Plantation: An Early History of the Governor's Palace Lands." The Colonial Williamsburg Foundation, August.

Franklin, Maria. 2019. "Enslaved Household Variability and Plantation Life and Labor in Colonial Virginia." *International Journal of Historical Archaeology* 241 (1): 115–55.

Franklin, Maria, and Larry McKee. 2004. "African Diaspora Archaeologies: Present Insights and Expanding Discourses." *Historical Archaeology* 38 (1): 1–9.

Fuentes, Marisa. 2016. *Dispossessed Lives: Enslaved Women, Violence, and the Archive.* Philadelphia: University of Pennsylvania Press.

Gallien, Charles Stanley. 1966. "Melrose: A Southern Cultural and Literary Center." MA thesis, Northwestern State University of Louisiana.

Gates, Laura (Soulière). 2002. "Frankly, Scarlett, We Do Give a Damn: The Making of a
    New National Park." *The George Wright Forum* 19 (4): 32–43.
Genovese, Eugene D. 1976. *Roll Jordan Roll: The World that Slaves Made*. New York:
    Vintage Books.
Gijtano, Liza. 2007. "A Comparison of Invasive and Non-Invasive Site Location Methods
    at Oakland Plantation." Natchitoches, LA: The Society for Historical Archeology.
Giley, Shelby R. 2000. *Painting by Heart: The Life and Art of Clementine Hunter, Louisiana
    Folk Artist*. Baton Rouge: St Emma Press.
Glymph, Thaviola. 2003. "'Liberty Dearly Bought': The Making of Civil War Memory in
    Afro- American Communities in the South." In *Time Longer than Rope: A Century of
    African American Activism*, edited by Charles M. Payne and Adam Green, 111–49. New
    York: New York University Press.
Glymph, Thaviola. 2008. *Out of the House of Bondage: The Transformation of the
    Plantation Household*. Cambridge: Cambridge University Press.
Glymph, Thaviola. 2020. *The Women's Fight: The Civil War's Battles for Home, Freedom,
    and Nation*. Chapel Hill: University of North Carolina Press.
Gomez, Michael A. 1998. *Exchanging Our Country Marks: The Transformation of African
    identities in the Colonial and Antebellum South*. Chapel Hill: University of North
    Carolina Press.
Graves, R. A. 1930. "Louisiana, Land of Perpetual Romance." *National Geographic* 57 (4):
    393–482.
Hadden, Sally E. 2001. *Slave Patrols: Law and Violence in Virginia and the Carolinas*.
    Cambridge, MA: Harvard University Press.
Hahn, T. H. G., III, and T. Wells. 1991. *Archaeological Investigations of the Magnolia
    Plantation Slave Quarters*, Natchitoches, LA: Coastal Environments, Inc., Baton Rouge.
Hall, Gwendolyn Mildo. 1992. *Africans in Colonial Louisiana: The Development of Afro-
    Creole Culture in the Eighteenth Century*. Baton Rouge: Louisiana State University
    Press.
Hall, Stuart. 1997. *Representation: Cultural Representations and Signifying Practices*.
    London: Sage Publications.
Handler, Richard, and Eric Gable. 1997. *The New History in an Old Museum. Creating the
    Past at Colonial Williamsburg*. Durham: Duke University Press.
Handley, Fiona. 2007. "Memorializing Race in the Deep South: The 'Good Darkie' Statue,
    Louisiana, USA." *Public Archaeology* 6 (2): 98–115.
Harris, Leslie M., James T. Campbell, and Alfred L. Brophy, eds. 2019. *Slavery and the
    University: Histories and Legacies*. Athens: University of Georgia Press.
Harrison, Alisa Y. 2008. "Reconstructing Somerset Place: Slavery, Memory and Historical
    Consciousness." PhD diss., Duke University.
Harvey, Chance. 2003. *The Life and Selected Letters of Lyle Saxon*. Gretna, GA: Pelican
    Publishing Company.
Haynie, Sandra Prud'homme. 2002. *Legends of Oakland Plantation*, edited by Mary
    Breazeale Cunningham. Shreveport, LA: LaPressCo Printing.
Hine Darlene Clark. 1994. *Hindsight: Black Women and the Reconstruction of American
    History*. Bloomington: Indiana University Press.

Historic Natchitoches. 2007. A Free Guide to Leisure and Attractions Courtesy of The Natchitoches Times Since 1970. August.

Historic Structure Report, Oakland Plantation, The Cottage. 2002.

Historic Structure Report, Oakland Plantation, Gin Complex. 2004.

Historic Structure Report, Oakland Plantation, Prud'homme's Store. 2004.

Historic Structure Report, Oakland Plantation, The Big House. 2004.

Historic Structure Report for Yucca House, Melrose Plantation. 2005. Eean McNaughton Architects, August.

Hodes, Martha. 1997. *White Women, Black Men" Illicit Sex in the 19th Century South*. New Haven: Yale University Press.

Hodes, Martha, ed. 1999. *Sex, Love, Race: Crossing boundaries in North American History*. New York: New York University Press.

Horton, James, and Lois Horton, eds. 2006. *Slavery and Public Memory: The Tough Stuff of American Memory*. New Press: New York.

Hunter, Henley Alexander. 2005. *Magnolia Plantation. A Family Farm*. Natchitoches, LA: Northwestern State University Press.

Jackson, Antoinette. 2012. *Speaking for the Enslaved: Heritage Interpretation at Antebellum Plantation Sites*. Walnut Creek, CA: Left Coast Press.

Jacobs, Harriet A. (1861) 1999. *Incidents in the Life of a Slave Girl*, edited by George Hendrick and Willene Hendrick. New York: Brandywine Press, St. James.

Johnson, David C., and Elaine G. Yodis. 1998. *Geography of Louisiana*. New York: The McGraw-Hill Companies, Inc.

Johnson, Michael P., and James L. Roark. 1984. *Black Masters: A Free Family of Color in the Old South*. New York: W. W. Norton & Company.

Johnson, Walter. 1999. *Soul by Soul: Inside the Antebellum Slave Market*. Cambridge, MA: Harvard University Press.

Jones, Jacqueline. 1986. *Labor of Love, Labor of Sorrow: Black Women, Work, and the Family, From Slavery to the Present*. New York: Vintage Books.

Jones-Rogers, Stephanie. 2019. *They Were Her Property: White Women as Slave Owners in the American South*. New Haven: Yale University Press.

Jordan, Winthrop D. 1968. *White Over Black: American Attitudes towards the Negro, 1550–1812*. Chapel Hill: University of North Carolina Press.

Joyner, Charles. 1984. *Down by the Riverside: A South Carolina Slave Community*. Urbana: University of Illinois Press.

Kane, Harnett T. 1945. *Plantation Parade. The Grand Manner in Louisiana*. New York: William Morrow & Company.

Keel, Bennie C. 1999. *A Comprehensive Subsurface Investigation at Magnolia Plantation*, Tallahassee, FL: Southeast Archeological Center, National Park Service.

Keel, Bennie, and Christina E. Miller. 1997. *Research Design for Archeological Investigations at Oakland Plantation, Cane River Creole National Historical Park and Heritage Area, Natchitoches Parish, Louisiana*. Tallahassee, FL: Southeast Archeological Center, National Park Service.

Keel Bennie, Christina E. Miller, Lynn Shreve, and Marc A. Tiemann. 1997. *Summary Field Report: 1997 Archeological Investigations, Oakland Plantation Unit, Cane River National*

Historical Park, Louisiana. Tallahassee, FL: Southeast Archeological Center, National Park Service.

King-O'Riain, Rebecca C., Stephen Small, Minelle Mahtani, Miri Song, and Paul Spickard, eds. 2014. *Global Mixed Race*. New York: New York University Press.

Kolger, Larry. 1995. *Black Slaveowners: Free Black Slave Masters in South Carolina, 1790–1860*. Columbia: University of South Carolina Press.

Landers, Jane, G. 1996. *Against the Odds: Free Blacks in the Slave Societies of the Americas*. Portland, OR: Frank Cass & Co Ltd.

Landers, Jane, G., ed. 2000. *Colonial Plantations and Economy in Florida*. Gainesville: University Press of Florida.

Landrieu, Mitch. 2018. *In the Shadow of Statues: A White Southerner Confronts History*. New York: Viking Press.

Leslie, Kent Anderson. 1995. *Woman of Color, Daughter of Privilege: Amanda America Dickson, 1849–1893*. Athens: University of Georgia Press.

Levine, Lawrence. 1977. *Black Culture and Black Consciousness: Afro-American Folk Thought from Slavery to Freedom*. New York: Oxford University Press.

Lord Gifford, Wally Brown, and Ruth Bundey. 1989. *Loosen the Shackles. First Report of the Liverpool 8 Inquiry into Race Relations in Liverpool*. London: Karia Press.

Louisiana Creole Heritage Center. 2006. *Badin Roque House: A Creole Story—Circa 1770*. Natchitoches; St. Augustine Historical Society.

Lyons, Mary E. 1998. *Talking with Tebé. Clementine Hunter, Memory Artist*. Boston: Houghton Mifflin Company.

MacDonald, Kevin C., and David W. Morgan. N.,d. *Melrose Plantation. The Archeological Geophysics Survey of 2001*. Natchitoches, LA: Association for the Preservation of Historic Natchitoches.

MacDonald, Kevin C., David W. Morgan, and Fiona J. L. Handley. 2006a. "The Cane River Africa Diaspora Archaeological Project: Prospectus and Initial Results." In *African Re-Genesis: Confronting Social Issues in the Diaspora*, edited by B. Haviser and Kevin C. MacDonald, 123–44. Abingdon: University College London Press.

MacDonald, Kevin C., David W. Morgan, Fiona J. L. Handley, Aubra L. Lee, and Emman Morley. 2006b. "The Archeology of Local Myths and Heritage Tourism: The Case of Cane Rivers' Melrose Plantation." In *A Future for Archaeology*, edited by Robert Layton, Stephen Shennan, and Peter Stone, 127–42. London: University College London Press.

Malone, A. P. 1996. *The Magnolia Plantation Overview*. Report submitted to the Southeast Region. Atlanta: National Park Service.

Malone, Ann Patton. 1992. *Sweet Chariot: Slave Family and Household Structure in Nineteenth Century Louisiana*. Chapel Hill: University of North Carolina Press.

Matrana, Marc. 2005. *Lost Plantation: The Rise and Fall of Seven Oaks*. Jackson: University Press of Mississippi.

McDaniel, George W. 1982. *Hearth & Home: Preserving a People's Culture*. Philadelphia: Temple University Press.

McDonald, Roderick A. 1993. *The Economy and Material Culture of Slaves: Goods and Chattels on the Sugar Plantations of Jamaica and Louisiana*. Baton Rouge: Louisiana State University Press.

McElya, Micki. 2007. *Clinging to Mammy: The Faithful Slave in Twentieth-Century America*. Cambridge, MA: Harvard University Press.

McGowan, James Thomas. 1976. "Creation of a Slave Society. Louisiana Plantations in the Eighteenth Century." PhD diss., University of Rochester, New York.

McLeod, Ruth Mullins. 1936. "The History of Natchitoches." MA thesis, Louisiana State University.

Menn, Joseph Karl. 1964. *The Large Slaveholders of Louisiana—1860*. New Orleans: Pelican Publishing Company.

Messner, William F. 1978. *Freedmen and the Ideology of Free Labor: Louisiana 1862–1865*. Lafayette, LA: Center for Louisiana Studies, University of Southwestern Louisiana.

Mignon, François. 1972. *Plantation Memo: Plantation Life in Louisiana 1750–1970 and Other Matters*. Baton Rouge: Claitor's Publishing Division.

Miles, Tiya. 2015. *Tales from the Haunted South: Dark Tourism and Memories of Slavery from the Civil War Era*. Chapel Hill: University of North Carolina Press.

Miller, Christina E., and Bennie C. Keel. 1999. "Gabe Nargot's Cabin—Investigations at a Nineteenth Century Slave Domicile in Northwest Louisiana." Paper presented at the Society for Historical Archaeology Conference, Salt Lake City, UT.

Miller, Christina E., and Susan E. Wood. 2000. *Oakland Plantation. A Comprehensive Subsurface Investigation*. Tallahassee, FL: Southeast Archeological Center, National Park Service.

Mills, Elizabeth Shown, and Gary B. Mills., 1978. *Tales of Old Natchitoches*. Natchitoches, LA: Association for the Preservation of Historical Natchitoches.

Mills, Gary B. 1977. *The Forgotten People. Cane River's Creoles of Color*. Baton Rouge: Louisiana State University Press.

Mills, Gary B., and Elizabeth S. Mills. 1973. *Melrose*. Natchitoches, LA: The Association for the Preservation of Historic Natchitoches.

Miri, Ali A. 1998a. *Historic Structures Assessment Report. Oakland Plantation: Cooks House, Corn Crib, West Pigeonnier, East Pigeonnier, Carriage House, Carpenter's Shop, Chicken Coop, Setting Pen*, vol. 3. Atlanta: National Park Service,

Miri, Ali A. 1998b. *Historic Structures Assessment Report. Oakland Plantation: Overseers house, Store and Post Office, South Slave Cabin, North Slave Cabin*, vol. 2. Atlanta: National Park Service.

Mitchell, Koritha. 2020. *From Slave Cabins to the White House: Homemade Citizenship in African American Culture*. Urbana: University of Illinois Press.

Modlin, E. Arnold, Stephen P. Hanna, Perry L. Carter, Amy E. Potter, Candace Forbes Bright, and Derek H. Alderman. 2018. "Can Plantation Museums Do Full Justice to the Story of the Enslaved? A Discussion of Problems, Possibilities, and the Place of Memory." *GeoHumanities* 4 (2): 335–59.

Moody, Jessica, and Stephen Small. 2019. "Slavery and Public History at the Big House: Remembering and Forgetting at American Plantation Museums and British Country Houses." *Journal of Global Slavery* 4 (February): 34–68.

Mooney, Barbara Burlison. 2004. "Looking for History's Huts." *Winthur Portfolio* 29 (1): 43–70.

Moore, Dianne M. 1984. *Their Adventurous Will: Profiles of Memorable Louisiana Women*. Lafayette, LA: Acadiana Press.

Morgan, D. W., K. C. MacDonald, and A. Lee. 2003. Interim Summary Report of Excavations at Yucca House, Melrose Plantation. Natchitoches, LA.

Morgan, Jennifer L. 2004. *Laboring Women: Reproduction and Gender in New World Slavery*. Philadelphia: University of Pennsylvania Press.

Morrison, Toni. 1992. *Playing in the Dark. Whiteness and the Literary Imagination*. Cambridge, MA: Harvard University Press.

Natchitoches Parish Resources and Facilities. N.d. Survey by Natchitoches Parish Development Board, Department of Public Works, Planning Division.

Natchitoches Times. 1978. April 16, 1978, 4B.

Nimako, Kwame, and Glen Willemsen. 2011. *The Dutch Atlantic, Slavery, Abolition and Emancipation*. London: Pluto.

Nimako, Kwame, and Stephen Small. 2012. "Collective Memory of Slavery in Great Britain and the Netherlands." In *New Perspectives on Slavery and Colonialism in the Caribbean*, edited by Marten Schalkwijk and Stephen Small, 92–116. The Hague: Amrit Publishers.

Oakland Plantation Historic Furnishing Report. December 2004.

Olmsted, Frederick Law. (1854) 1969. *Journey in the Seaboard States in the Years 1853–1854*. Reprint, Westport, CT: Negro Universities Press.

Phillips, Ulrich B. 1920. *Life and Labor in the Old South*. Boston: Little, Brown and Company.

Poesch, Jessie, and Barbara SoRelle Bacot. 1997. *Louisiana Buildings 1720–1940: The Historic American Buildings Survey*. Baton Rouge: Louisiana State University Press.

Potter, Amy E. 2015. "'She Goes into Character as the Lady of the House': Tour Guides, Performance, and the Southern Plantation." *Journal of Heritage Tourism* 11 (3): 250–61. DOI: 10.1080/1743873X.2015.1100626.

Pustz, Jennifer. 2010. *Voices form the Back Stairs: Interpreting Servants' Lives at Historical House Museums*. Dekalb: Northern Illinois University Press.

Rawick, George, ed. 1972. *The American Slave: A Composite Autobiography*. 19 volumes. Westport, CT: Greenwood Publishing Co.

Rehder, John B. 1999. *Delta Sugar: Louisiana's Vanishing Plantation Landscape*. Baltimore: Johns Hopkins University Press.

Ripley, C. Peter. 1976. *Slaves and Freedmen in Civil War Louisiana*. Baton Rouge: Louisiana State University Press.

Rodrigue, John C. 2001. *Reconstruction in the Cane Fields: From Slavery to Free Labor in Louisiana's Sugar Parishes, 1862–1880*. Baton Rouge: Louisiana State University Press.

Roland, Charles P. (1957) 1997. *Louisiana Sugar Plantations During the Civil War*. Reprint, Baton Rouge: Louisiana State University Press.

Sartain, Lee 2007. *Invisible Activists: Women of the Louisiana NAACP and the Struggle for Civil Rights, 1915–1945*. Baton Rouge: Louisiana State University Press.

Savage, Kirk. 1997. *Standing Soldiers, Kneeling Slaves: Race, War, and Monument in Nineteenth-Century America*. Princeton, NJ: Princeton University Press.

Saxon, Lyle. 1939. *Children of Strangers*. Boston: Houghton Mifflin Company.

Saxon, Lyle. 1948. *The Friends of Joe Gilmore and Some Friends of Lyle Saxon*. New York: Hastings House.

Saxon, Lyle. 1950. *Old Louisiana*. New Orleans: Robert L. Crager & Company.

Scarborough, Dorothy. (1925) 1962. *On the Trail of Negro Folk-Songs*. Reprint, Cambridge, MA: Harvard University Press.

Scarborough, William Kauffman. 2003. *Masters of the Big House: Elite Slaveholders of the Mid-Nineteenth-Century South*. Baton Rouge: Louisiana State University Press.

Schafer, Daniel L. 2013. *Zephaniah Kingsley Jr. and the Atlantic World: Slave Trader, Plantation Owner, Emancipator*. Gainesville: University Press of Florida.

Schweninger, Loren. 1996. "Socioeconomic Dynamics among the Gulf Creole Populations: The Antebellum and Civil War Years." In *Creoles of Color in the Gulf South*, edited by James H. Dorman, 51–66. Knoxville: University of Tennessee.

Schweninger, Loren. 1990. "Prosperous Blacks in the South, 1790–1880." *American Historical Review* 195 (3): 31–56.

Scott, Rebecca J. 2005. *Degrees of Freedom: Louisiana and Cuba After Freedom*. Cambridge, MA: Harvard University Press.

Sexton, Richard, Eugene Darwin Cizek, and Alex MacLean. 1999. *Vestiges of Grandeur: Plantations of Louisiana's River Road*. Vancouver: Chronicle Books.

Shiver, Art, and Tom Whitehead, eds. 2005. *Clementine Hunter: The African House Murals*. Natchitoches, LA: Northwestern State University Press.

Shiver, Art, and Tom Whitehead. 2012. *Clementine Hunter. Her Life and Art*. Baton Rouge: Louisiana State University Press.

Shugg, Roger W. 1937. "Survival of the Plantation System in Louisiana." *Journal of Southern History* 3 (3): 311–25.

Shugg, Roger W. 1939. *Origins of Class Struggle in Louisiana: A Social History of White Farmers and Laborers during Slavery and After, 1840–1875*. Baton Rouge: Louisiana State University Press.

Shuler, Marsha. 1980. "Women of Cane River Country." *Shreveport Times*, August 21.

Singleton, Theresa. 1985. *The Archaeology of Slavery and Plantation Life*. Orlando: Academia Press.

Sitterson, J. Carlyle 1953. *Sugar Country: The Cane Sugar Industry in the South, 1753–1950*. Lexington: University of Kentucky Press.

Small, Stephen. 1994a. "Racial Group Boundaries and Identities: People of 'Mixed-Race' in Slavery across the Americas." *Slavery and Abolition* 15 (3): 17–36.

Small, Stephen. 1994b. "The General Legacy of the Atlantic Slave Trade." In *Transatlantic Slavery: Against Human Dignity*, edited by Tony Tibbles, 122–26. Liverpool: Merseyside Maritime Museum.

Small, Stephen. 1997. "Contextualizing the Black Presence in British Museums: Representations, Resources and Response." In *Museums and Multiculturalism in Britain*, edited by Eilean Hooper Greenhill, 50–66. Leicester: Leicester University Press.

Small, Stephen. 2002. "Racisms and Racialized Hostility at the Start of the New Millennium." In *The Blackwell Companion to Race Relations*, edited by David T. Goldberg and John Solomos, 259–81. Oxford: Blackwell.

Small, Stephen. 2004a. "Mustefinos Are White by Law: Whites and People of Mixed Racial Origins in Historical and Comparative Perspective." In *Racial Thinking in the United States. Uncompleted Independence*, edited by Paul Spickard and G. Reginald Daniel, 60–79. Notre Dame: University of Notre Dame Press.

Small, Stephen. 2004b. "Researching 'Mixed-Race' Experience Under Slavery. Concepts, Methods and Data." In *Researching Race and Racism*, edited by Martin Bulmer and John Solomos, 78–91. London: Routledge.

Small, Stephen. 2011. "Multiple Methods in Research on 21st Century Plantation Museums and Slave Cabins in the South." In *Rethinking Race and Ethnicity in Research Methods*, edited by John H. Stanfield, II, 169–89, Walnut Creek, CA: Left Coast Press.

Small, Stephen. 2012. "Still Back of the Big House: Slave Cabins and Slavery in Southern Heritage Tourism." *Tourism Geographies: An International Journal of Tourism Space, Place and Environment* 15 (3): 405–423. DOI 10.1080/14616688.2012.723042.

Small, Stephen. 2015. "Social Mobilization and Public History of Slavery in the United States." In *Eurocentrism, Racism and Knowledge: Debates on History and Power in Europe and the Americas*, edited by Marta Araújo and Silvia Rodríguez Maeso, 229–46. London: Palgrave Macmillan.

St. Clair, JoAnn. 2008. *A Preliminary Report on the 2008 Archaeological Excavation of the Magnolia Plantation Blacksmith's Shop*. Natchitoches Parish, LA: Cane River Creole National Historical Park.

Stanfield, John H, II, ed. 2011. *Rethinking Race and Ethnicity in Research Methods*. Walnut Creek, CA: Left Coast Press.

Stanonis, Anthony J. 2006. *Creating the Big Easy: New Orleans and the Emergence of Modern Tourism, 1918–1945*. Athens: University of Georgia Press.

Starling., Marion Wilson. 1988. *The Slave Narrative: Its Place in American History*. Washington, DC: Howard University Press.

Sterx, H. E. 1972. *The Free Negro in Ante-Bellum Louisiana*. Rutherford, NJ: Fairleigh Dickinson University Press.

Strutt, Michael. 2010. "Slave Housing in Antebellum Tennessee." In *Cabin, Quarter, Plantation. Architecture, and Landscapes of North American Slavery*, edited by Clifton Ellis and Rebecca Ginsburg, 223–32. New Haven: Yale University Press.

Taylor, Joel Gray. 1963. *Negro Slavery in Louisiana*. New Orleans: Louisiana Historical Association.

Taylor, Joel Gray. 1974. *Louisiana Reconstructed, 1863–1877*. Baton Rouge: Louisiana State University Press.

Teal, Rolonda D. 2007. *Natchitoches Parish. Black America Series*. Charleston, SC: Arcadia Publishing.

Thomas, James W. 1991. *Lyle Saxon: A Critical Biography*. Birmingham, AL: Summa Publications, Inc.

Thompson, Ginger. 2000. "Reaping What Was Sown on the Old Plantation. A Landowner Tells Her Family's Truth. A Park Ranger Wants a Broader Truth." *New York Times*, June 22.

Tibbles, Tony, ed. 1994. *Transatlantic Slavery: Against Human Dignity*. Liverpool: Merseyside Maritime Museum.

Toth, Emily. 1990. *Kate Chopin*. New York: William Morrow and Company, Inc.

Toth, Emily. 1999. *Unveiling Kate Chopin*. Jackson: University Press of Mississippi.

Trouillot, Michel-Rolph. 1995. *Silencing the Past: Power and the Production of History*. Boston: Beacon Press.

Tunnell, Ted. 1984. *Crucible of Reconstruction: War, Radicalism and Race in Louisiana, 1862–1877*. Baton Rouge: Louisiana State University Press.

Upton, Dell, and John Michael Vlach, eds. 1986. *Common Places. Readings in American Vernacular Architecture*. Athens and London: University of Georgia Press.

Upton, Dell. 2010. "White and Black Landscapes in Eighteenth-Century Virginia." In *Cabin, Quarter, Plantation. Architecture and Landscapes of North American Slavery*, edited by Clifton Ellis and Rebecca Ginsburg, 121–39. New Haven: Yale University Press.

Vlach, John Michael. 1986. "The Shotgun House: An African American Legacy." In *Common Places. Readings in American Vernacular Architecture*, edited by Dell Upton and John Michael Vlach, 58–78. Athens: University of Georgia Press.

Vlach, John Michael. 1993. *Back of the Big House. The Architecture of Plantation Slavery*. Chapel Hill: University of North Carolina Press.

Vlach, John Michael. 1995. "'Snug Li'l House with Flue and Oven': Nineteenth-Century Reforms in Plantation Slave Housing." *Perspectives in Vernacular Architecture* 5: 118–29.

Vlach, John Michael. 1997a. "Plantation Landscapes of the Antebellum South." In *Before Freedom Came. African American Life in the Antebellum South*, edited by Edward D. C. Campbell Jr. and Kym S. Rice, 21–50. Charlottesville: Museum of the Confederacy and the University Press of Virginia.

Vlach, John Michael. 1997b. "'Without Recourse to Owners': The Architecture of Urban Slavery in the Antebellum South." *Perspectives in Vernacular Architecture* 6: 50–60.

Wade, Richard C. 1964. *Slavery in the Cities: The South, 1820–1860*. Oxford: Oxford University Press.

Walcott-Wilson, Emma Jay. 2020. "Tour Guides as Place-makers: Emotional Labor, Plantation Aesthetics, and Interpretations of Slavery at Southern House Museums." PhD diss., University of Tennessee, Knoxville.

Wallace-Sanders, Kimberly. 2008. *Mammy: A Century of Race, Gender and Southern Memory*. Ann Arbor: University of Michigan Press.

Washington, Booker T. 1901. *Up from Slavery: An Autobiography*.

Wells, Carol, ed. 1990. *War, Reconstruction and Redemption on Red River: The Memoirs of Dosia Williams Moore*. Ruston, LA: Louisiana Tech University.

West, Patricia. 1999. *Domesticating History: The Political Origins of American's House Museums*. Washington, DC: Smithsonian Institution Press.

White, Sophie, 2019. *Voices of the Enslaved: Love, Labor, and Longing in French Louisiana*. Chapel Hill: University of North Carolina Press.

Wilkie, Laurie A. 2000. *Creating Freedom: Material Culture and African American Identity at Oakley Plantation, Louisiana 1840–1950*. Baton Rouge: Louisiana State University Press.

Wilson, James L. 1990. *Clementine Hunter: American Folk Artist*. Gretna, GA: Pelican Publishing Company.

Winters, John D. 1963. *The Civil War in Louisiana*. Baton Rouge: Louisiana State University Press.

Woods, Frances Jerome, Sr. 1972. *Marginality and Identity: A Colored Creole Family through Ten Generations*. Baton Rouge: Louisiana State University Press.

Woodward, Van C. 1957. *The Strange Career of Jim Crow*. New York: Oxford University
     Press.
Yocum, B. A. 1996. *Magnolia Plantation: Building Materials Assessment and Analysis,
     Cane River Creole National Historical Park and Heritage Area, Natchitoches, Louisiana.*
     Lowell, MA: Northeast Cultural Resources Center, National Park Service.
Yuhl, Stephanie E. 2005. *A Golden Haze of Memory: The Making of Historic Charleston.*
     Chapel Hill: University of North Carolina Press.

INDEX

136–38, 142–43, 147, 172, 176–76, 179, 183, 221n2; elite whites in, 32, 39, 47, 50–51, 60, 62, 84, 98–100, 108, 110, 125, 132–34, 151, 176, 183–87, 189, 195; founders, 21; French in, 10, 17, 21, 24–25, 29, 46, 51–52, 57, 143, 179, 181, 187; *gens de couleur libres* (free people of color), 23–30, 34, 38–40, 42–43, 45–46, 54, 98, 125, 135, 138, 141–44, 151–52, 154, 172, 178, 181, 185–86, 195; heritage tourism in, 10–12, 15, 21–58, 72, 176, 178–82, 187, 196; National Historic Landmark district, 22, 55; Native Americans, 10, 12, 21, 24; population in 1776, 25; population in 1785, 24; population in 1810, 24; population in 1820, 25; population in 1840, 25; population in 1850, 25, 29; population in 1860, 4, 10, 25, 29; population in 2009, 10; postbellum, 17, 38–39; slavery in/enslaved people living in, 6, 10, 21–58, 179; Spanish in, 10, 21, 24–25, 52, 181, 187; twentieth century through 1970s, 43–46
Natchitoches Art Colony, 54, 147
Natchitoches Enterprise, 49
Natchitoches Historic District, 56
Natchitoches National Historic Landmark District, 57
Natchitoches Normal School, 47, 146, 156
Natchitoches Rotary Club, 49
Natchitoches Sheriff's Office, 77
Natchitoches twist, 16–17, 24, 195
National Mall, 204
National Museum of African American History and Culture, 204
National Park Service (NPS), 13, 18–19, 51, 111, 175, 179, 188–89, 196, 199–200; oversight of Magnolia Plantation, 102, 104, 113–14, 119–20, 123, 125–26, 134, 174, 179, 182, 193–94; oversight of Oakland Plantation, 57, 59–61, 72, 85, 87, 89, 91, 93, 100–101, 113, 123, 174, 179, 182, 193–94; National Center for Preservation Technology and Training, 57
National Register of Historic Places, 117, 161, 167–68

New Deal, 110
New Orleans, 13, 14, 21–22, 46, 148, 203–4; antebellum period, 26; port, 25; racial origins of population, 13; slave auctions, 25, 27; sugar production, 25; Union occupation, 37, 66
Newsom, Gavin, 207
North Carolina, 13–14, 180, 204
Northrup, Solomon, 36
Northwestern State University, 151–53
Nottoway Plantation, 223n15, 225b8

Oak Alley Plantation, 201
Oakland Plantation, 5, 10, 15, 19, 33, 38, 40, 52, 57, 59–102, 119, 123, 130, 133, 174, 176, 179, 182–86, 188; acetylene-gas lighting at, 69; archaeological research, 100; attic, 88; bedrooms, 86–88, 96; Big House Historic Structure Report, 95–96; blacksmith, 65, 68, 75, 88; bottle garden, 85–86; carpenter's shop, 61, 72, 77–78, 96–97; carriage house, 61, 72, 77, 96–97; Civil War, 60, 63, 66, 71, 78–79, 81, 89, 95, 222n11; continuum of coerced accommodations, 62, 76–77; cook's house/kitchen, 61, 66, 70, 72, 74, 76, 80, 88, 89, 92–95, 222n11; corn crib, 61, 72, 77–78; cotton, 69–70, 79; designation as a heritage site, 60; dining room, 87; doctor's cottage, 61–62, 72, 77–78; domestics at, 80, 95–96; exhibits at, 74, 82–84, 87, 91–92, 98, 224n2; founding, 63–64; gendered representations at, 98–100, 185; heritage tourism at, 60, 63, 71–76, 98, 99, 134, 192–96; Historic Structure Report, 83–84; involvement of Black people on site, 100–101, 194; language used at, 100; Live Oak Allée, 72, 80; livestock raised at, 69, 78, 80; main house, 33, 59–62, 66, 69, 74, 76–77, 80, 86–89, 91, 95–96, 98–100, 188, 222n11; main house, backyard, 77, 80, 84, 185; mammy/nanny's room, 33, 62, 76, 85–87, 89, 95–96; map, 61–62, 72–73, 75–77, 84, 89, 93–94, 96; mule barn/

ABOUT THE AUTHOR

Stephen Small is professor in the Department of African American Studies at the University of California, Berkeley. His most recent book is *20 Questions and Answers on Black Europe*. He is coauthor of *Representations of Slavery: Race and Ideology in Southern Plantation Museums* and coeditor of *Global Mixed Race, New Perspectives on Slavery and Colonialism in the Caribbean*, and *Black Europe and the African Diaspora*.